STUDENT MINISTRY

THAT LEAVES A MARK

CHANGING YOUTH TO CHANGE THE WORLD

GARY ZUSTIAK — JOHN MOUTON
KEVIN GREER — JOSH FINKLEA

COLLEGE PRESS PUBLISHING COMPANY
Joplin, Missouri

Copyright © 2003
College Press Publishing Company
www.collegepress.com
Toll-free order line 1-800-289-3300

Printed and Bound in the
United States of America
All Rights Reserved

Cover design by Mark Cole

Library of Congress Cataloging-in-Publication Data

Student ministry that leaves a mark : changing youth to change the world / by
Gary Zustiak . . . [et al.].
     p. cm.
Includes bibliographical references.
  ISBN 0-89900-916-6 (hardcover)
  1. Church work with youth.   I. Zustiak, Gary Blair, 1952–
  BV4447.S729 2003
  259'.23—dc21

                                       2003005394

DEDICATION

This book is dedicated to the men and women who have answered the call to serve God by serving young people. We hope you are ready for a roller coaster ride that will take you through incredible lows and exciting highs.

There is no greater joy than seeing a young person you have taught, discipled, and prayed for make a profession of faith and commitment to serve God. At the same time, there is nothing more frustrating than hearing someone say, "When are you going to get a 'real' job?" We want you to know that Youth Ministry is *more* than a real job—it is a passion and a calling even more than it is a profession. By investing your life in the lives of young people, you will leave a legacy that will long outlast all the things of this world. So take heart!

It is also dedicated to the churches, youth groups, and ministers who have allowed us to learn and share under your tutelage. Thanks for the patience when we weren't the most mature leaders we could be. Thanks for overlooking the mistakes we made in planning and organization. Thanks for your graciousness in putting up with our early sermons and lessons. You even found ways to be encouraging when others would have only criticized. May all who read this book be as fortunate and blessed as we were.

Change youth. . . change the world.

Josh Finklea, Kevin Greer, John Mouton,
Gary Zustiak
Christ In Youth

ACKNOWLEDGEMENTS

The writing of this book came about because of the combined efforts of many people. We are all thankful to our good friends at College Press who believed in this project and patiently encouraged us to see it to completion. Thanks to Mark Moore who first envisioned this project and got it started. Thanks, also, to Jessica Scheuermann who spent countless hours editing each chapter. We appreciate your patience and kindness.

We are all thankful for the common ministry that we share with Christ In Youth. What a great fellowship we share. It is a privilege to work alongside such men and women of great faith, vision, talent, insight, and experience. May this book be a resource and blessing for years to come for the ministry of Christ In Youth.

To all those who have been a mentor to me; to all those I have attempted to mentor; and especially to those close friends and brothers who challenged me in personal growth, faithfulness, and accountability in my walk with God, marriage, and ministry. . . Thanks. —Kevin Greer

Thanks to everyone who allowed me to "mess up" long enough that I've finally started to get about half the things I do right. —Josh Finklea

I would like to acknowledge a debt of gratitude to God, my family (Nancy, Joshua, Jonathan, and Sarah), and the Missions/Outreach Department at Christ In Youth. —John Mouton

To every student who has allowed me to share with you my passion for youth ministry and allowed me the privilege of mentoring and encouraging you, I am thankful. When I see you faithfully serving God it fills me with pride and assures me that my efforts have not been in vain. —Gary Zustiak

CONTENTS

FOUNDATIONAL ISSUES

PRACTICAL CONCERNS

PROGRAMS

MODELS FOR YOUTH MINISTRY

Writers

GZ = Gary Zustiak
JM = John Mouton
KG = Kevin Greer
JF = Josh Finklea

Introduction

Pursuing the Passion

"But if I say, 'I will not mention him or speak any more in his name,' his word is in my heart like a fire, a fire shut up in my bones. I am weary of holding it in; indeed, I cannot" —*Jeremiah 20:9*

Webster's Seventh New Collegiate Dictionary defines passion as: "intense or overmastering feeling; ardent affection; a strong devotion to some activity, object, or concept; synonyms = fervor, enthusiasm, zeal. An intense emotion compelling action; energetic and unflagging pursuit of an aim or devotion to a cause." Søren Kierkegaard, the Danish theologian/existentialist once wrote, "Let others complain that the age is wicked; my complaint is that it is wretched, for it lacks passion."[1] That would be quite an indictment for anyone, but it is especially sad when it can be applied to those in ministry.

Lately I come across an increasing number of youth ministers who have lost their passion for reaching and discipling youth and are just "marking time" until they can apply for a different position or until something opens up in the business world. Somehow they think a change in job description or responsibility will magically restore what they have lost inside. It won't.

I understand that the call to youth ministry does not come to everyone. I have no problem with those who leave for the right reasons, but my heart breaks for those who leave because their fire simply died out. There is nothing more pitiful than a hollow youth minister who has lost heart.

Not all of those who lack passion have lost heart; some never had it in the first place. These are those who saw youth ministry simply as a great "job." You get to hang around kids, do fun events, put in a minimum of office hours, and get paid for it. This is the "hired hand" that Jesus speaks of in John 10:12-13. From an outside perspective they are serving, but on the inside there is no passion driving them that would cause them to sacrifice for any compelling need or teen in their group. Lord, save us from such people!

I want to put out a call for youth ministers to regain their passion, their sense of call and destiny. I want to see youth ministry carried out with a sense of adventure and not simply as a duty or a job. It was Teddy Roosevelt who said:

> It is not the critic who counts; not the man who points out how the strong man stumbles, or where the doer of deeds could have done them better. The credit belongs to the man . . . in the arena, whose face is marred by dust and sweat and blood; who strives valiantly . . . who knows the great enthusiasms, the great devotions; who spends himself in a worthy cause; who at the best knows in the end the triumph of high achievement, and who at the worst, if he fails, at least fails while daring greatly, so that his place shall never be with those cold and timid souls who know neither victory nor defeat.[2]

One of my favorite lines from the movie *Braveheart* occurs when William Wallace faces torture and death and says, "All men die; few men ever really live." He is talking about living life with passion. Oh, God, revive us again with your fire from above so that we can serve you with zeal and passion. Let our lives count, and when we have looked back at the end of our days, let there not be regret but a deep satisfaction knowing that we spent our all and held nothing back in service to the King.

This book is written out of passion with the hope and prayer that it will inspire others to serve young people with a fervency of heart and spirit—to see ministry as an adventure with God. The authors have almost 100 years of combined youth ministry experience. The contents of this book are the result of insights gained through those years of faithful service. We are grateful to those who went before us and passed along their wisdom and insight. Out of gratitude, it is our desire to provide a practical resource for others which will serve as a foundation and compass for those answering the call to work with youth.

Understand that you do not have to be perfect in order to faithfully serve God in the area of youth ministry. In fact, it is better if you are not. A deep awareness of your need for daily grace will make your interactions with teens more compassionate and understanding as you deal with their shortcomings and failures. We are all broken vessels who have been restored by the gentle touch of Jesus. This awareness of our need and His provision can work as a catalyst to encourage us to serve in the same spirit in which He served.

May you find great satisfaction and joy in answering the call to ministry with young people and may this book serve as an encouragement and guide to keep you on course and pursuing with passion the destiny God has laid before you.

Dr. Gary B. Zustiak, Ed.
Josh Finklea
Kevin Greer
John Mouton

NOTES ON INTRODUCTION

1. Søren Kierkegaard, *The Present Age,* trans. by Alexander Dru (New York: Harper and Row, 1962), p. 33.

2. Theodore Roosevelt, *History as Literature* (New York: Charles Scribner's Sons, 1913).

Chapter One

The Three Greatest Movements in Youth Ministry

Dr. Gary B. Zustiak

An On-line Discussion

Mark Senter describes a very lively on-line discussion that took place on an America Online bulletin board concerning the correct way to practice youth ministry in the 21st century.[4] One person was adamant that the only way to reach kids was to "hang out with them—be real." Living a redemptive lifestyle is the key to gaining an entrance into the world of teens and earning the right to be heard.

The next person was adamant that much more was needed. The youth groups and parachurch agencies she had attended sounded more like a sociology class or a twelve-step program. She wanted an inductive study of the Scriptures.

"No, no no!" came the next reply. "It's neither relationships nor theology. It's not programs or boring Bible studies—it's action!" Youth ministry that is going to reach and change kids is a youth ministry that will find a way to help kids do genuine ministry. Service projects and short-term missions are what is needed.

Who's right? The problem with this on-line discussion is that everyone was right—to a degree. It is much like the proverbial blind men describing an elephant. One, feeling the animal's tail, described it as a rope. The second man put his hands on the legs of the elephant and declared that the animal was like a tree trunk. Yet another blind man, feeling the side of the great beast determined that the elephant was much like a wall. The confusion and error came about because each person was focusing on only one aspect of the animal.

The history of youth ministry suggests that when ministry to students is done well, it blends three elements—warm respectful relationships; appealing, conservative Bible teaching; and an aggressive bent for action. By contrast, when youth ministry begins to stagnate or institutionalize there comes a fragmentation of these aspects of ministry.[5]

Youth ministry that has been effective down through the ages has always been relational, theological, and action oriented.

Youth ministry that has been effective down through the ages has always been relational, theological, and action oriented. Before trying to decide which is the proper way to do youth ministry in the 21st century, it would be most helpful to look at where it has been first. If certain principles or patterns can be found, then these may be helpful in predicting the future of youth ministry.

The Birth of a New Ministry

The beginnings of youth ministry in America could be seen as early as 1724 when Cotton Mather organized societies to sustain the faith of young people. It was a time when impurity, infidelity, and intemperance were common. "Societies that formed as a result of Mather's proposals met weekly for prayer, Bible study, and singing."[6] While Mather saw the positive good that was provided by these societies with respect to young people, he also noted that these societies "were frowned on by the Puritan fathers who viewed them as a dangerous innovation."[7]

However, youth ministry, as we know it, did not come into being until late in the eighteenth century. Great social upheaval came about as a result of the Enlightenment and the Industrial Revolution.

With the rise of technology, the sheltered world of the village, extended family, and church was shattered. Industrialization caused jobs to be concentrated in urban centers. Families needing income left the nurturing environment of the small village and followed the promise of a better life to the city. Lost in the transition was the spiritual and moral accountability, which was present in extended family and parish life. Youth fell prey to the temptations that abounded in the city.[8]

It was in this spiritual vacuum that there arose a number of ministries that were focused on reaching out to the youth of their time. The first wave of these ministries came in the form of the Sunday school.

The Sunday School

Robert Raikes (1735–1811) is the man credited with establishing the Sunday school. He was a prosperous businessman who owned and edited the *Gloucester Journal*. His heart went out to the poor and uneducated in his city, especially to the children who worked in the factories and sweat shops during the week and spent their Sundays, "playing, quarreling, cursing and fighting"[9] in the streets of Gloucester. Believing that "vice was preventable" and that vice was caused by ignorance, Raikes decided that vice could be prevented by instructing the children.

> In 1780 he started his first Sunday School in Mrs. Meredith's kitchen in Sooty Alley . . . His pupils were from the lowest levels of society and from places of the worst reputation. . . . He paid Mrs. Meredith to instruct these wretched children. The boys were bad and the girls were worse, so she gave up after several months. Raikes then transferred the children to the kitchen of Mrs. King and Mrs. May Critchely as teacher. She seemed to be better able to handle them.[10]

The children were kept in school from ten to twelve in the morning and then returned at one o'clock for a lesson after which they were taken to church. After church they were taught the catechism and then sent home by about five o'clock. Rewards of Bibles, Testaments, books, games, clothing, and combs were given to well-behaved children as a source of encouragement and reinforcement.

> The design of Raikes' schools was not to teach the Bible but to teach reading, writing, and religion to poor children for the purpose of bettering their lot and bringing about reform in society. From the beginning, however, the Bible was used as a text in his school, as it was at that time in secular schools. The ultimate objective of the schools was to form character, and the Bible

was considered the essential means of doing this. Raikes' movement aimed at popular religious education for the poor whom the church was neglecting, and the Bible was the main textbook. The efficacy of religious education in cleaning up the slum life of a wicked city was demonstrated by his experiment. Out of it grew also a plan for national popular education.[11]

Raikes waited for three years before he made his work public. On November 3, 1787, he published a brief article in his newspaper about the success and nature of his program. This article was then copied by other newspapers throughout England. Many praised his efforts and soon his plan was adapted by others.

But not everyone received it with welcome arms. Some of the strongest opposition came from the clergy!

> Some . . . condemned them as dangerous and demoralizing institutions and agents of the devil. The Archbishop of Canterbury called together the bishops to consider what should be done to stop the movement. William Pitt thought seriously of introducing into Parliament a bill for the suppression of Sunday Schools. In Scotland, teaching on the Sabbath by laymen was pronounced a violation of the Fourth Commandment.[12]

John Wesley and William Fox both gave Raikes their support of the Sunday school and by the time of his death in 1811, the total attendance of pupils enrolled in Sunday school came to 400,000 students.

The Sunday school movement in America got off to a slow start for two reasons. First, it was held in suspicion by many American churches because it originated in England. Secondly, clergyman saw themselves as the chief leaders in the area of spiritual instruction and were very hesitant to give any leadership responsibility to laymen. But because eighteenth-century conditions in America were similar to those in England, the Sunday school was seen as a way to combat the moral problems of the day. From 1785 to 1815 a number of Sunday schools were established based on the English model. By this time the Sunday school also took a subtle change. "It became less and less a literacy program and increasingly a gospel agency."[13]

Several observations about the Sunday school movement are in order before moving on to the next major youth movement. First, it was established out of a profound need observed in society. Second, it was a grassroots movement started by a layman. Third, it met opposition by the established church at first, and then was incorporated into the church. These observations, or similar ones, will appear with other major youth movements.

Christian Endeavor

On February 2, 1881, Francis E. Clark, pastor of the Williston Congregational Church, invited his young people to the parsonage for cocoa and cookies. Clark "sensed the growing lack of spiritual vitality in Sunday Schools and YMCAs."[14] He felt "the failure of contemporary youth movements and local groups of the late nineteenth century was due to their expecting too little from the young. Most of these mistakes lay along the line of doing too much for the young people rather than allowing them to do what they could for themselves."[15]

The failure of contemporary youth movements and local groups of the late nineteenth century was due to their expecting too little from the young. Most of these mistakes lay along the line of doing too much for the young people rather than allowing them to do what they could for themselves.

Clark wanted to start something new and different that would correct the current failings of the previous youth movements. He laid out what was to become known as the Six Essential Characteristics of the International Christian Endeavor Society. At the weekly meetings, each member was expected to be present and to give a brief report on his or her endeavor to live as a Christian, especially in respect to the Six Essential Characteristics. The Six Essential Characteristics are:

1. The Pledge—an active commitment to the service of Jesus Christ as Lord and to actively participate in the Society's prayer meetings.
2. The monthly experience or consecration meeting.
3. Systematic, definite, and regular committee work—trained by doing.
4. Private devotion: daily prayer and Bible reading.
5. Denominational loyalty including attendance at midweek prayer and Sunday evening services.
6. Interdenominational fellowship—an early Protestant and Evangelical ecumenism described as "a very complete and beautiful system of unions."[16]

"It is amazing that this pledge, required in all Christian Endeavor Societies, did not deter but rather contributed to the organization's attractiveness."[17] The results of this society were so successful that other churches requested to be brought into the program. In just four months five other societies sprang up. In sixteen months a convention was held for the six societies. In a short time its popularity grew so fast that the convention held in Boston in 1895 could boast of registering 56,435 people.[18] Remember that this is a period without automobile and airline transportation!

Christian Endeavor began to experience a decline in general vitality and interest by local churches at the beginning of the 20th century. This was brought about in part, by the fact that many denominations simply copied the basics of the Christian Endeavor movement and modified it to suit their own denominational distinctives. "They feared the loss of loyalty among their own youth and a lack of affiliation with the denomination. So they organized and sponsored their own youth groups."[19] The Baptist Church established a national Baptist young peoples organization in 1891. The Methodist Episcopal Church developed their Epworth League. The Lutheran Church of the Missouri Synod founded its Walther League in 1893. The Presbyterian Church appointed a Special Committee on Young People in 1891 which observed that many of its churches had already adopted the Christian Endeavor constitution or had modified it in some way.[20]

Before leaving the Christian Endeavor movement, some observations should be made. Once again, this great youth movement started as the result of a perceived need in the lives of young people that was not being met by anything else. Secondly, it was basically a lay movement. Even though it was started by a minister, it began in his home, not the church building, and was set up with an emphasis upon lay leadership and involvement. Last of all, the church eventually copied and incorporated the ideals and program of the Christian Endeavor movement.

Youth for Christ Movement

The post-Depression Era and the universal high school along with theological liberalism, scientism, enlightenment philosophy, labor-saving devices, and materialism, all worked together to create the modern-day youth culture. This youth culture was enamored with the changes brought about by technology. Music, soda fountains, cars, cheerleaders, ball games, school dances, and drive-in movies all made the traditional church youth meeting seem pretty boring by comparison.

Out of this era came some visionary leaders: Percy Crawford, Jim Rayburn, and Lloyd Bryant to name just a few. Percy Crawford was a Philadelphia seminary student who was disillusioned by what the church had to offer and especially how they presented it. He was turned off by the strict rules of a Bible conference and did not appreciate the "bawling out" he received for skipping a meeting in order to spend time with a good-looking girl he had just met. Yet, while frustrated with the system, he still had a heart and passion to reach young people for Christ. His vision was to use current, popular music as a means of evangelism.

Percy Crawford was a Philadelphia seminary student who was disillusioned by what the church had to offer and especially how they presented it.

Percy and his wife Ruth were some of the first to bring the sound of swing into Christian music, especially in the new choruses that they would use at their camp. Percy Crawford hosted a radio program called the Young People's Church of the Air. He knew the drawing power of contemporary music and used it to attract many listeners. He also developed a camp and a conference center where young people were challenged with the gospel.

Lloyd Bryant began in New York City with youth centers. These youth centers would hold evangelistic meetings on weeknights. These rallies were focused on outstanding speakers and gospel musicians as well as unusual testimonies.[21] Soon the evangelistic rallies began to lose their effectiveness, and a new wave of youth ministry ideas hit the scene.

Jim Rayburn was a young engineering student who decided to change his vocation and answered the call to serve as a minister. His first assignment was to work with young Mexican-Americans. Upon the advice of a Dallas pastor, Rayburn did not try to duplicate the traditional youth group programs which required the young people to come to the church, but developed a new program which required the youth workers to go where the young people were and minister to them in their own environment.

Rayburn is best known for believing "it's a sin to bore a kid." Rayburn was willing to go to any extreme to build relationships with young people in order to share the gospel with them. He demanded that all of his workers "earn the right to be heard" by practicing the ministry of presence. Jim and his staff perfected the art of using contemporary music, humor, and telling the gospel in stories in order to reach teens. It was out of the Rayburn model that Young Life was born.

The purpose of the club meeting was to present the gospel in a nonthreatening way, in a nonthreatening setting, to nonchurched kids. The meetings were typically very low key with an emphasis on crowd breakers, singing, Bible quizzing, and competitions between clubs which were held at area rallies.

The methodological principles practiced by Young Life are worth noting as they have been copied and incorporated into most youth programs in the established church. The principles are:

1. Go where kids congregate.
2. Accept them as they are.
3. Learn how to walk in wisdom to those outside the faith.
4. See the dignity of each unique person.
5. Find a neutral setting for the club meetings.
6. Create a climate that is informal.
7. Speak naturally in terms familiar to the vocabulary of the kids.
8. Communicate your certainties rather than flaunt your doubts.
9. Consider it a sin to bore kids, especially with the gospel.
10. Build on their instinct for adventure.
11. Capitalize on the elements of good fun and music to establish an openness to the gospel.[22]

Even though the parachurch organizations such as Young Life and Youth for Christ were way ahead of the mainline church in methodological innovations, the church did not take long to copy their example. Faced with dwindling numbers in the Sunday school and traditional youth meeting, the church began hiring youth ministers who were copying many of the Young Life and Youth for Christ club ideas. Youth for Christ leaders, Wayne Rice and Mike Yaconelli, left the organization and founded Youth Specialties which supplied youth ministers with *Idea* books and day-long seminars on how to work effectively with teens.

Observations for Application

In looking back over the three great youth ministry movements, what universal observations can be made which would be readily applied to youth ministry today?

1. Youth ministry that is effective rises out of a great need that is not being met by any other institution or organization.
2. Effective youth ministry must acknowledge and utilize the insights, gifts, and contributions of nonprofessional youth workers.
3. Great youth ministry often begins outside the church, with the possibility of the church even opposing it at first, but later embracing it.
4. It must be highly relational and not just informational.
5. It must offer solid, conservative Bible instruction.
6. It should capitalize on young people's desire for adventure and purpose and involve them in student leadership, work projects, and mission endeavors.
7. It should utilize contemporary mediums for sharing the gospel message.

Let's go back to the on-line discussion from the introduction. The problem with the e-mail discussion was a lack of perspective. While each had a valid point to make and all could support their perspective from Scripture, they each missed the big picture. A historical perspective may have helped them find a strategic balance that would lead to a fruitful and long-lasting ministry.

When youth ministries are healthy, they have retained a balance among relational dynamics, theological thinking, and a bent for action—which in turn shapes a system of discipleship. A balanced system will include contacting unbelieving youth, attracting them to activities that result in a confrontation with the Christian gospel, and a training process by which the new believer is discipled. Whatever model you choose to develop, I hope that you will learn from history and not repeat the mistakes of the past, but build on the insights gained from studying the development of youth ministry in the evangelical church.

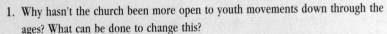

Time for Reflection 🕐

1. Why hasn't the church been more open to youth movements down through the ages? What can be done to change this?
2. If every significant youth movement down through history was started from an observed need in society, what are some needs today that demand attention? How could meeting these needs be the start of a new youth movement?
3. Historically the church has first opposed any new youth movement and then later adapted and embraced it. Why is this? What causes the church to feel threatened and to oppose most new innovations? Does it have to be this way?
4. What can be done to make the church more open to new youth movements and innovation?
5. What do you learn from a study of the history of youth ministry that you can use to help guide your development of a philosophy of ministry?

SUGGESTED READING LIST

Borthwick, Paul. *Feeding Your Forgotten Soul.* Grand Rapids: Zondervan, 1990.

Dean, Kenda Creasy, and Ron Foster. *The Godbearing Life: The Art of Soul Tending for Youth Ministry.* Nashville: Upper Room Books, 1998.

NOTES ON CHAPTER ONE

1. Herbert George Wells, *The Outline of History*, vol. 2 (New York: Garden City Publishing, 1930), ch. 40.

2. Abraham Lincoln, *Second Annual Message to Congress* (December 1, 1862).

3. Henry Kissinger, *The White House Years* (Boston: Little, Brown and Company, 1979), ch. 3.

4. Mark H. Senter III, "A Historical Framework for Doing Youth Ministry," in *Reaching a Generation for Christ*, ed. by Richard R. Dunn and Mark H. Senter III (Chicago: Moody Press, 1997), pp. 105-106.

5. Ibid., p. 106.

6. Merton Strommen, Karen E. Jones, and Dave Rahn, *Youth Ministry That Transforms* (Grand Rapids: Zondervan, 2001), p. 27.

7. F.G. Cressey, *The Church and Young Men* (Chicago: Fleming H. Revell, 1903), p. 85.

8. Senter, "Historical," pp. 107-108.

9. C.B. Eavey, *History of Christian Education* (Chicago: Moody Press, 1964), p. 224.

10. Ibid.

11. Ibid., p. 225.

12. Ibid., p. 226.

13. Ibid., p. 230.

14. Dean Borgman, "A History of American Youth Ministry," in *The Complete Book of Youth Ministry*, ed. by Warren S. Benson and Mark H. Senter III (Chicago: Moody Press, 1987), p. 64.

15. Ibid., p. 65.

16. Ibid.

17. Strommen, Jones & Rahn, *Youth Ministry*, p. 29.

18. F.E. Clark, *The Children and the Church* (Boston: Congregational Sunday School and Publishing Society, 1882); Amos R. Wells, *The Officer's Handbook* (Boston: United Society of Christian Endeavor, 1900), p. 140.

19. Strommen, Jones & Rahn, *Youth Ministry*, p. 29.

20. Charles Harvey McClung, *The Development of the Denominational Youth Program in the Presbyterian Church in the U.S.A., 1881–1954* (Ph.D. dissertation, University of Pittsburgh, 1957), p. 133.

21. Mark H. Senter III, *The Coming Revolution in Youth Ministry* (Wheaton, IL: Victor Books, 1992), p. 111.

22. Warren S. Benson, "A Theology of Youth Ministry," in *The Complete Book of Youth Ministry*, ed. by Warren S. Benson and Mark H. Senter III (Chicago: Moody Press, 1987), p. 19.

Understanding Youth Culture

Dr. Gary B. Zustiak

One Generation Passes to Another

It should come as no surprise that members of the youth culture have been misunderstood and criticized by their elders for centuries. Consider the following quote:

Youth have strong passions, and tend to gratify them indiscriminately. Of the bodily desires, it is the sexual by which they are most swayed and in which they show absence of self-control. They are changeable and fickle in their desires. . . . They are hot-tempered and quick-tempered, and apt to give way to their anger; bad temper often gets the better of them. . . . They love money . . . very little, not having yet learned what it means to be without it. . . . Their lives are regulated more by feelings than by reasoning. They are fonder of their friends, intimates, and companions than adults are, because they like spending their days in the company of others. . . . They overdo everything; they love too much and hate too much. They think they know everything, and are always quite sure about it. . . . They are fond of fun and therefore witty, wit being well-bred insolence.[4]

Who do you think is the author of that quote? I'm sure it could have been said by almost any irritated youth worker or by a frustrated parent who is trying to understand and work with today's teens. But this particular quote is from Aristotle who lived in the fourth century B.C.! It seems that every generation has been critical of the following generation. Let this be a warning to all who pass judgment on this generation of young people. So while much of what follows may seem alarming, it is important to keep it all in perspective. Plus, there is a growing body of evidence that indicates there is a positive turn in the characteristics and cohort personality of the Millennial Generation.

Generation	Birth Years
Lost	1883–1900
G.I.	1901–1924
Silent	1925–1942
Boom	1943–1960
Generation X	1961–1981
Millennial	1982–2002

Source: *Generations*

We have seen the last members of Generation X (those born from 1961–1981) graduate from high school and our youth programs. The Millennial Generation is upon us. How much has Generation X influenced the Millennial Generation? Are there any ways in which the Millennials are different from their predecessors?

The Millennial Generation is presently "coming of age," so data and demographics pertaining to them are just now being collected.[5] They are currently in the process of making their own unique contribution to the world, seeking their own path, and developing their own fads and styles. While much about the Millennial Generation is still to be revealed, there are some things that can be observed about them.

First of all their lives have been profoundly influenced by Generation X, who preceded them. One cannot understand the Millennial Generation without first understanding Generation X. Some of the characteristics of the Millennial Generation are simply a continuance of what was first started by Generation X. Other characteristics are a reaction against what was found in or experienced by Xers.

Similarities with Generation X

Like the generation that preceded them, the Millennial Generation is also a "visual" generation. While Generation X gave birth to MTV, the Millennial Generation takes it for granted. If the music video, concert, video game, or movie isn't filled with fast-paced action and technological wizardry, this new generation loses interest quickly. They are "visual junkies." They have grown accustomed to being bombarded by frequent images, and they are in need of continual "hits." Today's thrill has to outdo yesterday's or they are easily bored.

This desire for the visual has also affected their values. For the youth of today, "image is everything," as the commercial says. They are not so concerned about the substance of something as long as it looks good.

Closely related to their need for visual stimulation is their need for change. They are comfortable in a fast-paced world. "The remote control symbolizes their reality: change is constant, focus is fragmented."[6]

For the youth of today, "image is everything."

They live for the now. Decisions are made according to the moment. They do not think about future consequences, but simply what they "feel like doing." They decide on the basis of short-term pleasure rather than thinking about long-term consequences. "The art of reflection is lost on most Millennials. They have become used to rapid-fire media images, instant access to the Internet, fast food, and speed in almost every other area of their lives."[7]

They are jaded, having a "Been there-Done that" attitude; nothing shocks them. This is part of the reason for the rise and popularity of extreme sports. In everything they do they like to push the edge. What's thrilling today becomes blasé tomorrow. "Our fast-paced lives lead kids to seek ever-bigger thrills with ever-decreasing satisfaction."[8] Ronald Dahl describes the effects of this thirst for excitement:

> Parents seemed hard pressed to find new thrills for nonchalant kids. I saw this pattern in my family, in the sons and daughters of friends and neighbors and in many of my patients with behavioral and emotional problems. Surrounded by ever-greater stimulation, their young faces were looking disappointed and bored.[9]

They are a cyber-suckled community—they love e-mail, create their own web sites, and surf the net with abandon. They are very comfortable with technology. What took their teachers and parents a long time to master in the way of computers and the net is simply second nature to them.

One of the most serious issues surrounding Generation X, which has also been inherited by the Millennial Generation, is the loss of their moral base. Decisions for them are not made based upon what is right or wrong, but simply upon what works.

Decisions for them are not made based upon what is right or wrong, but simply upon what works. There is no universal set of ethical values or truths for all people for all time. For them everything is relative. It is simply a matter of the situation and personal opinion. Young people today do not believe there is such a thing as absolute truth. Rejecting the idea of absolute truth, they believe that everything in life is negotiable. A natural result of this loss of a moral base is an increase in crime and brutality.

The terrifying increase in the number of student shootings attests to the seriousness of this lack of a moral base.

Adults have always complained about their youth, but this is different. There have always been wild and rebellious kids who would go off the track and do something wrong. But they knew where the track was and what was wrong. Many of today's youth don't seem to know right from wrong. Children are robbing, maiming and killing on whims, and with no pity and no remorse.[10]

It is filtering down to the very young. In the May 11, 1998 issue of *USA Today* there was an article about a five-year-old boy who brought a loaded pistol to school with the intent of killing his teacher for disciplining him with a "time out." After becoming aware of the situation the teacher confiscated a .25-caliber semiautomatic pistol and called the police. The police learned the boy had also planned to kill several students. He was charged with carrying a weapon, but it was uncertain whether he would be prosecuted. The Juvenile Court Judge said, "A 5-year-old is not capable of forming criminal intent."

Before judging young people too harshly, think of who is really responsible for this lack or moral base. Millennials claim that the problem lies with the adult models to which they have been exposed.

In the words of 17-year-old Josh Lee in a letter to *Chicago Sun-Times*, "The biggest problem we have is the example adults show kids today." Millennials see national leaders and pop-culture celebrities as being vastly more spoiled and unethical than their own generation.[11]

Healthy Differences between Generation X and the Millennial Generation

One might conclude from the previous section that the upcoming generation of Millennials is as jaded, hopeless, and pessimistic as their predecessors, the Xers. But this is not true. In fact, most of the new data indicates that there are numerous differences that should cause us to hope. Millennials are showing a wide array of positive social habits which older adults thought would never again be seen in young people.

The first tough, cranky, pragmatic, independent Generation Xers are gonna start hitting 40 in the next couple of years, and rearing up behind them are the Millennials, the first batch of which are the high-school class of 2000. These kids are, as a group, pleasant, cheerful, helpful, ambitious, and community-oriented.[12]

Millennials are showing a wide array of positive social habits which older adults thought would never again be seen in young people.

They have a new commitment and focus on "teamwork, achievement, modesty and good conduct."[13]

The Millennials first arrived when "Baby on Board" signs appeared.[14] This signified a new "welcome" attitude towards children. The popular culture began stigmatizing hands-off parental styles and recasting babies as special.

Child abuse and child safety became hot topics. The government investigations into the safety of automobile airbags and young children are a great illustration of this concern for the welfare of children. I doubt whether this concern would have manifested itself twenty years earlier with Generation X. Today, politicians define adult issues (from tax cuts to deficits) in terms of their effects on children.

Another societal indicator of concern for the welfare of children is that cable TV and the Internet have cordoned off "child-friendly" havens. The invention of the V-chip allows parents to guard television watching. Ratings systems are enforced to protect children.

Internet programs to shield off detrimental areas from children are marketed and even encouraged.

There are some changes in education that are encouraging. Some educators are beginning to speak again of "standards." They are calling for kids to be taught *core values*, to do *good works*, and to meet *standards*, with *zero tolerance* for misbehavior. The new three R's are rules, respect, and responsibility. School uniforms are surging in popularity. With adults viewing children more positively and taking an active interest in their children's education, U.S. test scores are faring better in international comparisons.

Three-fourths of the nation's largest cities have enacted youth curfews. This has contributed to a significant decrease in the amount of juvenile crime.

State legislatures have changed child custody rules for the welfare of children and not for the convenience of parents as with the previous generation. Courts have become increasingly inclined to punish parents for child misbehavior. The rationale behind this move is to motivate parents to become more involved in the lives of their children and teens.

While Generation X was the most unwanted generation (birth control, abortion), the Millennials represent some of the newest and most popular areas in medicine; that is, infertility treatment and "preemie" care. From 1986 to 1988 the number of infertility related doctor visits quadrupled. In 1970, a two-pound baby had only a 5% chance of surviving; in 1990, 90% chance to survive—at an average cost of over $100,000 per child.

The stay-at-home parent is reviving as a popular choice among families able to afford it. Record numbers of men are stay-at-home dads. Promise-Keepers and other movements urge men to make commitments to be better fathers and husbands. Two of every three parents say they would take a pay cut in return for more family time. Thanks to new workplace trends such as job sharing, telecommuting, and career sequencing, parents are putting away the latchkeys and establishing a parental presence at home after school.

What Does All This Mean for the Church?

First of all, it emphasizes the need for family-based youth ministry. The church must offer programs, seminars, training, and mentoring on family issues. With a generation that was raised in the midst of tremendous dysfunction, healthy models are needed to direct them in godly principles concerning marriage and family. Youth programming should support the family, not be in competition with it.

The church needs to create a "user-friendly" environment. Many young people in today's culture do not have any church background whatsoever. They are totally unfamiliar with our traditions and rituals. In light of this, it is a good idea to explain everything you do so unchurched guests will have some idea of what is going on and be able to respond appropriately. Those in charge of leading the worship should eliminate "churchy" vocabulary and direct the congregation in easily understood, common terms.

Youth programming should support the family, not be in competition with it.

The nature of the worship service, youth meetings, and Sunday school will need to be revamped. The latest technology (such as computer-enhanced announcements and choruses) should be employed. The use of video, drama, and multimedia should be incorporated whenever possible. Not only does the worship service need to be of high quality, it needs to flow smoothly and quickly, without dragging on. The service will need to take on more of a "celebration" nature than a "liturgical" one. Today's youth culture is definitely more informal and casual in dress. They need to feel welcome and comfortable even if they are in blue jeans and a T-shirt.

The lack of absolutes in the worldview of Millennials touches every aspect of their lives, especially religion. For the typical Millennial no one religious denomination or religious belief is the only right one for all people at all times. It is more a matter of what works. Since they have rejected the concept of absolute truth, they have no objective standard by which to measure any one belief. Their judgment, then, is based upon feelings, experience, and practicality. If they have participated in a religious event sponsored by a local church and experienced some kind of emotionally moving encounter or received some practical help, they would say that proved the church and whatever beliefs it held are true because "they were helped by it." Pragmatism is the rule of the day. If it works, it must be right.

For the most part Millennials find it difficult to accept the exclusive truth claims of Christianity because of their postmodern belief that there are no absolutes. The relativism and tolerance of Millennials causes them to see all religions as having equal authority and validity and anyone who claims to have exclusive insight to spiritual truth or God is "intolerant."

Because of this pragmatism and lack of absolutes, if a Millennial was seeking a religious faith, he probably would not commit to any orthodox view of Christianity, but would develop a religious belief of his own. He might borrow something from Christianity, something from Islam, a little something from Native American religion with a dash of New Age philosophy and combine it together to form his own custom-made religion. As long as it works, that is all the proof that is needed to consider it valid.

In light of this, it is obvious that we must help young people realize that there are absolutes and that truth is not a matter of opinion or preference, especially with respect to God and His plan of salvation (John 14:6; Acts 4:12). But what is the best way to go about this?

You should follow the example of Paul in Acts 17:22-34 where Paul addressed the philosophers and influential leaders of Athens by first commending them for their interest in spiritual matters and then finding some common ground as a starting place. Affirm the Millennials' abandonment of the rationalist belief system as the *only* source of truth. For this allows for the existence of realities that science cannot measure—thus opening up the possibility for the supernatural and the spiritual. Understand you will probably not be successful in "arguing" them into the kingdom. Such an attempt would most likely be met with a cynical "whatever." Millennials will be open to what you have to share with them when you demonstrate authentic love and concern. They are searching for a community of acceptance and affirmation. When they experience this in the context of the church body, they will be open to accepting the beliefs of the Christians who have lived them out in their presence.

Maybe we should instead invite our young people to accept the challenge to become heroes and change the world.

Last of all, we need to challenge and involve Millennials in meaningful service. For too long we have relegated our young people to the arena of spectators. This is a grave mistake for it has been proven that Millennials respond enthusiastically when the church expects more of them and challenges them by offering genuine opportunities for service and involvement. Low expectations result in a weak commitment. I would quote Tony Campolo who said:

We must inspire young people to greatness. By helping young people see themselves as agents of God's revolution, commissioned to a vocation of ultimate importance, we can provide them with a sense of calling that generates unparalleled enthusiasm for life. . . . We in youth work have mistakenly assumed that the best way to relate to young people is to provide them with various forms of entertainment. . . . Maybe we should instead invite our young people to accept the challenge to become heroes and change the world.[15]

Time for Reflection

1. How do the characteristics and needs of Millennials affect your programming?
2. What is your ministry doing to promote family health and stability? Do you have a specific plan to hook up kids from broken or dysfunctional homes with a healthy model?
3. How willing is your church to involve youth in genuine ministry? What needs to take place in order to expand opportunities?

SUGGESTED READING LIST

Howe, Neil, and William Strauss. *Millennials Rising: The Next Great Generation.* New York: Vintage Books, 2000.

McAllister, Dawson. *Saving the Millennial Generation.* Nashville: Thomas Nelson, 1999.

Strauss, William, and Neil Howe. *The Fourth Turning: An American Prophecy.* New York: Broadway Books, 1997.

NOTES ON CHAPTER TWO

1. Neil Howe and William Strauss, *Millennials Rising: The Next Great Generation* (New York: Vintage Books, 2000), p. 7.

2. Dean Borgman, *When Kumbaya Is Not Enough* (Peabody, MA: Hendrickson, 1997), p. 1.

3. Howe and Strauss, *Millennials Rising*, p. 5.

4. Aristotle, *The Art of Rhetoric*, trans. by Richard McKeon, in *The Basic Works of Aristotle* (New York: Random House, 1941), pp. 1403-1405.

5. Much of this material is taken from "The Millennial Generation" chapter from my book: *The NeXt Generation: Understanding and Meeting the Needs of Generation X*, rev. ed. (Joplin, MO: College Press, 1999), pp. 225-237.

6. Wendy Murray Zoba, "The Class of '00," *Christianity Today* (February 3, 1997): 20.

7. Dawson McAllister, *Saving the Millennial Generation* (Nashville: Thomas Nelson, 1999), p. 63.

8. Ronald Dahl, "Burned Out and Bored." *Newsweek* (December 15, 1997): 18.

9. Ibid.

10. Rowland Nethaway, "Missing Core Values," Cox News Service, *Hamilton (OH) Journal-News*, 3 November 1993.

11. Howe and Strauss, *Millennials Rising*, p. 18.

12. MaryAnn Johanson, film critic, quoted in: Howe and Strauss, *Millennials Rising*, p. 4.

13. Howe and Strauss, *Millennials Rising*, p. 4.

14. William Strauss and Neil Howe, *The Fourth Turning: An American Prophecy* (New York: Broadway Books, 1997), p. 137.

15. Anthony Campolo, *Growing Up in America: A Sociology of Youth Ministry* (Grand Rapids: Zondervan, 1989), p. 53.

"We live in the Postmodern world where everything is possible and almost nothing is certain." —*Vaclav Havel,* *"Adrift in a Post-Modern World"*[1]

"A massive intellectual revolution is taking place that is perhaps as great as that which marked off the modern world from the Middle Ages." —*Diogenes Allen,* Christian Belief in a Postmodern World[2]

"The old paradigm taught that if you have the right teaching, you will experience God. The new paradigm says that if you experience God, you will have the right teaching." —*Leith Anderson,* A Church for the Twenty-First Century[3]

Chapter 3
Working with Youth in a Postmodern World

Dr. Gary B. Zustiak

The Times They Are A-Changing

Several years ago there was a GM commercial that had as its catch phrase, "This is not your father's Oldsmobile!" I could say something very similar about youth ministry. "This is not your father's youth group." Starting with Generation X and including the Millennials, the young people of today share a postmodern world-view. However, as Brad Cecil points out, this mind-set is not just found in the younger ages:

> I heard recently that postmodernity is just another fad consuming the conference circuit that will soon pass. I totally disagree . . . postmodernity is the most significant cultural shift we've seen in the last 500 years. It's not a generational issue exclusive to Gen-X or Millennials. In fact, it's fast becoming the adopted epistemology of all adults. Everyone in ministry—not just youth and young adult pastors—will have to wrestle with this phenomenon.[4]

This postmodern view affects their perception of everything from truth to leadership.

The postmodern mind views truth from a totally different perspective from that of the modern mind. In the modern worldview,

Postmodernists reject the idea that truth is rational and absolute. They believe that truth can be nonrational and even emotional and intuitive.

truth is rational—it is objective, absolute, and can be ascertained through human intellect and study. Postmodernists reject the idea that truth is rational and absolute. They believe that truth can be nonrational and even emotional and intuitive. For the postmodern man, truth is at best relative and possibly even nonexistent. Truth may just be a mental construct, something that man creates in his mind, but not something that "really exists" as a universal absolute. Since truth is no longer considered an absolute concept, it follows that there may be many truths. There is your truth, my truth, his truth, and her truth. No one truth is more valid than any other. It is even possible for these truths to be diametrically opposed to one another.

The premise of postmodernism is, then, to question all premises. All assumptions are out the window for a postmodern philosopher, who's on a quest to show that all is relative and nothing can be taken for granted. Skepticism and cynicism rule the day.[5]

This seismic shift in thinking brought about by postmodernism has touched virtually every aspect of daily living. This is best seen in a comparison/contrast with modernity.

Modern Value	Postmodern
Rational	Experiential
Scientific	Spiritual
Unanimity	Pluralistic
Exclusive	Relative
Egocentric	Altruistic
Individualistic	Communal
Functional	Creative
Industrial	Environmental
Local	Global
Compartmentalized	Holistic
Relevant	Authentic
Truth	Preference
Scientific discovery	Virtual reality
Human progress	Human misery[6]

Where the Rubber Meets the Road in a Postmodern World

Postmodernism has permeated everything from education, justice, arts, and architecture to medicine.[7] One of the ramifications of this is that the Millennials will continue to feel the effects of the "political correctness" movement in many facets of their lives. The correctness police will attempt to control what students and employees say in the schools and corporate world. This will make it hard for young people raised in this atmosphere to be comfortable with the Bible's judgments that some are saved and others are not. It may also make them less willing to share their faith with others lest they offend someone.

The concept of absolute truth is denied by postmodernism. This has had the devastating effect upon the Millennial Generation of taking away any foundation for a moral base. Decisions for them are not made based upon what is right or wrong, but simply upon what works. They do not believe that there is a universal set of ethical values or truths for all people for all time. For them everything is relative. It is simply a matter of the situation and personal opinion.

> What I want and what I choose is not only true (for me) but right (for me). That different people want and choose different things means that truth and morality are relative, but "I have a right" to my desires. Conversely, "no one has the right" to criticize my desires and my choices.[8]

Rejecting the idea of absolute truth, Millennials believe that everything in life is negotiable.

With the loss of absolutes, tolerance is the demand of the day. Especially in the media and universities, tolerance has been taken to the extreme. It is the increasingly common view that we should never criticize another culture or question an individual's moral decisions because all views deserve equal respect. To do so is to invite official censure or punishment.

The elimination of absolutes and the demands for tolerance has even changed the way that medicine is practiced. Your next visit to a doctor may drop you into the lap of occult healing techniques. Postmodern rhetoric has eased the introduction of alternative medicine into nursing and medical schools, where superstition is now taught as being no less credible than proven scientific principles. There is a declining emphasis in schools on helping students master the literature, history, values, and philosophy of Western culture, and a growing emphasis through multicultural education on students determining their own standards of literacy accepting, for example, nonstandard or "street English" as its own legitimate language, a.k.a. "ebonics." Histories that purposely leave out major events of the past in order to further the agendas of oppressed special-interest groups (examples: feminist or gay and lesbian histories) are becoming standard fare. History class has simply become a platform for radical political and social agitation. History is no longer the search for "what happened," but an opportunity for formerly excluded and silenced groups in society such as gays and lesbians to finally be heard. Postmodern analysis of history makes it possible.

Closely related to the demand for tolerance and the rewriting of history is the fresh attack on Christian missions, claiming that missionaries are unrelenting "destroyers of culture." As a result of this vilifying of Christianity, there has been a resurgence in the interest and practice of native religions and medicine.

In a postmodern world, people no longer accept the words of a written text, including the Bible, at face value or as authoritative in any way. Thanks to the current style in literary interpretation, postmodern "deconstruction," everything is open to the interpretation of the one reading who inserts his or her own experience and understanding into the text.

In a postmodern world, people no longer accept the words of a written text, including the Bible, at face value or as authoritative in any way.

The effect of postmodernism on society is that your neighbors think your Christian faith is "just fine for you"—just don't try to force it upon them. Unlike modernism, which treated religion as superstition, postmodernists are comfortable with any religion, as long as it makes no claims to universal truth or authority.

Postmodernists aren't against religion. They are only against religious teaching that holds to objective truth and the usefulness of reason. Religion based only on personal experience and "what's true for me" is perfectly compatible with the postmodern worldview.[9]

Religious beliefs are severely affected by the postmodern revolution. How does a Christian live and share his or her faith in a gullible, undiscerning world?

Sharing the Gospel with the Millennial Generation

Sharing the gospel with one who is raised in a postmodern world will require a special sensitivity to his or her own pilgrimage, good listening skills, and a great deal of patience. Here are some general principles to follow that will serve to guide your presentation of the claims of Christ to the Millennial Generation.[10]

- Listen respectfully and carefully to their position first and learn the reasons they hold the views they do.
- Be sure to clarify the particular issues that you are discussing.
- Try to use illustrations whenever possible.
- Arguments that get out of control are rarely helpful.
- Stick to the issue at hand.
- Never lie or "fake it."
- You do not have to be the one who is always on the defensive.
- Resist the desire to "win."
- Understand the futility of trying to share with a person who has a closed mind.

Implications for Ministry

Dean Borgman, professor of Youth Ministry at Gordon-Conwell Theological Seminary describes the Millennials as "the second great watershed for youth culture."[11] The repercussions of their values and experiences will cause churches to rethink how youth ministry is to be done. One of the key areas where change must take place is in the area of leadership, for the Millennials demand a different style of leader. Traditional or modern leadership has tended to be more positional and authoritative while postmodern leadership is relational and transparent. Millennials do not want to be told what to believe, but desire mentors who will come alongside and help them discover God for themselves.

Traditional Leadership	Postmodern Leadership
Positional	Earned
Perfect	Wounded Healer
Supervisory	Mentoring
Product Oriented	Process Oriented
Individual	Team
Dictatorial	Participatory
Aspiring	Inspiring
Controlling	Empowering

Youth ministry in a postmodern world requires a change in how it is programmed and facilitated. The planning of lessons and events must take into consideration the mind-set of postmodern youth. Compare the differences between a traditional youth ministry and a postmodern one.[12]

The main goal of the traditional youth ministry was to communicate knowledge about God with the belief that young people would understand the ramifications of that knowledge and apply it to their lives.

Traditional Youth Ministry	Postmodern Youth Ministry
Knowledge	Intimacy with God
Communicate content	Facilitate experience
Entertain and teach	Equip people to notice, name, and nurture God's hand at work
Youth minister as hub	Team of mentors

Postmodern youth ministry focuses on helping a young person experience God. It must never bypass knowledge, but strive to make biblical knowledge real through genuine and valid experiences. This is a wide-open opportunity to involve young people in service projects and short-term missions. I believe you will find most Millennials open and eager to take advantage of such an opportunity because they have been entertained to death. The novelty of hi-tech video games and extreme sports is gone. "They want to go beyond entertainment to genuine experience."[13]

In order to take advantage of this opportunity in the best way possible, the recruitment of adult volunteers who will be willing to act as mentors and guides will be indispensable to the success of the program. One person, the youth pastor, simply cannot find enough minutes in a day to spend quality time with all of the teens in the youth group. In fact, even if he did have the time, his personality and personal preferences would not allow him to relate to all of the different subgroups of young people. He cannot be a jock, skater, computer geek, artist, and intellectual all rolled into one. It makes much more sense to recruit adult volunteers who already have personal experience with a particular subgroup and support their efforts to disciple those teens they are drawn to.

The greatest apologetic for Christianity is not a well-reasoned argument but a wildly loving community. Our Lord did not say that they will know us by our truth—as important as this is—but by our love. At the very heart of the gospel is not a proposition but a person, Jesus Christ, who is made manifest in and through his called-out ones in their life together.[14]

Time for Reflection

1. What are some ways you have noticed the influence of postmodernism in your community?
2. Would you say that the youth program in your church more closely follows a traditional youth ministry or a postmodern one? Why?
3. What kinds of opportunities do you regularly make available for young people to have a genuine experience with God?
4. Would the teens in your group describe your leadership as more positional or relational?

SUGGESTED READING LIST

Jones, Tony. *Postmodern Youth Ministry*. Grand Rapids: Zondervan, 2001.

McAllister, Dawson, with Pat Springle. *Saving the Millennial Generation*. Nashville: Thomas Nelson, 1999.

McCallum, Dennis. *The Death of Truth*. Minneapolis: Bethany House, 1996.

NOTES ON CHAPTER THREE

1. Vaclav Havel, "Adrift in a Post-Modern Word," *Charlotte Observer* (24 July 1994), quoted in Jimmy Long, *Generating Hope* (Downers Grove, IL: InterVarsity, 1997), p 62.

2. Diogenes Allen, *Christian Belief in a Postmodern World* (Louisville, KY: John Knox Press, 1989), p. 2.

3. Leith Anderson, *A Church for the Twenty-First Century* (Minneapolis: Bethany House, 1992), p. 20.

4. Brad Cecil in Tony Jones, *Postmodern Youth Ministry* (Grand Rapids: Zondervan, 2001), p. 11.

5. Tony Jones, *Postmodern Youth Ministry* (Grand Rapids: Zondervan, 2001), p. 22.

6. Adapted from Jones, *Postmodern*, pp. 30-39.

7. For a complete and scholarly analysis of how widely postmodernism will affect society, see the excellent book by Dennis McCallum: *The Death of Truth* (Minneapolis: Bethany House, 1996).

8. Gene Edward Veith Jr, *Postmodern Times: A Christian Guide to Contemporary Thought and Culture* (Wheaton, IL: Crossway Books, 1994), p. 195.

9. McCallum, *Death*, p. 203.

10. The ideas for these principles come from an article by Gary DeLashmutt and Dennis McCallum entitled: "Apologetics and Worldviews Critique Communication Points" which I found on the Internet at: http://www.xenos.org/classes/papers/apocor.

11. Wendy Murray Zoba, "The Class of '00," *Christianity Today* (February 3, 1997): 18.

12. Dawson McAllister with Pat Springle, *Saving the Millennial Generation* (Nashville: Thomas Nelson, 1999), p. 104.

13. Ibid., p. 123.

14. Kevin Offner, "American Evangelicalism: Adrift with Amnesia," *Regeneration Quarterly* (Winter 1995): 9.

"The philosophy behind any ministry should be thoroughly based in biblical revelation." —*Doug Stevens*[1]

"The theology of the youth worker is ultimately more important than his or her strategy or methodology. . . . Your personal theology will have an effect on everything you do in youth work." —*Jay Kesler*[2]

"Youth ministry should also be built upon a more substantial foundation than the whims of contemporary culture. The motives that shape our philosophy of youth ministry must be built on the solid bedrock of biblical theology." —*Wesley Black*[3]

Chapter 4

The Need for a Theological Perspective of Youth Ministry

Dr. Gary B. Zustiak

A Well-Grounded Theology

Most youth ministers are more concerned about learning the latest "tricks of the trade" or thinking about their next "encounter" with the kids in the youth group rather than worrying about exegeting Scripture and working out a personal theology on youth ministry. But this is a grave mistake. As Donald Bloesch has stated: "content rather than methodology is to be the centerpiece in our paradigm of ministry."[4]

In our rapidly changing era of technology, it is easy to become enamored with all of the latest "bells and whistles." But fads and trends are short lived.

> Scripturally generated principles for youth ministry should be given primacy because they are always relevant. The Bible provides an unchanging yet dynamic base. Scripture retains its contemporaneity and transcultural character; it does not place us in a methodological restraint.[5]

A biblically informed theology of youth ministry will endure and remain stable through any number of societal changes.

We face today both a youth crisis and a cultural crisis. The natural tendency is to overreact to the trends and either uncritically jump on the bandwagon of the latest craze (like the WWJD, the Prayer of Jabez, The Left Behind series, etc.) or take a position against it by oversimplifying and separating ourselves from it as "dangerous."

> Jesus astounded the teachers and theologians of his time by defying the current categories in his lifestyle and teaching. His radical entrance into the subcultures of sinners and outcasts brought inside wisdom to outsiders. Today we seek a practical wisdom with the same radical boldness—for the sake of those oppressed or confused. We best help young people discover God's way by loving them, not by judging them. In so doing we bring back the central message of God to fractured cultures and individuals, whatever their situation.[6]

It's cheaper to buy books than it is to move! Those who are not learning and growing are beginning to die. I have tried to pound into the heads of youth ministry students for years that "it is cheaper to buy books than it is to move." By that I mean that it is easier to be a continual learner and have something new to say, than to teach the same old tired lessons over and over again from ministry to ministry. But the sad fact is that most people quit reading once they graduate. Oh, they may read *Sports Illustrated, Rolling Stone,* or *Group* looking for some novel idea, but they do not read anything of real substance. Learning demands humility and openness to challenge and change.

A theology of youth ministry does not derive its norms from popular consensus or from cravings for fulfillment or from easy "how tos." "Its quest for truth begins in the mystery of the triune God and in God's revelation through creation, Christ, and Scripture. It does attempt new insights into popular culture from God's perspective— expecting to find relevancy and fresh challenges."[7] Richard Dunn says in his book, *Reaching a Generation for Christ,* "Youth ministry becomes more experientially meaningful, spiritually vibrant and relationally effective when leaders commit themselves to the construction of a disciplined theological framework for doing ministry."[8]

The Practical Theologian

The youth minister may not be a systematic, biblical, or historical theologian, but if he is reflecting seriously upon Scripture and how it applies to the present struggles of the families and teens he works with, then he is already a practical or pastoral theologian. Many of the questions and issues that the youth minister is commonly faced with demand insight into Scripture and wisdom in making application to life. If Bob and Mary are living together, how can you minister to them while at the same time remaining true to biblical and church teaching? If Andy is caught up in a gang that demands that he participate in a drive-by-shooting, how do you approach him and his group regarding the basic worth of all human life? If Jennifer is addicted to television, obsessed with images of fashion magazines, or seems bordering on anorexia, what can you do to help her? These are all theological as well as sociological questions which demand a well-thought-out theology of youth ministry in order to properly address them.

Many times the idea of exploring theology can seem intimidating, overwhelming, and insurmountable to the youth minister. How does one delve into such issues as predestination and free-will, Calvinism and Arminianism, the attributes of God and soteriology and make it seem applicable to the typical teenager?

When the youth minister spends most of his time dealing with kids whose parents are getting divorced, whose friends are getting pregnant, and whose dreams are being dashed by economic realities, youth leaders may not think that spending the extra time sorting through deep theological issues is all that practical.

Traditionally youth ministry has been one of those areas where denominational and ministerial distinctives have been able to be set aside for common youth outreach and community functions. Youth ministry conferences and training seminars sponsored by organizations such as Youth Specialties and Group have long been ecumenical, bringing together people from all kinds of church backgrounds. Fearing that theological issues would split apart the friendly cooperation that exists among local youth ministers, most youth ministers shy away from dealing with the subject.

Discouraged by these issues most youth leaders may conclude that the best approach is to simply deal with any theological concerns as they surface. A preferred response is to pursue theological learning before, during, and after the emergence of critical questions that explicitly demand insight from God's word.

Why is it important for the youth minister to pursue theological studies? Because the purpose of theology is to better acquaint oneself with God. J.I. Packer said in *Knowing God*:

> What were we made for? To know God. What aim should we set ourselves in life? To know God. What is the "eternal life" that Jesus gives? Knowledge of God. "This is life eternal, that they might know thee, the only true God, and Jesus Christ, whom thou hast sent" (John 17:3). What is the best thing in life, bringing more joy, delight, and contentment, than anything else? Knowledge of God.[9]

A key reason why theological pursuits have been left out of the youth minister's priorities is because they have limited their concept of theological learning to the formal, systematic theological studies found in Bible colleges and seminaries. When asked to give a theological perspective on a particular topic of interest or to critique a particular event from a theological perspective, many youth ministers get that "deer in the headlights" look. In other words, they have not been taught to make theology practical—they lack the ability to make application to the issues that make up a teen's daily life.

They must learn that the whole of theology is not contained in formal statements, sophisticated systems of interpretation, and technical terms. The understanding and formation of a worldview is part of one's theological formation. This provides a bridge between what is revealed in Scripture and the world that we live in.

> Sound theology should lead to positive ministry. Our theology and ministry ought to be true to Scripture, faithful to our Christian traditions, and relevant in our current situations. No theology confined to an ivory tower can be relevant. You are seeking a theology that is true to God, faithful to your Christian community, and relevant to the times—especially to the young people you serve.[10]

While many shy away from a traditional study of systematic theology because they feel that it is too intellectual and "heady," it is just as dangerous to swing to the opposite pole and allow one's subjective, limited, experiential perspective to form one's understanding of God. What usually happens is that God becomes my idea of what I think God should be instead of the reality of who God is.

Systematic and practical theologians need each other. The ivory towers of academia need to be in touch with the streets, and the streets need the resources of scholarship and reflection. The cries of the world need to be heard; the lessons of historical analysis must be remembered. Such interdependence will not happen if academia does not appreciate the full meaning of contextualization.[11]

The bottom line for many youth ministers is "What difference would a study of theology make in my youth ministry?" If it only resulted in an increased accuracy in the teaching of the Bible, it would well be worth it (2 Tim. 2:15). Youth ministers should take seriously the warning from James about the strict judgment that will be placed upon all teachers (Jas. 3:1). Because accuracy in interpreting and communicating God's Word is an essential goal for all youth ministers, mastering the tools of biblical interpretation is crucial.

The impact of theological learning is not limited, however, to proper exegesis and teaching. The depth of one's personal relationship with God is directly affected by the authenticity of one's factual knowledge of Him. A youth minister's theological understanding pervades everything he is involved in. As Jay Kesler says,

> The theology of the youth worker is ultimately more important than his or her strategy or methodology. It is not that theology will replace the study of methods, but that methods must flow out of sound theology. Your personal theology will have an effect on everything you do in youth work. It will influence the type of message you bring, the response you expect, the progress of the youth among whom you minister, your method of counseling, your attitude towards others, and how you measure results. In short, all we do relates to what we actually believe.[12]

Everyone has a worldview which is formed and shaped by one's theology. Through this worldview all the events of life are interpreted. "Youth leaders cannot be *atheological* about life or ministry. Explicitly or implicitly, their internalized beliefs emerge."[13]

A theological framework for doing youth ministry consists of three components: theological foundations, personal implications, and ministry applications. Theological foundations are the raw materials necessary for developing a life and ministry that reflect a biblical knowledge and understanding of God. Personal implications address the impact basic theological foundations should have on the life of the youth minister. As students will learn a great deal about faith and God simply by observing the life of the youth minister, it is important for the youth minister to be aware of how his theology shapes his life. Ministry applications are general principles and practices that flow out of the youth minister's theology and life. "The youth minister should seek to make the 'why' of youth ministry explicit in the 'what' of youth ministry."[14] Borgman believes asking the questions can direct us in our study of theology.

> Every youthful quest for truth (whether at a youth group, the movies, or listening to rap) is a theological question. To ask why is human; theology directs us to the source of all meaning. Children ask the basic questions, adolescents ask the difficult and ultimate questions, and adults get tired of questions.[15]

There are several key subjects which make up the basics of one's theological study. Those subjects are: God, Scripture, humanity, sin, salvation, and the church. Each of these subjects naturally flows into and influences one's belief about the others. Once a youth minister has researched what he believes about each subject and how they relate to one another, he is ready to form his worldview which will influence how he lives life and carries out ministry.

A well-thought-out theology will answer such important questions as: What is the nature of humankind? What is our purpose in living? What is the nature of reality? What is the origin of the universe and man? What is the nature of knowledge, and how does one come to know (epistemology)? What is the ultimate destiny of man and the world?

Loving kids is not your first responsibility as a youth worker. Loving God must come first.

Ministry must first start with God. "Loving kids is not your first responsibility as a youth worker. Loving God must come first."[16] Far too many youth ministers have shipwrecked their lives and ministries because they reversed that order. A proper view of God reminds us that our relationship with Him is our highest calling.

The regular and systematic study of the Scriptures must be our main source for understanding God and His creation. While it is true we can gain partial insight about God through the study of His creation, we would be left with only subjective answers to the question of "What is God like?" if it weren't for His revealed word.

"Having devotions is one thing; building devotion is another. Examining a text to interpret its meaning is one task; allowing that text to examine one's heart is another."[17]

Youth ministers often fall victim to the trap of reading God's word only with the intention of preparing a lesson or sermon. They must daily be open to being instructed and convicted by it first.

Theology is a work of translation: the wisdom of God must be translated into a given culture in a particular time and place. "Inspiration" describes the initial work of translating the word of God into human languages, those of Hebrew, Aramean, and Greek cultures. But further translations—into tribal and techno- logical societies—are needed. The Word must be encountered, in flesh and in word, in each new culture. A living witness, a written Word, and a contextualized theology are the results.[18]

Youth Minister Theologian Checklist

The following list is provided to help you in your self-analysis of your theological perspective. It is one thing to think that you apply theological practices and insight to your youth ministry, but it is another to prove it. My intention is not to be critical, but to provide a realistic assessment tool.

	Yes	No	Sometimes
I continue to read theological books even after graduation.			
I have a regular time of reading the Bible for devotional insight and not just for lesson preparation.			
I am involved in continuing education through graduate school programs, seminars, and/or conventions.			
I have a sound library of biblical and theological books and I continue to add to my collection on a regular basis.			
I meet regularly with a group of peers to discuss theological issues and how they apply to youth ministry.			
I subscribe to several theological magazines or journals, e.g., *Christianity Today* or *Discipleship*, and read them.			
I evaluate a new program idea first in terms of "Is this biblical?" rather than "Will this work?"			
I practice several spiritual disciplines such as fasting, prayer, solitude, silence, meditation, etc. on a regular basis.			
When asked, I can easily define my theological beliefs and the practical and ministerial implications of them.			

If you are serious about having a theologically sound ministry, then you must think through how your understanding of key theological issues affects your personal choices and priorities in youth ministry programming. Some key theological tenets or beliefs that must be thought through for ministry would include:

- A view of God
- A view of Christ
- A view of man
- A view of eschatology

- A view of Scripture
- A view of the Holy Spirit
- A view of soteriology

Time for Reflection

1. What makes a youth minister's theology so important?
2. Why do many youth ministers neglect or downplay the importance of theology in their youth ministries?
3. How does one's theology directly affect all youth ministry programming?
4. What are some creative ways you can find more time to read good books which will stimulate your thinking about theological issues and how they pertain to youth ministry?
5. What was the essence of Jesus' theology of ministry? How does it compare to what you are currently practicing in ministry?

SUGGESTED READING LIST

Borgman, Dean. *When Kumbaya Is Not Enough: A Practical Theology for Youth Ministry*. Peabody, MA: Hendrickson, 1997.

Dean, Kenda Creasy, Chap Clark, and Dave Rahn. *Starting Right: Thinking Theologically about Youth Ministry*. Grand Rapids: Zondervan, 2001.

NOTES ON CHAPTER FOUR

1. Doug Stevens, *Called to Care* (Grand Rapids: Zondervan, 1985), p. 19.

2. Jay Kesler, "Determining Your Theology of Youth Ministry," in *The Youth Leader's Sourcebook,* ed. by Gary Dausey (Grand Rapids: Zondervan, 1983), p. 23.

3. Wesley Black, *An Introduction to Youth Ministry* (Nashville: Broadman Press, 1991), p. 13.

4. Warren S. Benson, "A Theology of Youth Ministry," in *The Complete Book of Youth Ministry,* ed. by Warren S. Benson and Mark H. Senter III (Chicago: Moody Press, 1987), p. 17.

5. Ibid.

6. Dean Borgman, *When Kumbaya Is Not Enough* (Peabody, MA: Hendrickson, 1997), p. x.

7. Ibid., p. xi.

8. Richard R. Dunn, "A Theological Framework for Doing Youth Ministry," in *Reaching a Generation for Christ,* ed. by Richard R. Dunn and Mark H. Senter III (Chicago: Moody Press, 1997), p. 65.

9. Quoted by Jim Wilhoit in *Christian Endeavor and the Search for Meaning,* 2nd ed. (Grand Rapids: Baker, 1991), p. 37.

10. Borgman, *Kumbaya,* p. xxi.

11. Ibid., p. 20.

12. Benson, "Theology," p. 21.

13. Dunn, "Framework," p. 50.

14. Ibid., p. 51.

15. Borgman, *Kumbaya,* p. 12.

16. Dunn, "Framework," p. 53.

17. Ibid., p. 56.

18. Borgman, *Kumbaya,* p. 19.

Chapter 5

Developing a Philosophy of Youth Ministry

Dr. Gary B. Zustiak

The Sad Neglect

Duffy Robbins presented a great illustration concerning the problems associated with trying to minister to youth without first developing a carefully thought out philosophy of ministry. Several years ago Rhode Island's *Provident Journal* ran a story that exposed how poorly the state had used the taxpayer's money. The findings of the article were almost amusing (except to Massachusetts taxpayers). Among the case studies that were exposed, the following are some of the highlights:

- The Boston State College has a thirteen-story tower, which is one of the largest buildings ever built by the Commonwealth. Its top five floors, intended as a library, have been shut off since 1976 because the designer failed to include any centralized security checkpoints. Accordingly, the five floors had been heated, air-conditioned, and unused for four years.
- The same college's auditorium was so constructed that one cannot see the stage from the balcony.
- The Haverhill, Massachusetts, parking deck was so poorly designed it can only be demolished and rebuilt. Apparently some ramps in this magnificent structure weren't large enough to admit cars.

- The multimillion-dollar University of Massachusetts power plant was built too far from the buildings it was designed to serve. It has never been used.[4]

While these blunders may be amusing to the reader, they represent a huge waste of taxpayers' money. Ironically, they may also be typical of what goes on in many youth ministries across the country. Considerable amounts of money, time, and energy are given to programs and structures so that we can say, "This is the largest ever built." Yet, half the time the finished product isn't even used, or if it is, it really doesn't accomplish what it was designed to do. It is as if we're building power plants that don't deliver power.

The standard practice in youth ministry seems to be for the youth minister to piece together a program and then, later, decide why he is doing what he is doing.

The standard practice in youth ministry seems to be for the youth minister to piece together a program and then, later, decide why he is doing what he is doing. If he is fortunate, he has done some things right by accident. But this approach seems backward. If one is to take youth ministry seriously, then one is obliged to articulate and apply a philosophy of youth ministry that conscientiously avoids just doing a program for program's sake. "To build the kind of youth ministry program that accomplishes the purpose for which it was built, serious consideration needs to be given to the blueprint."[5]

In an on-line article, Graeme Codrington put it this way: "Christian youth ministry in a local church must be intentional, incarnational, relational, integrated, holistic, pastoral ministry, based firmly on Scripture, and for the purpose of equipping young people for worship, discipleship, service, outreach and fellowship."[6]

The Importance of a Philosophy of Youth Ministry

Most youth ministers are very pragmatic in their approach to youth ministry. They are more concerned with "what works" in programming than with the "whys" of youth ministry. With trying to schedule all the Bible studies, camps, retreats, social activities, service projects, choir tours, etc., most youth ministers don't see the need to think through the philosophical and theological aspects of youth ministry.

Youth ministers may even reject the notion of developing a philosophy of youth ministry. The attitude is, "I don't have a youth ministry philosophy and I don't need one." But this is a grave error. Everyone in youth ministry has a philosophy of youth ministry. It just may not be articulated in so many words.

The theology of the youth worker is ultimately more important than his or her strategy or methodology.

Someone has said, "What you believe is the most important thing about you." In fact, the apostle James has reminded us that our conduct eventually will verify or deny what we say we believe. For this reason, the theology of the youth worker is ultimately more important than his or her strategy or methodology. Of course, the study of theology does not eliminate the need for the study of methods, but methods must flow from a sound theology.

Your personal theology will have an effect on everything you do in youth work. It will influence the type of message you bring, the response you expect, the progress of the youth among whom you minister, your method of counseling, your attitude toward others, and how you measure results. In short, all we do relates to what we actually believe.[7]

Why is it important to develop a philosophy of youth ministry? Because it will enable the youth minister to make better, more informed choices, and help define what he is doing. The youth minister will be able to set outcomes and goals that are driven by values and truly important things, rather than by the need to meet timetables.

A philosophy of youth ministry is a personal "North Star," giving guidance to program implementation and development and help for evaluation. Ultimately, a philosophy of youth ministry will answer the dual questions: What is worth dying for? and What is, therefore, worth teaching and leading? A philosophy of youth ministry goes for the passion and values that drive a youth ministry.[8]

Graeme Codrington also expresses the necessity of a well-developed philosophy:

Youth ministry must be planned. What happens in a youth ministry must be the result of deliberate strategy, based on a vision for a desired future amongst young people. . . . Youth ministry will never be effective if it just happens haphazardly, with no forethought or strategy. This is not to say that every aspect of youth work is meticulously programmed, but rather that each aspect of the ministry is carefully considered within the whole, and that there are genuine goals attached to each part of youth work.[9]

What Is the Basis of a Philosophy of Youth Ministry?

Youth ministry should be based upon a more substantial foundation than the latest fad or pragmatic discovery. The motives that shape our philosophy of youth ministry must come from a thorough study of the Scriptures, sensitivity to the leading of the Holy Spirit, and the needs of young people. There are several critical elements that should be integrated into a philosophy of youth ministry. Those elements are:

- A view of God
    - A view of Scripture
        - A view of man
- A view of learning
    - A view of ministry
        - A rationale for youth ministry
- Purposes and outcomes of youth ministry
    - Leadership roles
        - Program elements[10]

Doug Stevens, in *Called to Care*, suggests the following criteria for an adequate philosophy of ministry:

- It must be *biblical*. It must be explicitly grounded in Scripture and theologically sound. This implies that we must do more than select a few isolated verses as favorite proof-texts; we must be deeply interested in assembling a truly biblical theology, one that is faithful to the whole of the Bible and cognizant of its central themes.
- It must be *relevant*. Historical awareness and theoretical abstraction are not enough. We must find ways of meeting young people in their own environment and responding to them as they are. Our philosophy must be realistic as well as idealistic and vitally related to the personality and culture of our time and place. Youth ministry must be contextualized.
- It must be *comprehensive*. It must provide sufficient discussion of all the crucial issues and major elements of youth work. All of the tools of the trade should be considered.

- It must be *practical.* It must translate into a form that accomplishes what it is supposed to do. We need a philosophy that works when faced with life's real limitations and pressing demands.[11]

Ultimately the goal of youth ministry is to bring about transformation in the life of young people so that their lives are patterned after the life of Christ. In order to accomplish this desire, the youth ministry must have as its ultimate goal youth who:

Youth ministry should be based upon a more substantial foundation than the latest fad or pragmatic discovery.

1. Own their own faith in Christ. —
2. Are being led by the Spirit of God into his truth and holiness. —
3. Continue to feed their spiritual needs, growing more Christlike. ⌐
4. Practice Christian morality and ethics in the power of the Holy Spirit. —
5. Seek, find, and follow the will of God for their lives. —
6. Bring Christian values and motivation to all of their life experiences. –
7. Function interdependently with family, peers, church, and society at large. ⌐
8. Develop the means to feed their own cognitive capacities, social relationships, affective needs, and moral judgments. —
9. Develop a proper view of and care for their bodies as the temples of God. —
10. Determine effective and balanced relationships to authorities in their lives. —
11. Are developing their own Christian view of life and the world. ⌐
12. Begin to narrow their understanding of what they are called to in vocation. ⌐
13. Develop a biblical view of sex and their roles in society.[12]

Dettoni also states that the church body must encompass the youth ministry as a whole. He believes the church must see youth and the youth ministry as a necessity.

Ministry with youth belongs to the whole church. A church without a youth ministry is a church without a future. Tragically, youth ministry is too often seen as an "add-on" ministry that could be dropped if the circumstances demanded it. Rather, youth ministry is an integral part of the total church's ministry. Youth ministry that has a church focus helps adolescents recognize that they are part of a larger body of believers composed of others both younger and older than they. Youth are accepted as they are since Jesus has called them into his body and into the fellowship of believers.[13]

In light of the fact that the church needs a youth ministry, it should also be emphasized that a church's youth ministry should not be treated as a separate entity. It must be fully integrated into the rest of the church. The "adult" church must be vitally aware of the youth ministry, and how it will affect the rest of the church. Youth ministry should never be seen as an entity unto itself, but as an integral part of the whole.

Youth ministry should never be sold short, nor should it sell itself short. It is not an entertainment center, nor is it a baby-sitting service. It is to be a spiritual ministry, involving the modeling and teaching of spiritual disciplines, by spiritually gifted and spiritually mature people. This is not to say that it will not be fun, but only that the ultimate purpose is spirituality, not entertainment.

The ultimate goal of youth ministry is not to do things *for* young people, but rather to *equip* them to effectively minister for Christ (Eph. 4:11-16). Young people need to be encouraged to get involved and to minister as their gifts, personality, and spirituality allow. Effort must be made within the ministries of the church to not merely allow but also to encourage this to happen.

All youth workers, regardless of age and experience, can become more effective by rethinking their philosophy of youth ministry. Sometime during my ministry, I came across the following questions that will help you develop or fine-tune your own philosophy of youth ministry.

1. What is your philosophy of youth ministry? Why do you think youth ministry is important? What should the general goals be of youth ministry? What should the role of the youth leader be in the youth program? How does youth ministry relate to the larger ministry of the whole church?

2. What are the key elements of a youth program? How do they relate to each other?

3. Describe the major components of your view of youth ministry.
4. What is effective teaching? How do you define teaching? How does the Holy Spirit enter into your concept of teaching and learning?
5. If you don't learn and grow spiritually, whose fault is it? What can you do about helping youth to learn?
6. Describe your leadership style. Are you casual, intense, a director, model, coach, or something else?
7. How do you go about planning?
8. Describe some of your best teaching experiences, experiences in which you felt you did very well as a teacher. What made it a good experience for you and the learners?
9. What do you feel are the important theological issues of youth and how would you address them?
10. Of what does good youth programming consist? What does a good youth ministry look like? Describe attitudes, activities, and behaviors.
11. What are the relationships between organization, administration, programming, and leadership in youth ministry?
12. What will you look for to determine if youth ministry is successful?

Creating a Purpose Statement

Once the youth minister acknowledges the importance of developing a philosophy of ministry, the essence of it should be captured and stated in a brief mission/purpose statement. The mission/purpose statement not only reflects the purpose of ministry in and through the local church, but it also reflects the process of ministry that is implemented. "A clear purpose statement will help you: make sense of your programs, utilize your volunteers more effectively, and provide direction for your students' spiritual maturity."[14]

Once you have communicated your purpose for doing ministry, then you won't have to ask the "why" question again. The new question will be "how." A good, clear purpose statement will answer the "why" question. Doug Fields, author and youth minister, has as his youth ministry's purpose statement: "Our youth ministry exists to reach nonbelieving students, to connect them with other Christians, to help them grow in their faith, and to challenge the growing to discover their ministry and honor God with their life."[15]

Practical Application

I challenge you to study the following Scriptures and then develop a philosophy of youth ministry that captures the essence and essential teaching of the following passages. Your philosophy of youth ministry should clearly state the goals of your ministry and how you aim to accomplish them. Understand that these Scriptures are by no means exhaustive, but merely represent a starting place. Please feel free to add some of your own selections that you feel to be crucial to a biblical, well-rounded philosophy of ministry. Deut. 6:5-8; Micah 6:8; Luke 2:52; Acts 2:42; Rom. 12:4-8; Eph. 4:11-16; Phil. 3:7-13; 2 Tim. 2:1-2; 3:14-17; 4:2-5.

The following is an example of one philosophy of youth ministry based on the preceding Scriptures.

A PHILOSOPHY OF YOUTH MINISTRY

Purpose statement: The purpose of my youth ministry is to support parents in the spiritual, emotional, intellectual, and social development of their children so that the youth in my care will come to love God wholeheartedly and desire to grow spiritually while serving God and seeking to evangelize the lost.

I. The Goal of Youth Ministry

The ultimate goal of youth ministry is to prepare young people so that in the proper time they will reach "unity in the faith and in the knowledge of the Son of God and become mature, attaining to the whole measure of the fullness of Christ" (Eph. 4:12-13). In order to accomplish this goal, the youth minister looks for reliable leaders from among both adults and youth in whom he can entrust the message and purpose of the gospel so that ultimately they "will also be qualified to teach others" (2 Tim. 2:2).

II. Family-Based Youth Ministry

The youth minister realizes that the most important people in the accomplishing of this goal are the parents of the young people. It is their God-given responsibility and privilege to pass on a love for God and obedience to His word (Deut. 6:1-25). Recognizing the importance of the family, the purpose of the youth ministry is to support and aid parents in understanding the needs and concerns of youth and helping them to become strong links in the chain of faith as they pass on their love for God to their children.

III. A Balanced Youth Ministry

An effective youth ministry must be a balanced youth ministry. It seeks to meet the varied needs of youth by ministering to their physical, spiritual, social, intellectual, and emotional needs (Luke 2:52). In striving to accomplish a balanced ministry, programs will be offered in the areas of study, socials, service, fine arts, and athletics (Acts 2:42). Care will be given so that the overall program is balanced in the level of intensity and commitment that each program requires from the student. The goal is to take students where they are and lead them to maturity in Christ. The program starts with some low-key evangelistic programs to interest and win the non-Christians. This is designed to mature them through the growth track so that eventually they arrive at the ministry track which challenges them with in-depth Bible studies and service programs requiring intense commitment designed to stretch students spiritually.

IV. A People-Oriented Youth Ministry

Because young people come with a multitude of different needs and personalities, it is imperative that the youth program involve as many different volunteers as possible. This provides a variety of leadership models for the young people to choose from. A creative pool of resources is formed which provides a broad look at the possibilities for programming and ministry. This allows people to use their strengths and gifts in positive ways that add quality programs to the youth ministry and enable them to serve God by being good stewards of the gifts that He has provided (Rom. 12:4-8; Eph. 4:11-13). I will require my volunteers to be people of integrity because young people need flesh and blood heroes whom they can imitate. The volunteer's job is to strive to demonstrate the mind of Christ and imitate the example of Jesus in all aspects of their lives—religiously, vocationally, within the church and the community.

V. The Word of God in Youth Ministry

Because the Word of God is the powerful tool that brings about conviction and faith in the lives of people (Heb. 4:12-13; Rom. 10:17; Ps. 119:9-11), an emphasis will be placed on providing a variety of classes and studies where young people will be exposed to the message of the gospel in creative and sound ways and taught proper principles of biblical interpretation so that they can study and learn on their own.

VI. The Spiritual Life of the Youth Minister

In order to properly oversee and contribute to an effective youth ministry program, the youth minister must take care and nurture his own spiritual life. "To attempt to lead a person spiritually while at the same time neglecting one's own spiritual life would be a travesty. Any leader who fails to take nourishment daily from the Word of God will most certainly degenerate into a voice from a vacuum."[16] Personal purity must always be the standard and the goal for the youth minister. You cannot exert a godly influence on others if you yourself are not godly.

VII. The Overall Church Program and Youth Ministry

The youth ministry program must supplement and compliment the overall goals of the church at large. Youth ministry must not be done in isolation but in connection with the larger body of Christ. The overall goals of the church should not be man-made goals, but the goals of God for His church. These are revealed through a study of God's Word.

VIII. A Commitment to Youth Ministry

A proper philosophy of youth ministry has at its heart the belief that youth ministry is exactly that—a ministry. It is not glorified baby-sitting, recreational programming, or fun and games. It is a ministry that concerns itself with the spiritual welfare and development of the young people who have been entrusted to the oversight of the youth minister (Ezek. 34:1-16). As such, the youth minister must not see youth ministry merely as a "stepping stone" to greater and more important ministries. He should be committed to persevere in the task to which he has been called as long as he feels it is God's will for him. The youth minister must realize effective youth ministry cannot be accomplished if you only spend one hour a week with teens on Sunday morning. It will cost an investment of time. The motivation for being in youth ministry must be the love of God from a pure heart. You must love kids and serve them, not expect them to serve you. While working with kids can sometimes be frustrating, the youth minister must always remember, "failure is an event—not a person."[17]

Time for Reflection

1. Why is it that most youth ministers cannot clearly articulate their philosophy of youth ministry? What can be done to remedy the situation?
2. How does having a clear philosophy of ministry help in programming?
3. Why is it important that the youth minister's philosophy of ministry coincide with the philosophy of ministry for the church at large?
4. What are the essential elements that should go into the development of a philosophy of youth ministry?

SUGGESTED READING LIST

Dettoni, John M. *Introduction to Youth Ministry.* Grand Rapids: Zondervan, 1993.

Fields, Doug. *Purpose Driven Youth Ministry.* Grand Rapids: Zondervan, 1998.

Stevens, Doug. *Called to Care: Youth Ministry for the Church.* Grand Rapids: Zondervan, 1985.

Notes on Chapter Five

1. Doug Fields, *Purpose Driven Youth Ministry* (Grand Rapids: Zondervan, 1998), p. 44.

2. John M. Dettoni, *Introduction to Youth Ministry* (Grand Rapids: Zondervan, 1993), p. 18.

3. Graeme Codrington, (1998), On-line, "A Spiritual Growth Model of Local Church Ministry," **http://www.youth.co.za/genxthesis/ch4.htm.**

4. Duffy Robbins, "More Than a Meeting: Programming as Discipleship," *Youthworker* (Summer 1992).

5. Robbins, "More."

6. Codrington, "Spiritual Growth."

7. Jay Kesler, "Determining Your Theology of Youth Ministry," in *The Youth Leader's Sourcebook.*, ed. by Gary Dausey (Grand Rapids: Zondervan, 1983), p. 23.

8. Dettoni, *Introduction,* p. 18.

9. Codrington, "Spiritual Growth."

10. See Dettoni, *Introduction,* pp. 19-21.

11. Doug Stevens, *Called to Care: Youth Ministry for the Church* (Grand Rapids: Zondervan, 1985), p. 14.

12. Dettoni, *Introduction,* p. 23.

13. Ibid., p. 27.

14. Fields, *Purpose Driven,* p. 56.

15. Ibid., p. 57.

16. Dewey Bertolini, *Back to the Heart of Youth Work* (Wheaton, IL: Victor Books, 1989), p. 19.

17. Miriam Neff, *Helping Teens in Crisis* (Wheaton, IL: Tyndale House, 1993), p. 133.

> "Every resume is a one-of-a-kind communication. It should be appropriate to your situation and do exactly what you want it to do."
> —*Nicholas Lore,* The Pathfinder[1]

> "Resumes tell an employer a great deal about you. Where you have been, where you are and where you are headed. However, the story must be told quickly and clearly. You only have a few moments to convince the employer that your resume deserves further attention before it's trashed."
> —*Resume Writing*[2]

Chapter 6
Getting Hired— Landing That First Big Opportunity

Dr. Gary B. Zustiak

First Impressions

Once you have responded to God's call and have received the proper training and education, you are ready to begin serving. But even if you have received an outstanding education and preparation for ministry, you may have a difficult time securing the best position if you don't know how to write a proper resume and prepare for an interview.

A resume is your chance to make a first impression. You never get a second chance to make a first impression. Therefore, you must give attention to every aspect of it—content, form, and appearance. A sloppy looking resume or one filled with typos communicates a negative message about you and your ability to serve.

When preparing a resume, you want to communicate much more than your previous work experience. You are a person with personal qualities, gifts, and interests that suit you to your calling. Your past accomplishments and involvement indicate what kind of person you are. Choose a format that stresses your strengths. If you have no idea how to prepare a resume, it would be worth your while to check out some books from your local library which will assist you in your preparation.

A resume is your chance to make a first impression. You never get a second chance to make a second chance to make a first impression.

Preparing a Resume

In the old days, it was worth the investment to take your resume to a professional typesetter and have it printed, but in the day of the computer and laser printer there is no need. Do, however, spend the extra money to purchase some quality resume paper. This is made from a heavier bond than your typical typing paper. Avoid extreme colors such as fluorescent, dark red, purple, blue, or green. These might make your resume stand out, but may also communicate that you need to be the center of attention. It is better to stick with beige, off-white, and gray.

The Heading

Your resume should have a heading that is centered on the top of the page. Included in the heading should be:
- Your full name
- Current address
- E-mail address
- Phone numbers (work, home, and mobile)

Objective

Your objective is a brief statement of the general position you are seeking. Your objective should be stated in terms likely to be identical with the church's objective. Focus on emphasizing your strongest abilities as proven by the record of your experience or training to date. Stress abilities you have already demonstrated you can do that would be especially beneficial to the church, especially if they do not have it or if they need a particular skill you possess.

Education and Training

Your education should be first under your objective if it is your *most* qualifying experience to date. Show your *highest level* of educational achievement first. Be sure to show the dates of graduation. List specific courses taken that would uniquely qualify you for this position. If you have sufficient room, you may give a brief description of the course. List any special honors or outstanding scholastic achievements you received as a part of your educational experience. You may want to include your involvement in any clubs, student organizations, or extracurricular activities.

Personal Data

While this is not a requirement in the business world because it may be misconstrued and used as a basis for discrimination, it is still the current practice in the church. People on a search committee want to know your age (show it in date-of-birth style), marital status (name of your spouse), family data (names, number, and ages of your children), hobbies, and personal interests. This may be placed in the heading or at the end of the resume.

Experience

Once you have stated your objective, your next aim in writing your resume should be to *prove*, then and there, your strong qualifications to turn in an outstanding performance in the position you have applied for. In doing this, show your best experience first. Include the *scope* and *effect* of your previous work. Include specific *examples* of successful performance and the results produced whenever possible.

Mention *accomplishments, results* produced, and things that *changed* for the better because of your leadership and ability. Include *skills* that you possess that would be beneficial to the church, e.g., computers, graphic design, musical ability, mechanical, and all areas of expertise.

List *all* of your work experience (both ministry and nonministry related), full-time and part-time, military history, and volunteer work in related field. List your experience that is the most closely related to the position that you are applying for first, e.g., previous full-time position, weekend youth ministry, summer internships, camp team, etc. Next list work experience that you have done that is not related directly to the job being applied for. List the jobs in chronological order from the most recent to the oldest.

Finishing Touches

Be sure to include your references at the end of the resume. (It is considered proper etiquette to ask a potential reference for permission to use his/her name *before* placing it on a resume!) You should include at least three, but no more than four references. With each reference be sure to include their correct mailing address, phone number, e-mail, and a brief description of who they are (employer, elder, professor, etc.). Try to include a variety of references. Hint: Do not write, "References available upon request." This gives the impression that you have something to hide, and to a member of a search committee it also means more valuable time must be spent searching out the references. More than likely they will pass your resume by in favor of one with all the data supplied.

The Final Product

When your resume is completed it should look neat and professional. Be sure to keep your sections brief and orderly. Single space your data and double space between sections. Use marginal descriptions, underlining, capitalization and centered headlines to stress information on your accomplishments that you most want interview committees to see. The length of your resume should be limited to 1-2 pages. A good quality photograph is also helpful.

Remember that a resume is designed to get you an interview, and the interview is designed to get you the job.

Remember that a resume is designed to get you an interview, and the interview is designed to get you the job. A poor resume can disqualify you for a position that you may be qualified to handle. Be sure to proofread your final copy before printing and have someone other than yourself check it for errors.

Writing a Cover Letter

A cover letter is your personal introduction to the search committee of your desire to apply for the current position that is open. All of the information regarding your qualifications, skills, and work history can be found in your resume. The cover letter should simply sum up all that you have to offer and act as an introduction for your resume. You should note that you have supplied a resume along with the cover letter.

The cover letter should be fairly short and relaxed in manner. In writing your cover letter make certain that you have expressed yourself in a way that will engage the attention of the reader to what you have to offer, and will continue to hold his attention as he reads your resume. Let your letter reflect your individuality, but avoid appearing familiar, pushy, or overly "cute."

The Heading

The heading should include your address and the date. It appears in the upper right-hand corner.

The Introductory Address

The introductory address consists of the name and address of the church and the person to whom the letter is written. It should be flush with the left-hand margin.

The Salutation

The salutation is your greeting and you can choose from any number of acceptable salutations. Your choice may be determined by the recipient of your letter—is it a specific person or a committee? Some commonly used salutations would be: "Dear Sir," "Dear Madam," "Gentlemen," "Dear Mr. . .". Do *not* address it: "To Whom It May Concern." This comes across as uncaring and impersonal. Learn enough about the church you are applying to so that you can make a more personal greeting.

The Body of the Letter

This is the main message. The arrangement in the body should look well-balanced on the sheet of paper. Depending upon how much content you have, make sure it is centered on the page. Each left-hand line should be flush, except for the first line beginning each paragraph, which you may indent. Leave two spaces between each paragraph if you single-space the body. The body of the letter should include:

- Introductory paragraph (Greeting, introducing yourself)
- Statement of purpose (Your reasons for writing)
- Statement of job objective
- Brief summary of qualifications
- Philosophy of ministry (Especially if not included in the resume)
- Brief doctrinal statement (Position on key issues, e.g., salvation, inspiration of scripture, baptism, spiritual gifts, etc.)
- Anything about yourself you feel is pertinent but did not fit in the resume
- Statement of willingness to provide additional information if needed

- Request for a response
- Thank-you for considering

The Closing

This should be typed two or three spaces below the last line of the body. Some of the most commonly used closings are: "Sincerely," "Yours truly," "In Christ," and "By His grace."

Some Don'ts When Writing a Cover Letter

- Don't use sympathy or any sense of urgency as a lever for forcing the interview.
- Don't use gimmicks or any form of boasting (Jas. 4:10; 1 Pet. 5:5).
- Don't write overly long letters; just present the important facts. Let your resume speak for you.
- Don't mail a resume without a cover letter.
- Don't forget to adapt your letter to the facts in the resume, or the specific situation for which you are applying.
- Don't fail to tap what is best in your resume by drawing attention to it.
- Don't fail to reread your resume and cover letter before mailing. Check appearance, grammar, and spelling.

Winning Them Over through the Interview

The purpose of the cover letter and resume is to sufficiently draw attention to your qualifications, experience, and desire so that the search committee wants to interview you. The interview is going to determine whether they extend a call to you or not so you want to make sure that everything is in place so that you can make your best impression.

Try to find out as much as you can about the church, the community, and the position that you are applying for before the interview. Talk to other ministers/youth ministers in the area. Get their general impressions of the church, staff, and ministry. If possible, talk to the previous youth ministers. Find out how long they served and their reasons for leaving. If the church has a job description for the youth ministry

The interview is going to determine whether they extend a call to you or not so you want to make sure that everything is in place so that you can make your best impression.

position, request that it be sent to you before the interview. You might request figures regarding past attendance, budget, and missions giving. Be careful that you don't request so much information ahead of time that they begin to see you as a "nuisance."

On the day of the interview, be sure that you arrive early. There is nothing that makes a poor first impression like being late. Be sure you have adequate directions on how to locate the church so you don't get lost on your way to the interview.

Always dress your best for the interview. Even if the daily attire of the youth minister is going to be blue jeans and a T-shirt, it is important that you look sharp for the interview. It communicates to the search committee that you are serious about the position. I would suggest that a dark suit is still your best choice for the interview. While I understand that everything is becoming more "casual" in the church, a suit is still the uniform of choice in most of the business world. You can always take your jacket and tie off if they invite you to be more comfortable, but you cannot become more dressed-up if you show up underdressed for the interview. If you do not own a suit, then khakis and a button-down shirt with tie is your best bet.

When you arrive at the church and first meet with the members of the search committee, be sure to shake everyone's hand and introduce yourself. Offer a firm handshake that communicates confidence, but don't try to impress anyone with the strength of your grip. Try to remember everyone's name. If you repeat their name back to them and engage them in conversation using their name at least three times in one minute it will help you to remember it.

Come to the interview prepared. You may be asked any question imaginable that might pertain to doctrine, youth ministry, or your personal character and qualifications. It would be helpful if you printed out your philosophy of ministry ahead of time and provided copies for the members of the committee. If you have any samples of lessons, newsletters, or original work you have done in the past that you could show the committee, this would be extremely helpful. A picture is worth a thousand words and it may communicate more than your responses to specific questions during the interview.

After they have had sufficient time to interview you, it would be appropriate for you to ask the committee some pertinent questions. Take care that you do not come across as demanding or pushy, but proceed with tact and courtesy.

Ministry Questions:
1. Camp involvement, CIY?
2. Curriculum for Sunday school, youth group. Who chooses?
3. Youth Meetings — time and places, any rooms off limits?
4. Youth budget — Part of church budget? How determined? Fund raising allowed? Youth allowed to control their own checking? Who approves purchases? What comes out of the youth budget? Curriculum, conferences, supplies, etc.? Scholarship for camps, CIY, retreats? Money for training staff?
5. Resources available — Church van or bus? Video, music equipment?
6. Previous programs — Positive, negative, needs.
7. Church history — splits or recent moral issues with staff, doctrinal issues, interchurch involvement, overall church budget.

Personal Considerations
1. Job description — specific and reasonable?
2. To whom are you responsible — committee, minister, board?
3. Staff meetings — when, where, content, responsibilities?
4. Board meetings — attend, vote, required?
5. What other church duties will you share with the other staff — hospital calling, newsletter, worship service?
6. Vacation — when and how much?
7. Days off — when and how much? Fixed or flexible? Comp days for special events?
8. Conference, revival, or other speaking leave — Policy? When and how much?
9. Salary considerations — How much, upon what is it based? Housing allowance? Insurance? Professional expenses? Travel reimbursement? Convention expense? Retirement or pension? How often reviewed?

After you have finished the interview, be sure to thank them for their time and consideration. You should both agree upon a reasonable amount of time when you will contact one another and discuss whether you intend to accept the position if it is offered to you.

June 23, 2002

Joe Brown
2819 Caldwell Drive
Joplin, MO 64804

Mr. Ron Jones
First Christian Church
2354 Main Street
Anywhere, USA

Dear Mr. Jones,

I am very happy to supply the search committee with my resume and the appropriate references. Youth ministry is my passion and I believe that my philosophy of ministry and experience would very well meet the needs of First Christian Church.

It is my desire to fill the position of youth and family minister with a growing church that has a heart for evangelism. My gifts and abilities are especially suited for working with young people, both in evangelism and discipleship. The youth programs I have been associated with have grown in number under my leadership and direction. Not only have the youth programs grown in numbers, but I have increased the level of involvement among the adult sponsors.

My philosophy of youth ministry is based around the concept of balance. An effective youth ministry will meet the social, spiritual, emotional, intellectual, and physical needs of young people. This is accomplished through the development of both student and adult leaders, dynamic programming, and focused discipleship.

My doctrinal beliefs can be summed up in this way:
- I believe in God the Father as the creator of the universe, manifested in three personalities: the Father, the Son, and the Holy Spirit.
- I believe that the death of Jesus Christ upon the cross is the only means of salvation. This salvation cannot be earned, but is given as a free gift by God's grace.
- Man must accept God's free gift of Christ through, faith, repentance, confession, baptism, and faithful obedience.
- I believe in the bodily resurrection of Jesus Christ and in his physical return at the time of the second coming.

Thank you for taking the time to look over my resume and to consider me for the position of youth and family minister. If you have any questions that I may be able to answer, please do not hesitate to call.

In Christ,

Joe Brown

Joe Brown
1234 Maple Street
Anywhere, USA 64804
417-555-1234 (Home) 417-555-4567 (Work) 417-555-7890 (Cell)
E-mail: *Jbrown@hotmail.com*

Occupational Objective: Position of Youth Minister

Education
- 2002 – Lincoln Christian Seminary, M. Div in Marriage and Family
- 1998 – Ozark Christian College, B. Th. in Youth Ministry

Ministry Experience
- 1999–2002 – Youth Minister at First Christian Church, Bloomington, IL
- 1998–1999 – Youth Ministry Intern at Southeast Christian Church, Louisville, KY
- 1997–1998 – Camp team member for Ozark Christian College
- 1994–1997 – Weekend Youth Minister at Hume, MO
- 1998 – Inner City trip to Chicago with Christ In Youth during Spring Break

Work Experience
- 1996–1998 – Sears – Salesman in electronics department
- 1994–1995 – McDonald's – cook

Areas of Expertise
- Computers – Data entry, desktop publishing, web development
- Organization – Dean of Junior High week of camp at Little Galilee in charge of recruiting teaching staff, speakers, special events, and daily schedule
- Musical ability – play guitar and lead worship
- Teaching – Taught Sunday School and youth group for 8 years
- Speaking – Main speaker for Illinois Teen Convention

Honors and Awards
- Recipient of Eastern Star Scholarship
- Dean's list at Ozark Christian College and Lincoln Christian Seminary
- Graduated Magna Cum Laude

Personal Information
- Marital status – Married
- Wife's name – Mary
- Children – Josh and Alicia

Interests
- Tae Kwon Do, chess, guitar, reading, soccer

References
Kenny Boles (Professor) 1000 Walnut, Anywhere, MO 64804 Phone: 417-555-3456
E-mail: *kboles@occ.edu*
Mike Baker (Minister) 2000 Main St., Anywhere, IL 62656 Phone: 217-555-1212
E-mail: *whatapreacher@aol.com*
Ed Thomas (Employer) 3000 North St., Anywhere, MO 64804 Phone: 417-555-6767
E-mail: *mistered@att.net*

> ## *Time for Reflection* 🕐
>
> 1. Are you aware of your strengths and abilities, and are you able to articulate them well?
> 2. Does your resume have good eye-appeal, and has it been proofread by someone other than yourself?
> 3. Have you prepared a list of questions to ask a search committee?
> 4. Are you sufficiently prepared to answer any questions concerning your status as a potential youth minister?

SUGGESTED READING LIST

Lore, Nicholas. *The Pathfinder: How to Choose or Change Your Career for a Lifetime of Satisfaction and Success.* New York: Simon & Schuster, 1998.

There are a number of excellent free web sites that will help you with the writing of your cover letter and resume. One such site is: http://www.careerbuilder.com/index.cfm

NOTES ON CHAPTER SIX

1. Nicholas Lore, "How to Write a Masterpiece of a Resume." http://www.rockportinstitute.com/resumes.html This web site is an excerpt from the book: *The Pathfinder: How to Choose or Change Your Career for a Lifetime of Satisfaction and Success* (New York: Simon & Schuster, 1998).

2. "Why Your Resume Is Important," http://www.virtualville.com/employment_agency/resume_writing.html#1.

Chapter 7

The Planning, Power, and Purpose of Great Youth Events

Dr. Gary B. Zustiak

The Need for Youth Activities

Part of an effective youth program is the planning of great youth events where teens can get together, laugh, and have a great time. Teens are no different in this respect today than in the past. It doesn't matter what generational group you are from—everyone wants an opportunity to have a good time. Teens need the opportunity to laugh, play, and interact with one another in a casual nonthreatening environment.

In fact, teens today may even have a greater need for opportunities to socialize and have fun than some of the previous generations. With the rise in the divorce rate, many teens (especially the oldest in the family) end up having to take on parental roles in order to help out their single moms. This might mean getting their little brothers and sisters up and dressed for school. They may also be the chief caretakers of their siblings after school if their mother works late or has a second job. Many chores around the house such as cooking, cleaning, and washing fall upon them. With the need to "grow up and be responsible," some teens have forgotten how to play. Life has become entirely too serious for them— they are old beyond their years. Great

Teens need the opportunity to laugh, play and interact with one another in a casual nonthreatening environment.

youth events offer them a chance to be a kid once again—to laugh and be crazy (even if only for a short time).

While the need to laugh and have a good time is a legitimate need, it is important that the events and activities planned by the youth minister never come across as being beneath the age and dignity of the teen. Teens need opportunities to have fun without being juvenile. Never force a teen to participate in a game or activity he thinks is "lame." While you might think it is the greatest thing since sliced bread, it may only remind him of stupid junior-high antics that he is only too happy to be done with.

Self-esteem is such an important issue it is of paramount importance that any game, skit, or activity not challenge or harm their self-esteem or dignity in any way. For instance, in the early days of youth ministry, it was standard practice to involve students in skits or games that caused them to be the butt of a joke or some kind of water prank. This usually resulted in the group laughing their heads off at the one who had the prank pulled on him, but this was at the expense of the teen who was usually dying of embarrassment. Good planning will find a way to have fun without humiliating anyone—whether it is a young person or an adult sponsor.

Great youth activities provide the opportunity for teens to have a good time without getting into trouble or getting stoned—a first for some! The media and teen culture has perpetuated the myth that the only time teens can have fun is at some kind of party where various illegal or immoral activities are taking place. It is actually a great relief for most teens to know that you can have a good time and not have to wake up with a hangover or worry about having contracted some kind of sexually transmitted disease from the previous night's activities.

A well-planned youth event will enable the young person to create some great memories that will last a lifetime. One of the most rewarding things for a youth minister to experience is to overhear several members of the youth group talking about some previous youth event with great animation and excitement saying, "Do you remember when . . . ?" It validates all the effort and planning you put into the event because it ended up being significant to their lives.

Goals and Objectives for Youth Events

While providing an opportunity for teens to let their hair down and have fun in a safe setting is a legitimate part of youth programming, it should never be the sole reason for providing activities. Some activities should be specifically designed as evangelistic outreach. These events provide the youth minister and youth staff the opportunity to come into contact with some new teens and provide the possibility for follow-up later on. Because these contacts are so valuable, someone should always be assigned the responsibility of making sure that every teen who participates fills out some kind of attendance form that will provide sufficient information for a follow-up contact. Warning! Be very careful and sensitive as to how you go about getting this information. You do not want to come across as only caring about numbers or some kind of salesman who wants to sell them something.

You should never use a student event to trap teens. This is the old "bait-and-switch" trick. Countless numbers of teens have been turned off to the church because some youth minister invited them to a skating party or some other similar event and then after 30 minutes of skating forced them to sit in the middle of the roller rink and listen to an hour-and-a-half sermon telling them they are going to hell.

You should never use a student event to trap teens.

The purpose of evangelistic events should be for providing new contacts, not trapping kids. Don't misunderstand me! There is nothing wrong with planning an evangelistic crusade and inviting non-Christian teens, *if* the purpose of the event is openly shared with those who are invited before they come.

Another purpose for providing student activities is to return the strays that have wandered from the group. For various reasons, teens will drop out of regular youth group attendance. Sometimes it is due to conflicts in their schedule with school activities or a job. Other times they have chosen to leave the church because of sin in their lives, and they are struggling in their spiritual walk. Great youth events serve as a catalyst to bring them back to the church and to reacquaint them with the need for fellowship and spiritual growth.

Youth events, if planned correctly, can be a great way to build community within the youth group. Working together on the various tasks for an event helps the youth to get to know one another better and build trust as they laugh, play, and interact with one another. They can also be used as a tool in student leadership development.

When planning your youth events it is important that you plan a variety of events throughout the year. Don't just provide events that are athletic oriented or are centered on a theme park. Try to think of activities that will appeal to a wide variety of personalities.

Good Planning Is Essential to the Success of Any Event

Keep in mind the purpose of the event and plan accordingly. Be careful that the event you plan doesn't run counter to your purpose for having an event. For example, if you want an event that will help promote community and closeness within the members of the group, having the youth group invite all their friends on a trip to Six Flags is not going to accomplish that goal. As soon as you hit the parking lot, they are going to pair up with their best buds and scatter to the winds. If you want to have an evangelistic emphasis, then developing a Bible Bowl Team is not your best choice. Think through what you hope to accomplish with any event and then choose an appropriate activity.

When planning an activity, keep in mind the needs of the group. Think through the school calendar year. If it is right in the middle of testing for the SATs, you probably don't want to plan an activity like a lock-in or area youth rally that is going to further drain them and demand more of their time. Having a tutoring party the night before would be more appropriate and appreciated by the students.

If you want to plan a big-event that will have a large participation such as a state teen convention, then there are several key things you must do. First of all, realize that you cannot take on huge tasks alone. You must have some help. Form a committee from among youth ministers in the area and share your dream with them, and make sure they are on board and will support the program with their churches and youth groups. Delegate various responsibilities to the members of the committee. Work up a back-dated calendar that lists all the major tasks and the date by which they must be done. Follow up on everyone who has been assigned a specific duty to check on their progress. You may find that you have to reassign certain responsibilities because the person who first volunteered to do them has not

Keep in mind the purpose of the event and plan accordingly. Be careful that the event you plan doesn't run counter to your purpose for having an event.

proven faithful to the task. Some key elements that must be considered when planning a big event are:

- Location—is it a desirable place that teens and youth groups would want to come to? Is it centrally located so a good number of churches from all around the state could participate? Are there a sufficient amount of restaurants and hotels that could accommodate your group?
- Cost—you must work up a budget and then figure out how you are going to meet your budget. This can be from each church committing a certain amount of money and then charging each participant a registration fee, or it could all come from registration revenue. Items that need to be included in the budget would be: venue rental (hotel or convention center); speakers; worship band; publicity; postage; stage and lighting; tech crew; refreshments; meals; entertainment (concerts, comedians, etc.); and workshop leaders.
- Publicity—it must be done with quality. Who is going to design it? Mail it? Will it be designed in house or outsourced? Web site? E-mail?
- Staff—you must have a staff that will organize the event. This would include members of your committee. But in addition to them, you must have people to help with registration, setting up the stage, security, teaching workshops, etc.
- Theme—one that is easily conveyed and will excite teens to want to attend.
- Timing—don't plan an event that is in conflict with major school events such as state tournaments, prom, SATs, etc.

Understand that not every event you do in youth ministry needs to be huge. There is a lot to say in favor of the unique and intimate social that just involves the members of the youth group. Some things like scavenger hunts, video nights, and pizza parties will always be fun things to do. If you are someone who is devoid of ideas on the kinds of things you can do or you want to try something different, there are a number of books on creative social ideas that you can purchase from Group and Youth Specialties.

When choosing an event, try to plan ones where everyone can participate. Don't force participation, but encourage it. Keep things in good taste, and make sure you have taken adequate safety precautions to make sure no one is injured. Be prepared ahead of time for the event. Don't wait until the last minute to pull things together. Make sure you have adequate adult supervision. Keep a positive attitude during the event.

Don't have the adults do all of the planning and executing of an activity. It is much harder to promote if the adults do it all. If it bombs, it's all the adults' fault. When the adults plan it all, you lose out on a chance to involve the youth in a growth opportunity. Young people are capable of handling responsibility—in fact they are begging to be trusted and given real responsibility.

When young people are allowed to plan an activity, it insures that they will help promote it among their friends. They know if it fails, then it is their fault so they will work harder at making it a success. Involving the young people in the planning of an activity provides a great opportunity for leadership development. Teens are very capable of taking the responsibility for: publicity, transportation arrangements, decorations, devotions, refreshments, reservations, leading in the games, drama, setting up equipment, running the sound and lights, participating in the worship band, clean up, and writing thank-you notes.

Major and Minor Events

Major youth events only need to happen four to six times a year. You don't have to have a major youth event every month. If you try to do this, not only will you burn out your staff, but the teens will become jaded and lose interest. I consider a major event one that involves considerable planning ahead, greater expense, and a larger involvement of people and churches. Some major events would be: fall kick-off rally, state teen convention, area-wide crusade, missions trip, Christ In Youth Summer Conference, church camp, etc. A minor youth event involves less preparation and only needs a few hours of time to participate in the activity. Many of the events that we used to call "socials" would fall under this category, such as: video night, scavenger hunt, car rally, mini-golf, roller-skating, and concerts.

There are prefab and do-it-yourself youth activities. Each has its own advantages and disadvantages. A prefab youth activity is one where the activity is already available—all you have to do is organize the transportation and pick a date. Typical prefab activities would include: mini-golf, theme parks, water slides, roller-skating, concerts, etc. The advantage of a prefab event is that interest usually already exists for this activity and there is little preparation needed on your part. The disadvantage of a prefab social is that many times it spreads your kids out too thin and there is no sense of community or group identity developed. They can also be expensive and require long-distance traveling.

A do-it-yourself activity is one that you have to plan yourself and gather the materials that are needed in order to make it happen. A typical do-it-yourself activity would be: a bigger and better hunt, Polaroid scavenger hunt, hayride, video night, lock-in, Halloween fun house, etc. Advantages of do-it-yourself activities are that they are unique, cost less, involve kids in the planning, convenient, and may come about by popular demand. The disadvantages of do-it-yourself activities are that they take time to set up, may not be successful, and key personnel can fall through on responsibilities.

Using Games in Student Activities

When planning your various student activities, it is good to incorporate some crowd-breakers at the beginning of the event, especially if it is a do-it-yourself activity that you are holding at the church. These promote interaction between kids who would not normally do so. It is also a good way for sponsors to do some casual interacting with the teens. So often the teens only see the sponsors in their role as teacher or disciplinarian. It is good for them to see that the adult sponsors like to have a good time and are good sports throughout the various activities.

Depending upon the type of crowd-breaker or game that you choose, it could also be used to help build group unity as the group works for a common goal. Participation in a team game can also make better listeners of the kids, especially if there is some kind of penalty for not following instructions or bonus points for being good listeners.

Games can be used to help build positive character qualities in the participants. For example, if a student is very athletically gifted and is used to winning all the time, and if the particular game chosen involves some skill other than athletic ability (which this student does *not* have), it can be a good lesson in humility. It may also allow a student who does not get much recognition a chance to shine and have his/her moment in the sun. Games that require cooperation among the team members can be used to teach the importance of interdependence upon one another and the body of Christ. Through team cooperation people learn about one another in ways that they normally would not and come to appreciate one another.

While using games and crowd-breakers can be a very positive activity within the youth group, there are some dangers you need to be aware of. There is always the possibility that the competition between teams can become overemphasized and some individual or group of individuals gets their feelings hurt or ends up causing a scene because they do not handle losing very well. I have personally seen all of the spiritual blessings and growth that had taken place during a week of camp absolutely negated by the faculty-student softball game! Youth ministers and adults who feel they have something to prove will knock over students, argue about the calls, and display horrible temper tantrums when they strike out. The students observe this kind of activity and then question the validity of the lessons and spiritual truths these leaders have been teaching the entire week.

There is also the hidden danger of possible physical injuries. While teens love to "live on the edge," no self-respecting youth leader should ever plan or allow an activity that may cause physical harm to a participant. The old standby, the "Chinese fire-drill," may seem like great fun when sitting in the van at the stoplight, but when a student ends up hit by another vehicle and has to be taken to the hospital, it is obvious that better judgment should have prevailed. I have known youth ministers who have allowed the following:

- Jumping off a cliff into a lake without first checking the depth of the water or for hidden objects beneath the water
- "Hookie bobbing" (hanging on to the bumper of a car and being pulled along the back through the snow using their shoes like skis)
- Hood surfing (standing on the hood of a moving vehicle and "surfing")
- Holding a dunk contest by running and jumping onto a folding chair in the church gym
- Rock climbing without proper safety gear or belay ropes
- Pushing students off a moving hay wagon
- Rafting in flood waters without proper gear or training

The list could go on, but hopefully you got the point. Student safety is a must when planning any student activity. Hard as it is telling a kid "No" when he wants to do something adventurous, it is still much easier than having to call a parent and tell him/her that his child is at the hospital, or worse, the morgue.

A must for all those who participate in any and all youth activities sponsored by the church is a permission slip/liability release form. The youth minister should keep the permission slips and medical release forms on file and have them easily accessible at all events. It is advisable to have a new medical release form signed each year.

A SAMPLE MEDICAL RELEASE FORM

MEDICAL RELEASE FORM
FIRST CHRISTIAN CHURCH

Name of Student _____ Date of Birth _____

Address _____ Age _____

City/Town _____ State _____ Zip _____

Phone # (____) _____ Sex _____ Height _____ Weight _____

Social Security # _____

Emergency Contact Person

Parent/Guardian Name (Full name) _____

Address (if different from student) _____

Town _____ State _____ Zip _____

Phone # (Home) (_____) _____ (Work) (_____) _____

Alternate Contact Person

Name _____

Address _____

Town _____ State _____ Zip _____

Phone # (Home) (_____) _____ (Work) (_____) _____

If you have medical insurance, your carrier will be billed for medical charges in the case of illness or injury while your child is at the activity.

Do you have health insurance _____ Yes _____ No

Name of insurance company _____

Policy # _____ Group # _____

In whose name is the insurance? _____

Family Doctor _____ City/Town _____

Phone # (____) _____

If your child should require medical attention for injuries received or illnesses contracted prior to activity, please send us the necessary information to give him/her proper medical care during his/her time with the youth ministry activity.

Health History:

Any pre-existing or present medical conditions (e.g., diabetes, asthma, allergies)

_____

_____

Name and dosage of any medications that must be taken:

_____

_____

Reactions to any medications? ____Yes _____No If so, which ones? _____

___ Hay Fever   ___ Heart Condition   ___ Diabetes   ___ Insect stings

___ Epilepsy   ___ Nervous Disorders   ___ Asthma   ___ Ulcers

___ Physical Handicap (Specify: _____

___ Any major illnesses during the past year?

If any of the above are checked, please give details (e.g., normal treatment of allergic reactions)

_____

_____

Date of last Tetanus shot _____ Contact lenses? _____

Any swimming restrictions? ____ Yes ____ No What? _____

Any activity restrictions? ____ Yes ____ No What? _____

Parent Medical and Liability Release Statement:

I understand that in the event medical intervention is needed, every attempt will be made to contact immediately the persons listed on this form. In the event I cannot be reached in an emergency, I hereby give my permission to the physician or dentist selected by the youth minister or sponsors to hospitalize, to secure medical treatment and/or order an injection, anesthesia, or surgery for my child as deemed necessary.

I understand all reasonable safety precautions will be taken at all times by the First Christian Church and its staff during the events and activities. I understand the possibility of unforeseen hazards and know the inherent possibility of risk. I agree not to hold First Christian Church, its ministers, leaders, employees, and volunteer staff liable for damages, losses, diseases, or injuries incurred by participation in any youth activities sponsored by the church.

Parent/Guardian Signature _____ Date _____

Signature of Student (if over 18 years of age) _____

Notarized:

Good Promotion for All Events Is a Must

No matter how well planned or creative a student activity may be, it will all go for naught if the word doesn't get out to the students. Good publicity is a must. You should never rely on simply using one method of advertising for your student activities—you need to utilize as many as possible. Get the students involved in every aspect of promoting the activities. The responsibility is good for them, and they will amaze you at their skill and ability. Consider using the following for promoting your student activities:

- Use snail mail. Send out a special flyer. Have one of the students design it on his/her home computer. With all of the affordable desk-top publishing that is now available, this is a snap. They have more time than you do and will amaze you at their creativity and the quality of their final product.
- Use creative announcements. Utilize film, drama, television sitcoms, contemporary music, PowerPoint, etc.

- Have a youth web site with a spot devoted to upcoming student activities.
- Use mass e-mailings.
- Hang posters in the youth room at church.
- Set up a telephone chain. Have a youth group hot-line
- Print some hand-outs for school and friends if this is permissible.

Time for Reflection

1. Do you provide a variety of student activities throughout the year?
2. Do you have a well-defined purpose for every activity? Could others easily state what that purpose is?
3. Have you done all that you can to involve both adult sponsors and student leaders in the planning and execution of your activities?
4. Do you make student safety a priority? Do you have current medical release forms on file?

SUGGESTED READING LIST

Crabtree, Jack. *Better Safe Than Sued.* Loveland, CO: Group Publishing, 1998.

_____. *Quick Crowdbreakers and Games for Youth Groups.* Loveland, CO: Group Publishing, 1988.

Rice, Wayne, and Mike Yaconelli. *Creative Socials and Special Events.* Grand Rapids: Zondervan, 1986.

http://www.funandgames.org/

www.funattic.com/game_list.htm

http://www.pastor2youth.com/gamesindex.html

http://www.thesourcefym.com/games/index.asp

NOTES ON CHAPTER SEVEN

1. Dewey M. Bertolini, *Back to the Heart of Youth Work* (Wheaton, IL: Victor Books, 1989), p. 143.

2. Paul Borthwick, *Organizing Your Youth Ministry* (Grand Rapids: Zondervan, 1988), p. 125.

3. Bertolini, *Back,* p. 144.

The Need for Creative Bible Teaching Methods and Planning

Dr. Gary B. Zustiak

Warning! Famine in the Land!

It was fifteen years ago, but seems like yesterday. I was the dean of a high school week of camp. Instead of following the traditional programming that had characterized this particular camp for so many years, I decided to introduce some creative alternatives to the camping program.

One evening during the scheduled social hour I had planned to divide the campers up into teams and play Bible Family Feud, my variation on the then popular game show "Family Feud." The game is played by having the audience answer certain questions before the game begins and the answers the contestants must come up with are based upon the audience response. The number one answer is the answer given by the most people. (It doesn't matter if the answer is actually correct or not, just the fact that the majority of people give it as an answer makes it number one.)

I created a list of questions concerning general Bible knowledge and the campers were polled on Sunday during registration. The next day the answers were compiled and arranged in descending order according to the number of campers giving a particular response. The response given most frequently by the campers was the number one answer and so forth.

I was shocked and dismayed at the biblical ignorance displayed by these young people. For the most part these represented the cream of the crop from our churches. These were our best teens, the ones who had attended more Sunday school and youth group meetings than any of their peers. But you would never know it from their answers. For example, I instructed them to name a king found in the Bible. Some answers I expected and was looking for were; "David," "Saul," "Solomon," "Nebuchadnezzar" and so forth. The number one answer given by the campers? *King James!* Get it? The King James Bible.

"The days are coming," declares the Sovereign Lord, "when I will send a famine through the land—not a famine of food or a thirst for water, but a famine of hearing the words of the Lord." —Amos 8:11

Another question I asked was, "Name one of the fruits of the Spirit found in Galatians 5:22-23." Once again, I expected to find "love, joy, peace, patience, etc." The number one answer? Survey says: "Apple."

This would be hilarious if it didn't signify such a serious problem. Be reminded of the prophecy found in Amos 8:11. "'The days are coming,' declares the Sovereign LORD, 'when I will send a famine through the land—not a famine of food or a thirst for water, but a famine of hearing the words of the LORD.'"

Sadly enough, my experience was not unique. Research has shown that biblical ignorance is now the norm, not the exception. Consider the following:

- In a 1988 survey by The Gallup Organization, it was found that only 35% of the youth surveyed could name the four Gospels and only 66% knew the number of Jesus' disciples.[4] Only 35% could name four or more of the Ten Commandments and only 3% could name all ten. Only 9% of those same youth polled read the Bible daily, 10% read it two or three times a week, and 20% read it at least once a week.[5] It has only gotten worse since this survey in the late '80s.

- While a good number of teens consider themselves to be Christian in the U.S. and attend a Christian church at least occasionally, many of their beliefs are not consistent with biblical teaching. For instance, two-thirds stated that Satan is not a living being but merely a symbol of evil. Six out of ten argued that a good person can earn eternal salvation through good deeds. A majority (53%) said that Jesus committed sins while He was on earth.[6]

Knowledge of the word of God is the key in the conversion and growth process of all Christians (Ps. 119:9-11; John 6:63; Rom. 10:17; Heb. 4:12-13; 1 Pet. 1:23). How can conversion and growth take place if young people are not familiar with the word of God and given skills in which to exegete and understand it? Answer: It won't and it isn't.

How Did We Get Here?

It used to be that the Bible and the people and events recorded within it were common knowledge. The stories and values contained within were taught in public education. A few years back George Will reminded us of an incredible story that took place in the darkest days of World War II that illustrates this point.

In 1940, trapped on the beaches of Dunkirk, France, hundreds of thousands of British and French soldiers were near the point of surrender or certain death as Hitler's troops tightened the noose around them.

As the battle raged, one British officer was able to send a message back to London. He chose three simple words, "But if not . . ." Will writes that the message "was instantly recognized as a quotation from the book of Daniel, where Nebuchadnezzar commands Shadrach, Meshach, and Abednego to worship the golden image or be thrust into the fiery furnace."

The three biblical heroes answer defiantly, ". . . our God whom we serve is able to deliver us from the burning fiery furnace, and he will deliver us out of thine hand, O king. *But if not*, be it known unto thee, O king, that we will not serve thy gods, nor worship the golden image."

The message from Dunkirk was a pledge from the entrapped soldiers that they had faith in being rescued, *but if not* they would not cooperate, even at the price of death, with the evil conquerors of Europe. As such, the message was remarkable for its courage. But that the three words' significance was immediately understood "is stirring evidence of a community deriving cohesion from a common culture."[7]

Would anyone even recognize the phrase as a biblical quote in today's society aside from some ministers and Bible college professors? What a tragic loss. What changes led to this sad state of affairs?

The key to understanding the present situation is found in looking back into the past and identifying the forces that have shaped present-day youth education in the church. A critical look to the past will show there are three major issues that have adversely affected the Christian education of our youth.

The first has been the poor programming and priorities of many youth ministry programs. Don't get me wrong! I am in full support of youth ministry. I have been personally involved in youth ministry since 1972. But I am dismayed by many of the programs that I have encountered in our churches through the years. Many youth programs center around fun and games and not discipleship and growth. Not that there is anything wrong with fun and games. There is a place for them in youth ministry (Eccl. 11:9). But they must not become the focal point of the ministry with serious study, service, and discipleship relegated to a minor role.

It is easy to understand how this change in emphasis has taken place. When a church hires a youth minister, they make it very clear up front that they want to see results. Translate "results" into numbers. Most churches automatically see large numbers of students in attendance at a youth program as a successful program. The content of the program is often ignored in light of the large numbers and the excitement that is being generated.

Youth ministers feel this pressure to produce results. It is much easier to get large numbers of students to go to Six Flags or Wild Waters than it is to memorize Scripture. This trickles down into the weekly programming. If there is an emphasis upon fun and games and activities rather than study, it is easier to maintain the high numbers. It also takes less time to prepare a recreational activity than it does a well-crafted and relevant Bible study. Many youth ministers are just starting out their careers in full-time ministry and in their insecurity have a great need to feel liked by the teens in their church. They want to be known in the youth community as a "fun" guy. Thus, an emphasis upon youth ministry "lite" rather than serious programming is the result.

A healthy church will care enough to investigate the content of the youth program and support the youth minister who is serious about discipleship even if it means fewer numbers of teens are involved.

The local church needs to take responsibility for its part in this problem. It is not just the youth minister's fault. Church leadership must quit judging a program's effectiveness by numbers only. A healthy church will care enough to investigate the content of the youth program and support the youth minister who is serious about discipleship even if it means fewer numbers of teens are involved. After all, the size of Jesus' youth group was only twelve and I would call it a success.

The second contributing factor to the demise of Bible knowledge in our young people is our current educational crisis in the United States. About 13% of American seventeen-year-olds are functionally illiterate. For some minority groups, the figure rises to 40%. Only half of surveyed young adults can read and comprehend high school textbooks.[8] About 3 out of 10 teenagers (29.4%) drop out of high school. This figure rises to 40% of inner-city students and increases to 50% among urban blacks, 80% of urban Hispanics, and 85% of Native Americans.[9]

It is hard to get young people involved in Bible study when they cannot read or are embarrassed by their poor reading skills. When their public educational experience is negative, this influences any attempts at education in the church. For most teens, doing homework and attending school has probably never made the top ten list of fun things to do. If Sunday school and youth group just remind them of more school, then the youth minister's job is made even more difficult.

The third factor has to do with the effect that technology has had on our culture. The technological advancements of television, video games, and computers have all contributed to the demise of interest in Bible study among young people by making everyday life seem boring in comparison. Television holds people's attention through the use of technical changes. The picture scene changes back and forth from one angle and perspective to another so that the person's interest is held by the ever-changing screen. The average show will have about fifteen technical changes per minute and expensive advertisements (like Coke, Pepsi, McDonald's, etc.) will have as many as a hundred per minute.[10]

This phenomenon makes the teacher's job that much harder in trying to hold the students' attention. After all, the teacher's presentation doesn't change every five seconds. Students quickly lose interest and their minds' wander off to something they consider more entertaining.

How Do We Fix the Problem?

Churches and youth programs need to make a renewed commitment to the study of the Word. It must be a priority. The Scriptures must be taught with authority, credibility, and enthusiasm.

Students must study for change. Application is imperative. Too many young people equate and confuse spirituality with biblical knowledge. "Without application, all you have is biblical knowledge which is a sorry substitute for spirituality."[11] As J.I. Packer says, "You can know a great deal *about* God without knowing Him personally."

One way to ensure that teens will be interested in your lesson is to prepare lessons that meet a felt need. A felt need is characterized as a need that is current and relevant. While a study on the battle of the Jebusites might be biblical, it is not current or relevant unless some timeless principle is gleaned from the account and the teens are shown how to apply that principle to some struggle or problem they are currently engaged in. Sometimes you may have to cultivate that feeling before they will be open to receiving instruction in a particular area, but the results will be well worth the effort.

Too many young people equate and confuse spirituality with biblical knowledge.

The use of creative Bible study methods is another tool that will make Bible study more interesting for the students. The more the students are personally involved in the learning process the more they will retain and put to use in their everyday experience. The remainder of this chapter will be devoted to the use of creative Bible study methods.

The Need for Creative Bible Study Methods

A woman read somewhere that dogs were healthier if fed a tablespoon of cod liver oil each day. So each day she followed the same routine—she chased her dog until she caught it, wrestled it down, and managed to force the fishy remedy down the dog's throat. This went on for some time until one day when, in the middle of this grueling medical effort, the bottle was kicked over. With a sigh, she loosed her grip on the dog so she could wipe up the mess—only to watch the dog trot over to the puddle and begin lapping it up. You see, the dog just loved cod liver oil! It was just the owner's method of application the dog objected to.[12]

After more than thirty-two years of youth ministry and teaching in a Bible college, I have come to the conclusion that most teens want to learn more about God and the Bible—but they are turned off by our method of application. Even the most hardened, apathetic teenager can become interested in the Bible if approached correctly. God has placed the desire to know Him in our hearts and we are never truly satisfied or fulfilled until we come to know Him personally through the study of His Word.

If it is true that most teens have a great spiritual hunger, then what is the problem? Why aren't kids flocking to our youth groups and Sunday school classes? How come Bible study never turns up on a top ten list of fun things that teens like to do? Probably because they do not like our method of application. Accustomed to the ever-changing rapid pace of today's multimedia to hold their attention, they have been turned off by boring, predictable, unchallenging, irrelevant attempts to teach them God's word. Perhaps *Life* magazine was right, when in 1957 it called the Sunday school "the most wasted hour of the week."[13]

We must apply the findings of educational psychology which provides insight on *how* we learn and *what* motivates us to learn. Some of the ideas that will be presented in this chapter may immediately strike you as usable with your youth group or class while others will not seem as applicable to your situation. That's okay—not all ideas work with every group. But don't make the mistake of discarding ideas too quickly, tossing them aside before they have been given a fair chance. Some typical excuses that I hear are, "This is too expensive. . . . I don't have a large enough staff to pull this off. . . . My group is too small for this . . . too big for that. . . . I don't have the time needed to prepare. . . . My church doesn't support change. . . ."

Before rejecting a new idea or creative teaching concept, ask yourself, "Could this idea be adapted to make it usable in my situation?" "With some fine-tuning, an idea that would not work exactly the way that it is presented could be customized just right for your group."[14] The essence of creativity is the ability to copy. Take a good idea, tweak it, and make it uniquely your own.

Teaching can be frustrating, even for an excellent teacher. Consider this fictional scenario of Jesus and the disciples at the Sermon on the Mount.

Then Jesus took his disciples up onto the mountain, and gathering them around him, he taught them saying: "Blessed are the poor in spirit, for theirs is the kingdom of heaven; blessed are the meek; blessed are they that mourn; blessed are the merciful; blessed are they that thirst for justice; blessed are you when persecuted; blessed are you when you suffer; be glad and rejoice, for your reward is great in heaven."

Then Simon Peter said, "Are we supposed to know this?" And Andrew said, "Do we have to write this down?" And James said, "Will we have a test on this?" And Philip said, "I don't have any paper." And Bartholomew said, "Do we have to turn this in?" And John said, "The other disciples didn't have to learn this." And Matthew said, "Can I go to the bathroom?" And Judas said, "What does this have to do with real life?"

And Jesus wept.[15]

Some Points to Keep in Mind when Teaching the Bible

The Bible is a positive book. I never knew that growing up. All of the Sunday school lessons and sermons that I heard in my home church centered on the negative consequences of sin. Don't do this, and don't do that. The Bible is so much more than just a book full of rules, although that is the impression so often given to teens. We need to approach it once again as if we are about to discover together the greatest news ever heard.

The Bible was written with the idea in mind that it could be understood by its readers. True, there are parts that are complex and difficult to comprehend. It doesn't hurt to have a good commentary on hand to help you with some of the more difficult passages and to get the fullest meaning from a text. But it is important to understand that God intended the Bible to be a book for everyone. One does not have to be a seminary graduate in order to understand it. The unique way that the books of the Bible are arranged can intimidate young people. The Bible is full of terminology that is foreign to most non-Christians. (How often do you use the terms sanctification, regeneration, propitiation, and predestination in your everyday vocabulary?) Your job as a teacher is to present the Bible as an understandable book, a timeless book. It is more than just good literature—it is life changing.

Kids Are Motivated to Learn by Learning

Learning is a self-motivating experience; it feels good to learn. By successfully teaching someone, you are actually creating within the desire to learn more. California's department of education reportedly spent three million dollars to discover that high school students were motivated to learn when they were learning something.[16]

Motivation is increased even more when learning is followed by positive attention and feedback. One way a teacher can cultivate an interest in his students about almost any topic is by utilizing a truth discovered by William James, the father of American psychology. James found that "any object not interesting in itself may become interesting through becoming associated with an object in which an interest already exists."[17] In other words, if you as a teacher can find a subject or topic that already holds an interest to your students (such as a contemporary song, popular movie, or TV sitcom), and tie that in to a Bible story or spiritual truth, then your students are much more likely to find it appealing and have it hold their interest.

Any object not interesting in itself may become interesting through becoming associated with an object in which an interest already exists.
—William James

Kids Learn Better by Experiential Learning

Edgar Dale, an educational communicator, discovered that the more directly involved the student is in the learning process, the more the student retains. The more senses that are involved in the learning process, the more effective the method. This is best illustrated by Dale's cone of learning. The least effective teaching methods are those which use only verbal and visual symbols. The most effective method of teaching is direct participation (involving all the senses) by the student. According to Dale, after two weeks we tend to remember:

- 10% of what we read (reading a book or lesson)
- 20% of what we hear (hearing words from a lecture)
- 30% of what we see (looking at still pictures)
- 50% of what we hear and see (watching a movie, demonstration, exhibit)
- 70% of what we say (participating in a discussion, giving a report)

- 90% of what we both say and do (dramatic presentation, simulated experience, role-play, field trip, genuine participation, i.e., mission or service trip)

Dale's contention is that we learn best when we actually try something—when we get our teeth into an assignment or project where we are responsible for the outcome. If your students can "take part" in your lessons, through methods and techniques such as discussion, case study, and role play your lessons will be more real to them because you will be using a more direct method of teaching.

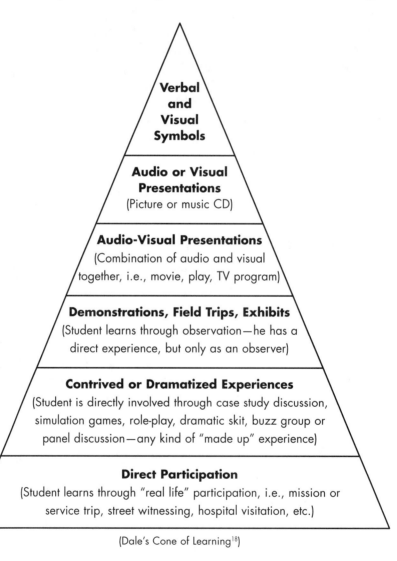

Verbal and Visual Symbols

Audio or Visual Presentations
(Picture or music CD)

Audio-Visual Presentations
(Combination of audio and visual together, i.e., movie, play, TV program)

Demonstrations, Field Trips, Exhibits
(Student learns through observation—he has a direct experience, but only as an observer)

Contrived or Dramatized Experiences
(Student is directly involved through case study discussion, simulation games, role-play, dramatic skit, buzz group or panel discussion—any kind of "made up" experience)

Direct Participation
(Student learns through "real life" participation, i.e., mission or service trip, street witnessing, hospital visitation, etc.)

(Dale's Cone of Learning[18])

Not only does a good teacher need to use creative methods, the teacher must take care to choose a method that will match the goal of the lesson. Not all experiences are equally educative. Teachers should choose the teaching method which best fits the type of learning desired.

Most Effective Methods for Basic Types of Learning[19]	
The development of knowledge	Purposeful reading. Lectures. Audio-visual aids. Field trips. Exhibits. Question and Answer. Recitations. Research projects. Depth Bible Encounters. Symposia. Symposium dialogues. Panels. Book Reports.
The development of understanding	Problem-solving discussions. Case studies. Team-inquiry projects. Writing assignments. Laboratory group analysis. Inductive Bible studies.
The development of skills	Demonstration. Role-playing practice. Discussion practice. Drill. Participant observation. Practice teaching. Laboratory experimentation.
The development of attitudes	Role-reversal role-playing. Free discussion. Feedback laboratory groups. Counseling. Field Trips.
The development of interests	Satisfying exposure to new interests: field trips, exhibits, demonstrations, assignments, group projects, visits.
The development of values	Biographical reading. Sermons. Visits with great personalities. Value-clarifying discussions.

Learning Is Best Facilitated in a Comfortable Environment

Teachers must constantly work to provide a learning environment that gives students space to learn without distractions, an environment that enhances rather than hinders learning. The first rule for selecting a location is to consider those who will attend.

- Homes have advantages: i.e., food, non-institutional, homey feeling, communicates caring and a sense of being welcome. Homes have disadvantages also: i.e., distractions of small children, pets, inadequate space, sporadic availability of host house, not so central location.
- Churches boast a central location, adequate meeting space, access to resources. Churches also have the disadvantage of feeling churchy.
- Ideas for creating physical comfort: temperature, distractions, seating, room selection, fatigue.

- A teacher's attitude is as important as the room's air conditioning in creating a positive learning environment. Honoring your students is essential to the learning environment. The chances for growth and a change of heart are much greater when students are treated with dignity.

People Believe What They Do
More Than They Do What They Believe

John Westerhoff said, "If we want people to be able to accept or reject the Christian faith, we have to turn our attention and emphasis from teaching about Christianity to offering within the church experiences which demonstrate our faith."[20]

People are more likely to behave their way into thinking than think their way into behaving.

Psychological study has found that people are more likely to behave their way into thinking than think their way into behaving. A distressing study found that one's attitude about church, for example, had little to do with his church attendance on any given Sunday. "Smith found that conservative Christian students who were orthodox in their belief about God and Jesus and active in groups like Campus Crusade for Christ and Navigators were as likely to cheat and as disinclined to volunteer as nonreligious and atheist students."[21]

Psychological research parallels the biblical and the theological idea that faith follows action. We come to know God by doing His Word. What this all means for the teacher is that instead of spending all our time trying to teach kids *about* Christianity, we should involve them in activities that enable them to *live* Christianity.

Kids are better at finding reasons to believe what they do than doing what they believe. When kids publicly act on their beliefs, they come to believe more strongly in their actions. All of this underscores the need for the use of creative teaching methods, especially ones that involve the student directly.

Time for Reflection

1. How has the technological revolution affected the way people learn?
2. Who was the most effective teacher you ever experienced? What made this teacher superior to all others?

3. How many different methods of teaching do you typically use? What would it take to motivate you to try some new methods?

4. What kinds of things can you do to actively involve your students more in the learning process?

SUGGESTED READING LIST

Dockery, Karen. *The Youth Worker's Guide to Creative Bible Study*. Nashville: Broadman & Holman, 1999.

LeFever, Marlene D. *Creative Teaching Methods*. Elgin, IL: David C. Cook, 1985.

McNabb, Bill, and Steven Mabry. *Teaching the Bible Creatively*. Grand Rapids: Zondervan, 1990.

NOTES ON CHAPTER EIGHT

1. Bill McNabb and Steven Mabry, *Teaching the Bible Creatively* (Grand Rapids: Zondervan, 1990), p. 29.

2. Marlene D. LeFever, *Creative Teaching Methods* (Elgin, IL: David C. Cook, 1985), p. 17.

3. Lawrence O. Richards, *Creative Bible Teaching* (Chicago: Moody Press, 1970), p. 96.

4. Robert Bezilla, ed., *America's Youth 1977–1988* (Princeton, NJ: The Gallup Organization, 1988), p. 141.

5. Ibid., p. 143.

6. George Barna, "Teenagers' Beliefs Moving Farther from Biblical Perspectives," Barna Research Online, **www.barna.org** (October 23, 2000). pp. 1-2.

7. James Dobson and Gary L. Bauer, *Children at Risk* (Dallas: Word, 1990), p. 184.

8. Eugene C. Roehlkepartain, ed., *The Youth Ministry Resource Book* (Loveland, CO: Group, 1988), p. 95.

9. Ibid., p. 101.

10. Anthony Campolo, "The Youth Culture in Sociological Perspective," in *The Complete Book of Youth Ministry*, ed. by Warren S. Benson and Mark H. Senter III (Chicago: Moody, 1987), p. 43.

11. Gary Dausey, *The Youth Leader's Source Book* (Grand Rapids: Zondervan, 1983), p. 158.

12. McNabb and Mabry, *Teaching*, p. 13.

13. Ibid., p. 14.

14. Ibid., p. 15.

15. Ibid., p. 19-20.

16. Ibid., p. 30.

17. William James, *Talks to Teachers* (George Ellis Press, 1899).

18. Adapted from: Ed Reed and Rex Johnson, *Sunday School Teacher's Planbook* (Glendale, CA: Gospel Light, 1975), p. 15.

19. H. Norman Wright, *Ways to Help Them Learn*, ICL, p. 86.

20. McNabb and Mabry, *Teaching*, p. 73.

21. Ibid., p. 75.

The Need for Creative Bible Teaching Methods & Planning

◆ 93 ◆

Chapter 9

Budgets, Finances, and Fund Raising

Dr. Gary B. Zustiak

The Troublesome Issue of Finances and Ministry

Billy Graham once warned an audience of pastors and youth ministers that the two main pitfalls of people in the ministry are sexual temptation and the abuse of money.

Not that money is evil in and of itself. Anyone involved in the nuts and bolts of youth ministry knows that both nuts and bolts cost money. What it does mean is that the way the youth minister handles his personal and ministry finances affects the way people view his ministry.[4]

Olson, Elliot, and Work remind youth ministers that their money management is an issue of character, "Keep integrity first, last, and always. Finances are an arena of spiritual warfare. Financial management, although admittedly only one small part of an effective ministry, is among the most critical of ministry tasks."[5]

One youth minister commented on the dilemma of budgeting this way, "Budget planning is not hard for my youth ministry. We don't get any!"[6] I think many youth ministers, especially those just starting out in small churches, can relate to this frustration. Even if no money is "officially" allocated from the church budget for the youth program, you cannot run a program without some kind of financing or support. A well-planned budget may lead to eventual financial support from the church body. The tighter the finances, the more important it is to have a well-thought-out budget.

The budget planning process begins with a good calendar planning process. Calendar plans that grow out of goals and priorities related to spiritual growth will reflect a min- istry-based approach to youth ministry. A church is more likely to underwrite such an approach. Many churches balk at providing funds for a youth ministry that is simply based on a series of social activities.[7]

The tighter the finances, the more important it is to have a well-thought-out budget.

Youth Ministry and Financial Management

While most youth ministers have a great concern for lost teens and have majored in theological studies in college, they are not high- ly trained handlers of money. In fact, most consider money matters boring or a nuisance. Quarterly financial reports and yearly budgets score low on their top ten list of fun things to do in ministry. Youth ministers are more interested in people than money. Unfortunately this shows in their lack of understanding and ability to handle finan- cial matters related to ministry.

This is especially disconcerting because it is not unusual for youth ministers to deal with a heavy cash flow. When collecting funds for an overseas mission trip, summer camp, CIY. conference, or a weekend retreat a large sum of money is generated that the youth minister is responsible for. Without an established procedure for han- dling and accounting for these funds, the youth minister is open to both temptation and accusation of mishandling the funds.

Money management is one of the main criteria by which the average congregation judges a youth ministry. Most people in the congregation won't know about the youth minister's creative Bible study techniques, his knowledge of contemporary Christian music, or the great retreats and Bible studies that he prepares and presents. But they will hear if the youth program overspends its funds, wants to increase its budget, or is always looking for a handout for some new program or activity.

Money management is one of the main criteria by which the average congregation judges a youth ministry.

Authority equals the power to spend funds. If you must get permission to purchase anything needed for your youth program, then you really do not have any authority over the finances. The person or committee who authorizes each request does. This is a cumbersome way to do things, but the benefit of it is that you will rarely be placed in a situation where you will be tempted or accused of mismanaging funds. If you *do* have the authority to purchase items without having it approved by someone first, then this makes it easier to plan and carry out events. But, it also means that the possibility for mishandling of funds is a reality. There needs to be a balance between *authority* to spend and *accountability* for spending.

"Youth ministry is an expensive proposition. Part of the nature of the beast is that it often costs more per person than any other ministry in the average local church."[8] Quality programming costs money. This is further complicated by the fact that most students don't expect to have to pay for church related activities. This means the youth minister must either learn how to stretch a budget in order to maximize the number of events his program offers or commit himself to a number of fund raisers throughout the year.

Planning a Budget

One of the first tasks a youth minister will be required to perform as a new staff member is to present a yearly budget to the board or finance committee. If you don't have any history in planning budgets, the best place to start is to simply ask, "What is the budget history of the youth program?" Have them provide you with copies of the previous years' youth budget. If possible, try to find out how much money has been allocated to the youth program in the past five years. Be sure to look for major areas of expense so that you will know what the church and youth have been accustomed to and what they consider a priority. Try to determine what the average percentage of increase (if any) has been in the budget.

Another key area of concern with respect to budget is to determine what the allotted money is supposed to cover. I heard of a church that advertised a $25,000 yearly youth budget. That sounded great until the youth minister found out his salary came out of the youth budget!

It is important in determining your budget that you find out exactly what items will come out of your budget and what items may be covered by another related budget (e.g., education, worship, building and grounds, transportation, office, etc.). The following list contains typical budget items that would come under the youth minister's responsibility and would require clarification as to which budget these items would fall under.

- Sunday school curriculum
- Guest speakers
- Refreshments
- Office expenses and mailings
- Office equipment (computer, scanner, color printer, digital camera, etc.)
- Printing and copying (youth newsletter, advertising)
- Sponsor training materials
- Staff leadership subscriptions to youth journals and magazines (*Group, Campus Life, Youthworker Journal,* etc.)
- Seminars and conventions for youth staff
- Curriculum for youth meetings
- Equipment for youth worship
  1. Laptop computer
  2. Video projector
  3. Screen
  4. P.A. System
  5. Lighting
  6. Music books
  7. Music CDs
- Scholarships for camp, CIY, mission trips
- Retreats
  1. Facility rental
  2. Transportation costs
  3. Food
  4. Speaker honorarium
- Mission trips
- Service projects
- Outreach and evangelism
- Transportation (vans or rented coaches)

- Rental (tapes, equipment, etc.)
- Athletic equipment
- Special events — Lock-ins, concerts, socials, etc.
- Internet and web site development
- Special program needs (Fine Arts—puppets, props, scripts, costumes, etc.)

To make wise planning decisions for your youth ministry, you need accurate information gathered through careful research. Winging it and estimations are a good way to crash and burn. The first step you must take is to prioritize which budget items are most important to your ongoing program. If the budget has to be cut back, which items will be erased first?

You must plan ahead. Maintain an ongoing file for ideas or needs of things that should go into the budget. Review your budget two or three months before your proposal is due. Break down your budget by the month. You should also break down your budget by individual expenses. Look over your youth ministry calendar for all projected and past events that need funding. Decide how budgeted items will be accounted for.

Creative Ways to Finance Your Budget Needs

While your total budget may look to you like the gross annual income of a third world country, there is no need to push the panic button. There are a number of ways to creatively finance all of your budget needs.

The first and most obvious place to begin is to request that the overall church budget include a certain percentage or dollar figure each year set aside for the youth program. Most churches are willing to include a certain portion towards the youth program especially if you can document exactly where the funds will go.

But I would caution against having the entire budget underwritten by the church, even if the church can afford it. I have found that if young people are given everything and there is no cost to them, then they do not appreciate it. In fact, they will take it for granted. It is better if the young people have to work at a fund raiser or pay a portion out of their own pocket than to have it given to them on a silver platter.

I would caution against having the entire budget underwritten by the church, even if the church can afford it.

Another source of income is to take up a weekly collection or offering at regular youth meetings. You would be amazed at the disposable income of today's teenagers! Just look at the cars they drive, the clothes they wear, and the number of CDs they buy each week. They have the money to give, they just need to be challenged and instructed on why giving is a part of worship and the Christian life. By challenging students to be regular givers, they learn what it costs to provide the various programs they enjoy through the church.

When you are trying to fund your budget, don't overlook specific organizations, Sunday school classes, and individuals within your church who would be willing to sponsor certain events or expenses. A Sunday school class probably won't want to be a regular contributor to the youth fund in general, but would be willing to cover the cost of several scholarships to camp, CIY, or a mission trip.

As the saying goes, "There is more than one way to skin a cat." Fulfilling your budget needs doesn't always mean that you have to bring in the exact dollar amount on the bottom line of your budget.

Fulfilling your budget needs doesn't always mean that you have to bring in the exact dollar amount on the bottom line of your budget.

Some of your line item needs could be met through donations of services or goods. Instead of having to rent your canoes, tents, camp stoves, etc. for the wilderness trip, several families in the church could loan the youth group their personal camping equipment. In fact, the best thing would be to recruit them as sponsors for the trip. They would best know how to use the equipment properly and would know the most about camping since it is their chosen form of recreation. They would love teaching the youth outdoor skills and survival tips.

Unfortunately, one of the realities of youth work is that many times sponsors, youth ministers, and parents end up paying out of their pocket for certain expenses related to youth activities. If you are in a small church or new youth ministry, this is just one of the hazards of the trade. Learn to see it as giving to Christ (Matt. 25:34-45). If this ends up causing bitterness, then you should find alternate ways of funding or plan more low-cost or no-cost activities.

You can plan your activities to have the students pay as they go. This means that each student simply pays a certain amount which will cover the cost for each event. This works out fine for most small activities, but may not be feasible for special activities such as mission trips or conferences which require a considerable cash outlay.

The most common solution to budget woes is for the youth minister and the youth group to hold fund raisers throughout the year. The money collected is then used to subsidize specific activities or individuals. While this is the most common solution, it is not without its own unique problems and blessings. These must be thoroughly studied before one embarks on planning a fund raiser.

A Look at the Pro's and Con's of Having Fund Raisers

The fact that youth groups have been holding fund raisers for years does not mean the endeavor is without pitfalls. There are some serious negative issues associated with fund raisers that the youth minister must consider before making plans to involve the youth group in the latest fast-bucks scheme.

There are some serious negative issues associated with fund raisers that the youth minister must consider before making plans to involve the youth group in the latest fast-bucks scheme.

The first and most serious issue is that some church board policies do not allow fund raising of any kind—either on or off the church property. A youth minister can find himself in deep trouble with the board if he initiates a fund raiser without first investigating if it is permitted by the church leadership.

The usual reason given for not allowing fund raisers in the church is that it is the equivalent of "money changing in the temple," which Jesus soundly condemned (Matt. 21:12-13; Mark 11:15-17; Luke 19:45-46; John 2:14-16). My home church would not allow gospel groups or evangelists to sell their wares in the church for this reason, but they were allowed to set up a table across the street and people were encouraged to support their ministry after church dismissed. This seemed hypocritical to me as a teen growing up. Whether Jesus' cleansing of the temple precludes selling of any kind associated with the church or whether there were other key issues, such as priests taking undue advantage of people with the exchange of currency and approval of sacrifices is a matter to be determined by sound exegesis of the key passages combined with some social and historical background studies. The conclusions of such a study should be presented to the leadership before attempting to initiate any fund-raising activities in a church which has previously banned it.

Another problematic issue with respect to fund raising is that it can easily be overdone. Young people can get burned out on fund raising as well as the people who are always being dunned to purchase their wares or services. The way to avoid this is by limiting the number of fund raisers the group does in a year and by carefully choosing the fund raisers which will bring in the most profit.

A personal pet peeve of mine is frivolous fund raisers. A frivolous fund raiser is one where youth groups try to gain support through being paid for a basically useless activity such as a "rock-a-thon" or "teeter-totter-a-thon." What good does a person accomplish for the world or the church by staying on a teeter-totter for 36 hours straight without falling off? Why should anyone want to pay them for an activity that neither helps him or others? If you want to hold some kind of an "a-thon" as a fund raiser, at least make it something substantial such as a "read-a-thon" where the Bible is read continuously at a nursing home where people who have lost their sight can still benefit from hearing the word of God. You could do a "trash-a-thon" where individuals or businesses would pay you for every bag of trash you picked up in their area of residence or business.

Fund raisers can have a negative witness to the community at large.

Another issue concerning fund raisers is that they can have a negative witness to the community at large. The church may be seen in the eyes of the community as always having its hand out begging. Jesus didn't take from the communities he preached in, but added to them by providing healing and forgiveness. If the only time the church shows up at someone's door is to solicit funds, it may make him gun-shy and negatively affect future witnessing possibilities.

Some of the products sold in fund raisers are overpriced, poor quality, or come under the category of "Jesus Junk." Do you really want the church associated with poor quality or bad service? Everything about the church should say "excellence" because we have a great God and selling inferior wares or services dishonors the name of our God and the church.

Fund raisers run the risk of placing teens in the position of feeling pressured to participate selling a product they are ashamed of, especially if it is an inferior product or "Jesus Junk." If they receive negative criticism from their peers for what they are being forced to sell, it may cause them to rethink their relationship with the youth program.

Not everything associated with fund raising is negative. There are a number of positive aspects to involving young people in fund raisers. The first is that it teaches teens the value of a dollar as opposed to the church always just giving them everything through the yearly budget. It is a universal truth that you appreciate something much more if it costs you something.

Kids receive more than just financial gain from participating in fund raisers. They learn about relationships, community, and ministry. As they work together on a project, friendships are deepened, and they begin to develop a sense of unity and identity as a youth group as they work towards a common goal. Also, more ownership is given to a project or program that you have personally invested your time and talents in.

Not only can participation in fund raisers help to develop a sense of unity and purpose among the members of the youth group, but it can teach young people some valuable skills—business procedures, salesmanship, service, responsibility, discipline, hard work. These are skills they will take with them into their chosen careers after graduation. The best way to learn these skills is on-the-job training, not in a classroom.

Kids receive more than just financial gain from participating in fund raisers.

Last of all, fund raisers can be a good witness to the community, because they provide a forum which allows the world to see that there are a number of young people who are still willing to work for a worthy project. Too often it seems to me that the only time teenagers are the focus of attention is when they do something bad. Seeing teens hard at work for a project they believe in helps to restore the confidence of adults in the emerging generation.

Do's and Don'ts of Fund Raising[9]

Do's

- Do begin your planning well in advance of the event. Allow at least twice as much time as you think you will need.
- Do be wise concerning the planning of a fund raiser and your own schedule.
- Do give ownership to young people, parents, and other adults by seeking their advice, assistance, and support from the start.
- Do be creative. Think of every possible angle of support for your young people. Consider every way to get what you need.
- Do keep people informed. Make sure the congregational members, staff, parents, and young people are fully aware of the projects, the expectations, the goals, and the time frame for every event.

- Do help young people see a purpose in their projects other than simply raising funds for their event.
- Do thank people who assist your projects—young people, adults, and businesses who donate goods and services. Everyone enjoys appreciation, whether it be public or private.

Don'ts

- Don't wait until the last minute to solicit adult help. Ask parents and other adults to get involved during the beginning stages of planning.
- Don't forget the busy lives of your teenagers. Remember to consider their schedules.
- Don't assume anything. Figure all costs of a project to their highest potential. It's better to be surprised if there's extra money left rather than disappointed because the project costs more than you expected.
- Don't move ahead with a project without proper approval from your church board or elders. Use the channels your church has established.
- Don't forget to pray for your young people and the benefits they can receive through the fund raising projects as well as the events they are raising money for.
- Don't build failure into projects by neglecting publicity, planning, and adequate personnel to carry out the event.
- Don't forget to have fun!

Guidelines to Ensure a Positive Experience with Youth Group Fund Raising

Above all you must keep the church staff, especially the senior minister, informed about your plans for the activity as well as the fund raisers to support it. Always get board approval before you begin any fund raiser. If you don't have the support of the senior minister and the rest of the church staff, you'll be fighting an uphill battle even before fund raising begins.

Form a fund-raising planning committee from your youth group and adult sponsors. Make sure individuals on the committee have gifts that relate to fund raising as well as creativity and wisdom. Don't just pick friends or people you like!

Organize a fun, informative evening for the entire youth group and their parents. Discuss the event being planned and ask the fund-raising planning committee to make an initial report about how funds can be raised to support the activity. If promotional videos, Power-Point, and other media are available, be sure to have them on hand to "sell" the idea. This kind of report will give added impetus to the suggested fund raisers. Invite questions and be prepared to answer them or find out the answers as soon as possible.

Next be sure to provide information to church members and the community about the specific details of the fund raiser in order to generate interest. Publicize the positive accomplishments of the young people in your church, especially those related to mission and service projects.

Encourage youth-group members to give a percentage of the funds they raise to a service organization outside the church. (For example, when raising funds to take a trip to Mexico to work at an orphanage, raise 10 percent more to leave as a donation to buy food for the orphanage after you leave.)

Whatever you choose to do as a fund raiser, make sure you maintain standards of excellence, not just in the products that you sell, but in the services that you offer. Give customers what they expect and were promised. Poor-quality products, items delivered late, and impolite salespeople leave people with a bad feeling about any project.

Some Possible Fund Raising Ideas

Keep in mind that not all fund raisers are the same! Be prudent in your selection. There are several good books and web sites which will offer you a number of choices in fund raising activities. Choose the ones that are best suited to your goals and group resources.

- A-thons: trash-a-thon, read-a-thon
- Food fund raisers: bake sales, salad fairs, ice cream socials, spaghetti dinners
- Selling door to door: greeting cards, magazine subscriptions, pizzas
- Car wash: regular outdoor, indoor, free by sponsor
- Slave sales
- Garage sales, rummage sales
- Spook insurance
- Kidnap the pastor
- Sample fairs
- Hugs for hire
- Party clowns
- '50s carhop
- Crazy auction

- Drive-in movie
- Creative calendars
- Bigger-and-better hunt
- Party clowns
- Project doorknob
- Parents' day off

A Sample Budget

Warning! When you first look at the amount needed for the total youth budget you may think, "No way a church is going to accept this!" It is important that you keep in mind some of the cost will be paid for by the students as they participate in a specific activity, e.g., mission trip, CIY conference, etc. Some of the expense will be covered by the yearly amount that comes from the general church budget designated for the youth program, and the rest will be covered through fund raisers. The entire budget does not come from just one source. I have provided a breakdown of how this might work out at the end of the sample budget.

1. Wednesday Evening Youth Program
   A. Curriculum for 50 students @ $1.00 a week per student $2,600
   B. Refreshments for 50 students @ $1.00 a week per student $2,600
   C. Supplies for crowd-breakers @ $10 per week $ 520
2. Sponsor Development
   A. *Group* Magazine & *Youthworker Journal* subscriptions $ 200
   B. One-day sponsor training retreat for 5 @ $50 each $ 250
   C. Youth Ministry resource books for sponsors $ 100
3. Office Expenses
   A. Scanner $ 75
   B. Digital camera $ 350
   C. Laptop computer $1,500
   D. Software $ 500
   E. Color Printer $ 100
   F. Printing & Copying (youth newsletter & fliers) $ 350
4. Special Program Needs
   A. Video projector $4,000
   B. Motorized screen $ 500
   C. Worship CDs $ 150
   D. Music for worship band $ 150
   E. Skit books for drama team $ 150
   F. Athletic equipment for church league softball $ 200

5. Retreats
   A. Facility rental $3,000
   B. Transportation costs $ 300
   C. Food $2,250
   D. Speaker honorarium $ 300
6. Scholarships
   A. Church Camp 15 @ $75 $1,125
   B. CIY (High School and Jr. High Believe) 15 @ $200 $3,000
   C. Adult Sponsors 5 @ $200 $1,000
7. Transportation
   A. Church Camp $ 100
   B. Summer Conference for High School $ 300
   C. Jr. High Believe $ 100
8. Mission Trip
   A. Transportation $ 500
   B. Food 15 @ $15 per day @ 7 days $1,575
   C. Housing 4 rooms @ $50 each two days $ 400
   D. Supplies (Tracts, balloons, candy, lesson materials) $ 300
9. Work Project
   A. Transportation $ 100
   B. Food 15 @ $15 per day @ 3 days $ 675
   C. Supplies (Paint, hammers, brushes, etc.) $ 500
10. Student Activities (Socials, concerts, etc.)
   A. Transportation $ 300
   B. Supplies (Video rentals, materials, etc.) $ 500

Total	**$30,620**

Amount paid for by students:	$ 9,500
Amount raised by fund raisers:	$ 8,500
Amount from church budget:	$12,620
Total	**$30,620**

Time for Reflection

1. Do you have a well-thought-out budget? If not, why not?
2. Is your budget prioritized so that if you had to make cuts, you would know which ones you would be willing to cut first?
3. Have you thought through all of the creative ways you might be able to fund your budget other than having the church subsidize it?
4. Have you thoroughly thought through all of the pros and cons to fund raising?

SUGGESTED READING LIST

Hinchey, Margaret. *Fund Raisers That Work*. Loveland, CO: Group, 1988.

http://www.fundraisinginformation.com/

http://www.fundraisingweb.org/

http://www.youthspecialties.com/central/view.php3?fund-raise

NOTES ON CHAPTER NINE

1. Paul Borthwick, *Organizing Your Youth Ministry* (Grand Rapids: Zondervan, 1988), p. 110.
2. Leland A. Hamby Jr. "Financing the Youth Program," in *Working with Youth*, ed. by Ray Willey (Wheaton: Victor Books, 1982), p. 88.
3. Ginny Olson, Diane Elliot, and Mike Work, *Youth Ministry Management Tools* (Grand Rapids: Zondervan, 2001), p. 110.
4. Duffy Robbins, *Youth Ministry Nuts & Bolts* (Grand Rapids: Zondervan, 1990), p. 179.
5. Olson, Elliot, and Work, *Management*, p. 99.
6. Wesley Black, *An Introduction to Youth Ministry* (Nashville: Broadman, 1991), p. 224.
7. Black, *Introduction*, p. 224.
8. Robbins, *Nuts & Bolts*, p. 181.
9. Margaret Hinchey, *Fund Raisers That Work* (Loveland, CO: Group, 1988), pp. 8-10.

Chapter 10

Staff Relationships

Dr. Gary B. Zustiak

The Problem No One Wants to Talk About

"You will find no more important relationship in all of your ministry than the one between you and your senior minister."[4] The single greatest problem facing men and women in youth ministry is probably the inability to communicate or develop a good relationship with the senior minister. Research has shown that the cause of most people leaving the ministry is interpersonal conflict. There are many reasons why this is so. Sometimes the different members of the staff end up in a power struggle, each one vying for control so his programs receive the needed funding or support he desires. Other times it is simply a matter of personality conflict, age differences, or a difference in philosophy of ministry. None of these issues *has* to be a problem—it is just that they often become one.

Your relationships with fellow church staffers will have a direct impact on whether or not your youth ministry is successful.

As the old saying goes, "Forewarned is forearmed." This is certainly true in the area of staff relationships. If you know that certain issues hold the potential for serious conflict, you can be proactive and deal with them ahead of time, before they become a problem. Developing positive staff relationships will pay dividends later on down the road.

Your relationships with fellow church staffers will have a direct impact on whether or not your youth ministry is successful. When other staff members and church leaders are interested and supportive of you and your ministry, they can be influential in ways you may never know. This support will not come naturally; it will have to be earned, but it will be worth more than you can possibly imagine.

How to Relate to the Senior Minister[5]

I have heard a number of youth ministers gripe and complain about their senior minister—that he doesn't spend any time with them or give any guidance or oversight. When I ask them if they have taken the responsibility to initiate a relationship with the senior pastor, most look at me like I am crazy. If time and oversight is something that you as a youth minister desire, then don't make it the pastor's responsibility to initiate this relationship—you initiate it! Pursue the pastor for his time. It is possible that he has had some bad experiences with previous youth ministers who didn't want his input and who made it clear that they thought he had nothing to offer. You may have some previous history to overcome, but don't let that stop you. The benefits of a great working relationship greatly outweigh any fears or obstacles that you both need to work through.

One of the best ways to develop a great relationship with the senior minister is simply to encourage him. Go out of your way to find things to compliment him on. It may be his sermon, the way he presides over a board meeting, the changes he has initiated in the worship service, etc. The possibilities are endless. But don't make up things or be dishonest because he will know the difference.

Make your senior minister your project. Go out of your way to make him succeed. Find ways to work in the background that will make him look good. Find out what his needs are and either try to meet them yourself or find other church members or staff who can fulfill them. One of the most important things you can do is to pray for your senior minister regularly. Pray for his ministerial duties, his spiritual life, and for his family.

Learn to love your senior minister. Don't come into a position thinking that the senior minister is the enemy, someone who is going to oppose every new and creative idea you have for youth ministry. Ask about his spiritual pilgrimage. Discover what his gifts and strengths are and be thankful for those contributions to the ministry team. See him as more than a pastor, but a human being with hopes, dreams, fears, and desires.

Above all, earn your senior minister's trust. This will come slowly, but it is one of the fundamental and indispensable building blocks of a healthy staff relationship. The first thing you can do to begin building trust is to keep the minister informed. Communicate clearly and often with him about your philosophy of ministry, program

Perhaps the most common and insidious evil that affects staff relationships is when church members with a personal agenda try to pit one minister against another.

ideas, and special events. Do not betray confidences. Make sure that what is said in private in the office, stays in the office.

Do not allow others to divide you. Perhaps the most common and insidious evil that affects staff relationships is when church members with a personal agenda try to pit one minister against another. Listen to the wise advice of veteran youth minister, Dewey Bertolini:

When someone comes to you for the expressed purpose of criticizing another staff member, refuse to hear him. Politely but firmly state, "I am sorry but I really don't want, nor do I need, to hear what you are saying. He is my friend and I stand with him in absolute loyalty."

Second, insist that the person go to the pastor to express his concerns with him face to face. The person obviously felt the seriousness of the situation justified his coming to you; therefore, it is serious enough for him to go to the pastor.

And then the kicker: tell the critic that you will be informing the pastor that he will be coming to see him with a serious concern within the week. You might add that if he doesn't make contact within the week, the pastor will be calling him.

Needless to say, the disgruntled critic feels stunned.[6]

A potential source of conflict between the youth minister and the senior minister is when there is a difference of opinion concerning a philosophy of ministry or a particular youth activity. For example, while the youth minister may believe the youth group is ready for an overseas mission trip, the senior minister may have some reservations and not give support or final approval for the trip. If something like this should happen, do not blame the minister for the change in plans in front of the youth group. Take responsibility for your own lack of preparation and communication and protect those in authority over you.

What should the youth minister do when he adamantly disagrees with a decision made by the senior pastor or the board? He must ask himself, "Does this issue constitute a nonnegotiable? In other words, does it violate a biblical conviction I would refuse to compromise no matter the cost?" If it is a nonnegotiable, then you must either stand and fight or leave.

An example of a nonnegotiable for me would be if the board and senior minister decided that kids of a different race were no longer welcome to attend youth meetings or church. That violates the biblical principle of salvation for everyone, regardless of race, sex, or social status (Gal. 3:27-28).

If the issue is merely one of preference, then it is a negotiable issue. For these kinds of conflict you should follow the example of Daniel. When he disagreed with the food situation ordered by the king, he respectfully requested an alternate plan that would still uphold the ultimate desire of the king. After carefully presenting his request, Daniel trusted God with the outcome.

If your appeal is refused, demonstrate flexibility concerning your own desires and preferences. Submit to the decision and by your humble and obedient attitude you will be storing up good will for future situations where there may be a difference of opinion concerning a program or activity.

An important lesson I learned in my first youth ministry is to adjust to the senior minister. The first minister I worked with was a fantastic preacher and very evangelistic minded. He had great vision and was a dynamic leader. He was very progressive and instituted many new changes in the church. His motto was, "Get on board or get run over." Needless to say he ruffled the feathers of some of the "old timers." I liked working with this man—we shared a kindred spirit and many of the same gifts.

Tom left to go to seminary, and Marvin replaced him. Marvin was called to ministry later in life. He had been a public school teacher for fifteen years before he went to Bible college. He only needed two years of theological classes on top of his liberal arts degree in order to receive a four-year ministerial degree. When he came to the church, I was in my third year of Bible college. It didn't escape me that I had more Bible training than this man and in my youthful arrogance I thought I was more qualified.

Not only did I have more theological training, I was a better preacher (in the eyes of many of the church members who purposely went out of their way to tell me so!). This man was not strong in the pulpit and neither was he very evangelistic. Needless to say, my personal opinion of him was not good in the first months of our ministry together.

But the problem was not the preacher—it was my lack of humility and immaturity. I soon learned that Marvin had gifts that Tom did not—gifts that were just as important to God and the church. During our time of ministry together I saw Marvin spend three days and nights at the hospital caring for a family who had been told their mother and grandmother was going to die any day. He never left their sides until she left this world for the next. I saw how much that meant to the family to have him there, and how he used the situation to teach about God's comfort and to trust in His promises. I saw the heart of a pastor in Marvin and have never forgotten that lesson. I am indebted to him for teaching me that very important aspect of ministry, and I would never have learned it if I hadn't adjusted to his style of ministry. Once I did that, we had a great ministry together learning to appreciate each other's strengths and adjusting to the differences.

The senior minister is the one who bears the ultimate responsibility for any problems or difficult decisions that must be made within the congregation.

One last observation that will help the youth minister relate in a positive way with the senior minister is for the youth minister to understand his place in the hierarchy of importance with respect to the leading of the church. The senior minister is the one who bears the ultimate responsibility for any problems or difficult decisions that must be made within the congregation.

> We understand we're not number one. We must face the fact squarely and honestly—as youth pastors we are not in charge of the church. We are under authority. We do not have the last word, we do not have the final say, and our great wisdom may not even be consulted on some church-wide issues.[7]

The youth minister and other staff members (important as they are) must remember that they make up the support staff.

Critical Concerns That Affect Staff Relationships

There are a number of key issues that may serve as catalysts for disagreements between the senior minister and the youth minister. A strained relationship can be avoided if these concerns are voiced ahead of time and a consensus reached before they become sources of contention.

One of the most common problem areas concerns the priorities of the youth minister and the youth ministry. Many times the church may have a hidden agenda by which they judge the effectiveness of the youth minister and his program. If the church has certain expectations, these need to be stated clearly in the job description. It is not fair to hire a youth minister who believes that discipleship and small groups is the key to effective ministry when the senior minister and congregation judge the effectiveness of the program by the number of students involved in "big" programs. This will inevitably lead to conflict.

Another possible source of conflict is in the area of professional standards for the ministerial staff. Some ministers want all the staff to "dress up" for the office each day—even if it means simply khakis and a button-down shirt. The youth minister may want to wear jeans and a T-shirt claiming that he relates to students better that way.

Hair styles—length and color—are a similar issue. The senior minister may not allow any "fad" hair cuts on staff members, but demand a "clean-cut" look. The same could be said for tattoos and body piercings. The youth minister may believe they help him to relate to the youth culture much easier while the senior minister may think they are only signs of conforming to the world and not allow them on staff members.

The issue of office hours would also fall under this heading. The senior minister may want the staff to keep regular office hours from 9:00 a.m. to 5:00 p.m. The youth minister may want to make a case for coming in later in the morning because he is so often up late counseling teens or that he needs to be in the schools at 3:00 when they let out to meet students instead of sitting in an isolated office.

The youth minister may find himself at odds with the powers that be because of his impatience with how long it takes the board to come to a decision about some simple youth-related request. He may be frustrated with the facilities that are assigned to the youth and with the amount of money they are allocated from the church budget.

It is inevitable that the youth minister will make some mistakes along the way. At some point in time, he is going to have some angry parents up in arms (whether justified or not it doesn't matter—it is going to happen). When this happens, he should inform the senior minister first. That way the minister is not surprised when the angry mob storms his office on Monday morning. He can then easily diffuse the situation by stating that he is already aware of the situation and has taken the proper steps to rectify it. The youth minister will gain the trust of the senior minister through these "growing pains" because he has kept the senior minister informed and has not tried to hide anything from him.

Expectations That Affect Staff Relationships

When you join a church staff, there are certain expectations that you have concerning various staff members. While there must be allowances made for individual gifts and skills, there are certain standards and behaviors that are expected in every ministry setting. When these are not met, tensions develop among the staff.

The youth minister has a right to expect certain things from the senior minister. Doctrinally the lead pastor must be a man who is committed to Christ and the church and who believes in the changing power of the Word. He must believe in the death, burial, and resurrection of Christ and in the judgment to come. He must teach that salvation is through Christ alone and that the free gift of eternal life is intended for all people, regardless of race, social position, or nationality.

From a leadership standpoint, he should be a man of vision, possessing the ability to inspire people to follow his lead. He needs to have the heart of a shepherd, caring for those entrusted to his care and willing to go out and bring back the strays. Since he heads up a multiple staff, he needs to be a team worker and not a Lone Ranger. This means he needs to be able to delegate responsibility to key staff members and not try to do everything himself. It also means that he trusts his staff and doesn't try to micromanage them. He must believe in the importance of every staff position and do what is necessary to support the minister called to fill that ministry.

With respect to youth ministry, the senior minister must believe in the importance of youth ministry and see it as an essential part of the total ministry of the church. He must not resent the youth minister or see him as infringing on his territory. With all the means available at his disposal, he should support the programs initiated by the youth minister, unless there is some doctrinal issue or other concern that may affect the total well-being of the church.

What kinds of things should the senior minister do in order to best facilitate good staff relationships? First of all, he should be willing to stand up for the members of his staff. He should insist on staff meetings where any interpersonal problems can get ironed out and where the direction the church needs to go is established through dialog and the input of the entire staff. Staff meetings should not be just business meetings, but time should be set aside for spiritual growth and prayer. The senior minister should never publicly criticize his staff. This does not mean that he will always agree with every decision or action made by his staff, but that he will handle any disagreements in the privacy of the office or during a staff meeting.

What Kinds of Things Make for Poor Staff Relationships?

Just as there are certain things that help build healthy staff relationships, there are also things that will hurt or destroy staff relationships. For example, if the senior minister undercuts the authority of his staff members with other leaders and adults, there will be no harmony or unity among the staff. This usually shows up in board meetings or times of crisis within the congregation.

If the senior minister does not trust his staff or encourage them, then the staff becomes discouraged and disheartened. This manifests itself when the minister does not stand behind new programs or encourage innovative change. Staff members do not like being taken for granted but need periodic words of encouragement as much as anyone else does. If the minister lacks respect for you and your position, then the motivation to "go the extra mile" is lost.

A common problem (especially among youth ministers) that is sure to cause tension within a staff relationship is the lack of a clear-cut job description. This causes problems because the youth minister either ends up at the mercy of everyone in the congregation who thinks of a job or program that the youth minister should be responsible for or the youth minister ends up doing everything the senior minister doesn't want to do. A detailed job description protects both the youth minister and the congregation. The lack of one invites problems because it is inevitable that the youth minister and senior minister are going to have different opinions on what constitutes the chief responsibilities of the youth minister and the focus of the youth ministry program.

Sometimes disagreement amongst the staff is the result of personality conflict. If the senior minister is oversensitive to suggestions or criticism and gets his feelings hurt easily, he may respond in a defensive and insecure manner. This may cause communication to break down between him and the other staff members. It is a fact of life that sometimes people's personalities simply clash and you just don't get along. It is not a matter of any party doing anything wrong—it is simply a matter of preference and choice. You just get on each other's nerves like The Odd Couple.

There are some senior ministers (although they are becoming fewer in number) who simply don't understand or care about youth ministry. These are the ones who love to talk about "the good old days" before there were youth ministers when the senior minister did it all. He went to camp, organized VBS, and directed the youth group meetings. He was a "one-man band." This minister sees the youth minister as an unwanted intruder, trespassing on his sacred territory. He will not give his support to the youth minister or his programs because he secretly resents his presence and is subtly trying to sabotage anything he does.

If the senior minister doesn't hold regular staff meetings, then small differences and conflicts never have a chance to get ironed out. They fester and grow until there is a major explosion. Also, it is through meeting together regularly that people get to know and appreciate one another. The more you know about someone, the more willing you are to try to work things out.

The good news is that everything mentioned in this section that contributes towards poor staff relationships is fixable! Nothing is laid in stone. As long as every member of the staff understands the importance of positive staff relationships and is willing to work and make changes, then any problems that might arise can be corrected.

Time for Reflection

1. What are you actively doing to promote positive staff relationships?
2. What could you do better that would help improve the quality of your relationship with the senior minister?
3. Do you have a detailed job description? If not, why not? What would you want included in a job description?
4. How do you handle conflict and criticism? What could you do differently?

SUGGESTED READING LIST

Ambrose, Dub. "Is It Possible to Team Up with Your Pastor?" *Youthworker* (Winter 1988): 50-56.

Nuechterlein, Anne Marie. *Improving Your Multiple Staff Ministry.* Minneapolis: Augsburg, 2001.

Stevens, Doug. "Looking over Both Sides of the Fence." *Youthworker Journal* (Fall 1985): 25-32.

NOTES ON CHAPTER TEN

1. Dewey Bertolini, *Back to the Heart of Youth Work* (Wheaton, IL: Victor Books, 1989), p. 128.

2. Ridge Burns, *Create in Me a Youth Ministry* (Wheaton, IL: Victor Books, 1986), p. 162.

3. Doug Stevens, "Looking over Both Sides of the Fence," *Youthworker Journal* (Fall 1985): 30.

4. Bertolini, *Back,* p. 128.

5. Many of the ideas for this section came from: William H. Stewart and William E. Yaeger, "The Youth Minister and the Senior Pastor," in *The Complete Book of Youth Ministry,* ed. by Warren S. Benson and Mark H. Senter III (Chicago: Moody, 1987), pp. 115-118.

6. Bertolini, *Back,* p. 136.

7. Len Kageler, *The Youth Minister's Survival Guide* (Grand Rapids: Zondervan, 1992), p. 69.

Chapter 11
Discipline in the Youth Group

Dr. Gary B. Zustiak

An Historical Perspective on Discipline in America

Tony Campolo gives some wonderful sociological insight into the problem of discipline as it relates to the family in his book, *Growing Up in America.*[4] It used to be that the discipline that took place in the home was very authoritarian and the responsibility of the father. The father set the rules and enforced them. This was easy in the preindustrial agrarian era because most families lived on the farm and the fathers were at home all the time and able to take care of any discipline problems directly.

But in today's family, the father is absent from the home most of the day due to our socio-economic changes. This is not so much by choice as it is a matter of forced practicality; the father often provides the majority of the family's income. Consequently, he has lost his position of authority and control in the family. In a number of families the father is absent because of the growing number of divorces and their resulting single-parent situations. Step-families often do not fare much better. These second marriages place the father, or step-father, in awkward situations where parental authority and discipline are needed. The desire to promote unity in the newly created family often leads to overly lax or harsh standards as the children and new step-dads try to work out the details of their relationships.

It would seem logical that the mother would then take over this role. But Tony contends that most American mothers feel caught in the double bind between being the chief caregiver or disciplinarian. They are not comfortable being both so they choose to love. The fact that many single-parent mothers are just too tired or emotionally drained after working all day to take on the rigors of disciplining the children only adds to this frustrating situation. So they simply choose to ignore improper behavior and the children go undisciplined.

If the fathers can't rule the home because they are absent and if the mother is afraid to for fear her children won't love her, who does rule the typical middle class family? The children do!

If the fathers can't rule the home because they are absent and if the mother is afraid to for fear her children won't love her, *who does* rule the typical middle class family? *The children do!* This leaves children growing up without proper boundaries being enforced in their lives. This lack of boundaries and direction causes many problems for these children as they grow up. Campolo draws upon Erik Erikson, the famed Harvard psychologist, who concludes that

> the demise of parental leadership in American families has left teenagers with the burden of making decisions they are ill equipped to make. The authority vacuum in American family life has forced young people to accept privileges and responsibilities they cannot handle. In short, the inability of families to cope with changes brought on by the urban industrial revolution has placed teenagers in a burdensome position. They are being forced into a state of freedom that their immaturity has not equipped them to handle. The depressions and despondencies so typical of contemporary teenagers are, in part, related to this. The rising rate of teenage suicide is also a likely concomitant.[5]

Moreover, drug use and alcoholism among teenagers are probably related to the *lack of regulations* in the teenage world. Young people need structure in their lives if they are to survive psychologically, and they seem incapable of creating that structure for themselves. A serious need exists for the church to take action in this area.

An interesting study was conducted with young school children. The school playground was once surrounded by a tall wire fence. When the teacher on playground duty would monitor the children, she would stand near the door of the school and look out over the playground. The children played in every quarter of the school playground—some on the monkey bars, some on the swings, others far away on the ballfield.

But someone complained that the tall wire fence was suggestive of a prison and unfit for a school yard. So the fence was taken down. Nothing else was changed in the school yard. All the other playground equipment remained where it had originally been. But there was a noticeable difference in where the children chose to play. They all huddled near the teacher. The absence of a solid boundary made them all feel insecure. What we learn from this is that rules can also serve as boundaries and provide a calming effect of structure.

Studies on cults and new religions show that young people will often join these groups seeking a parent substitute who will authoritatively direct their lives and deliver them from the uncertainties of an unstructured life. They find it comforting to have "parents" who can give direction to their lives and spell out in detail what should be said and done each moment of the day.

What Is Discipline?

What is meant by the word "discipline"? In the New Testament, the word that is usually translated as "discipline" is the Greek word *paideuo*. The lexicon defines *paideuo* as: "to bring up, instruct, train, educate; correct, give guidance to someone; discipline, punish, whip, scourge,"[6] "to train children, to be instructed or taught, to cause one to learn; to chastise or castigate with words, to correct; to mold the character of others by reproof and admonition; use employed of God, to chasten by the infliction of evils and calamities; to chastise with blows, to scourge."[7]

I would have you notice that there are two separate concepts contained within the meaning of the word "discipline": punishment and instruction. Both aspects of the definition must be present in order to give an accurate accounting of the word. Punishment is used to correct a present wrong behavior; it is the penalty for failing to do what is right when the right is known. Instruction focuses on future behavior, that which is proper and right. It has more of a preventive emphasis.

The problem I find when studying books about discipline, especially educational books which focus on discipline in the classroom, is that they only want to focus on the instructional aspect of discipline and totally ignore the punishment part. In fact, they will go so far as to say that instruction and punishment are polar opposites and should never be used together. Yet the biblical definition for discipline shows that instruction and punishment must go hand in hand.

Educational psychologists will argue that punishment teaches children to fear and increases the likelihood that they will resort to violence when they find themselves at odds with a peer. They claim it is damaging to the psyche of the developing child. But I would argue that the Bible presents God as using both instruction (Ten Commandments, prophets, and priests) and punishment (ten plagues, Babylonian captivity, drought, etc.) to guide the nation and people of Israel. Since God is the one who created us, He will best know how to train and correct us. He would never do anything that was ultimately harmful to His people, but only that which worked toward their ultimate good. It is true that discipline often brings temporary pain, but that is nothing when compared to the eternal reward that it brings (Heb. 12:5-11).

The ultimate goal of discipline is to train up a person who will make the right choices on his own because he wants to.

The ultimate goal of discipline is to train up a person who will make the right choices on his own because he wants to. Hopefully he sees the inherent value in the correct choice and makes his decision based on that and not because someone is going to punish him if he doesn't. This is the difference between internal versus external motivation.

Our goal is to develop young people capable of thinking and acting for themselves. Undue dependence on a disciplinary authority can cripple the personality and stifle progressive independence. Discipline that encourages independent thought and action, however, will produce personal freedom and confidence.[8]

When a child is young, he best responds to instructional discipline when it is accompanied by some form of external motivation such as a removed privilege, time out, or grounding, etc. However, the ultimate goal is that eventually the child will agree with the values being taught and internalize them so that he will choose the right action even if the threat of punishment is removed or no longer present.

Discipline goes beyond demands and intimidation. Its purpose is not only to achieve right behavior, but also to progressively lessen dependence upon the disciplinary authority. External discipline that fails to result in self-discipline fails altogether.[9]

Why the Need for Discipline?

Becoming a disciple of Christ requires obedience and self-discipline in every area of life.
- "Taking every thought captive," 2 Cor. 10:5.
- "I discipline my body and make it serve me," 1 Cor. 9:27.
- "Those whom the Lord loves, He disciplines," Heb. 12:6.

One of the great developmental and psychological inadequacies of today's youth is an "emotional softness" that comes from never having to pay the consequences for their own actions. Mom and Dad rescue the child from any trouble or problems, so he never learns to deal with his own pain. When he gets out into the real world and is forced to suffer the consequences for his own actions, he crumbles and folds under the pressure. Many turn to drugs or suicide because they have never learned how to handle pain or say "no" to themselves.

One of the great developmental and psychological inadequacies of today's youth is an "emotional softness" that comes from never having to pay the consequences for their own actions.

There are many purposes and benefits of discipline for the individual. Consider the following list. Keep in mind this list is not exhaustive but is merely representative of the many benefits of discipline found in the Bible and life. You discipline a student of any age:

- So he won't ruin his life, Prov. 19:18.
- To help him make wise choices, Prov. 22:6.
- To keep her from hell, Prov. 23:14.
- To train for maturity, Heb. 12:11.
- To give you peace of mind, Prov. 29:17.
- To communicate love, Prov. 13:24; Heb. 12:6.
- So she won't be given a more severe judgment later, 1 Sam. 24:11.

- Because deep down inside he really desires guidelines and security.
- Because obedience is not a natural instinct. It must be learned.
- Because teenagers are not equipped to know what is best for themselves; they must submit themselves to those adults who love and care for them.

Not only is discipline needed for the individual, but it must also be applied to entire groups such as a Sunday school class or youth group meeting. The reason for enforcing discipline upon the whole group is it is necessary for the development of a proper attitude toward all authorities. Discipline is a must because all students will learn good or bad from their class experience. It is never neutral! Discipline is essential to accomplishing an objective.

Preventive Discipline

Without a doubt the best thing you can do as a youth minister is to be as proactive as you can in the area of discipline problems. Try to prevent them from happening. There are some common problem areas that you should be aware of. First of all, I would encourage you to do a little self-analysis of you and your programming to make sure that you are not contributing to the discipline problems, even if unintentionally. You may be surprised to find out the kinds of things that may actually create discipline problems among the young people.

The youth minister needs to carefully examine how he uses the time allotted for teaching and the lesson itself. It used to be a constant struggle for me to get the high school class to settle down, quit talking, and pay attention to the lesson. I would work very hard preparing a relevant lesson, but I would end up frustrated because instead of presenting the lesson, I would spend an inordinate amount of time pleading with the students to quit talking and to listen to the lesson.

One day I was lamenting about my frustration with this situation with one of the leaders of the high school group. He gave me some great insight. Lance told me that most of the teens in the group had grown up together and in the church and were good friends, but hardly anyone had any of the same classes at school together. Most had after-school jobs or activities that kept them apart. Church was about the only time they were able to catch up on one another's lives. It was important relational time for them.

Once I understood this, instead of fighting it, I programmed for it. I built in a fifteen-minute sharing time at the beginning of the lesson. That still left me with thirty-five minutes for teaching, which was plenty of time considering the average attention span of most teens. It solved my "talking" problem during the lesson. I found that I was actually able to get more quality teaching in during the remaining thirty-five minutes than in the previous fifty minutes because I didn't have to constantly stop and chastise kids for talking.

You must also take into consideration the age factor when thinking of preventive discipline issues. The younger the student, the more critical it is that you have a balanced meeting time. By this I mean that you balance the amount of sitting time with the proper amount of physical activity time. For example, if you have one hour of junior church it will be absolutely impossible to expect four- to eight-year-olds to sit still for that entire hour. You need to divide up the time between having physically active times (action songs, games, working on a craft) with quiet times (sermon, prayer, communion, lesson).

The lesson you choose to present must be relevant to the students' needs if you expect to keep their attention. Understand that it is possible for a lesson to be biblical but not relevant. For example, I could base a lesson around Israel's battle with the Jebusites. That is biblical, but not relevant to teens growing up in the 21st century. (After all, how many Jebusites do *you* know?) The exception to this rule would be if I could find some timeless principle involved in the battle that might apply to teens' lives today.

Not only must your lesson be relevant, you must be sure to have a proper student/sponsor ratio. The rule is, the younger the student, the smaller the ratio needed. When teaching teens, you can get by on a 1-12 ratio, but you should not be any higher than 1-6 when teaching four- and five-year olds. The younger students simply demand more attention because their skills and attention spans are not as highly developed as older students.

If the students know that you truly care about their lives outside of the classroom arena, they will give you more respect and not cause as many discipline problems. This can only take place if you develop a relationship with the student outside of class. If the only time you see the student is in a class setting, then he may think that you are only interested in him as another number to fill a class. You might be amazed at how spending a little "Coke" time after school or cheering them on at an athletic contest affects their classroom behavior.

One of my pet peeves is with youth ministers who complain about discipline problems within the youth group but who are not examples of obedience and respect themselves. How can you expect your students to behave any differently than what you model for them? I know that some youth ministers do this unintentionally—they are just trying to be "fun" or "liked" by the students so they act up during the church service by passing notes or making faces while the minister is preaching the sermon. But the ultimate result of such actions is that you are modeling misbehavior so you should not be surprised when the students who attend your youth group meeting do the same to you.

The teacher needs to be aware of his physical state and how that affects classroom behavior. When I am tired or sick, I know I don't have the patience with students that I normally do. It seems that I am more sensitive and easily irritated during those times. So when I find myself irritated at a student, I need to ask myself, "Did this student *really* do something that deserves my attention, or am I just being supersensitive because of my own tiredness or illness?"

The last checkpoint that relates to discipline issues for the teacher is his own emotional state. If the teacher is feeling burned out, then there is little tolerance for minor infractions of the rules. If you had a confrontation at home before you got to church, your heart is not in the lesson but in the unresolved issue back home.

A related question is "Do you really like to teach or have you been forced into this situation?" If you do like teaching, do you like this age group? If you don't, it affects your emotional state to the point that the students know your heart is not in it, so they act out.

Not only does the teacher's emotional state and preparedness affect discipline issues, but the physical setting of the class can also contribute to discipline problems. The size of the meeting area is a significant issue. If you place too many students in a room that is too small, it is inevitable that they will begin to invade one another's space and begin misbehaving.

The temperature of the room also affects behavior. If the room is too hot or too cold, it is impossible to stay focused on the lesson. The students' main concern becomes their discomfort. That is why it is important for the teacher to arrive early and set the thermostat to a comfortable temperature so that when the students arrive the room is a desirable temperature.

Another issue that can adversely affect discipline is simply the room environment. Is it attractive and conducive to teaching? I remember holding youth meetings in a moldy, smelly church basement. The paint was peeling off the wall and bare pipes hung down from overhead. It was no wonder the students always wanted to horse around down there—they knew they certainly weren't going to hurt anything!

Even if the room itself is attractive, the way you arrange the chairs for teaching can help or hinder discipline issues. Instead of setting the chairs up in rows like a school classroom, forming them in a semicircle is much better. It allows for more interaction between the students and feels friendlier and less formal.

Try to keep your meeting areas free from any distractions, both inside and outside. One of the worst situations is when you have several classes that have to share the same large space with only portable dividers between them. The sounds of one teacher and classroom easily drift over to another and cause the students to lose their focus and wonder what is going on in the other classroom.

If the discipline problem does not originate with the youth minister or the environment, then it may have something to do with the youth themselves. Some young people bring with them their own unique home problems. This can be anything from having non-Christian parents to simply being overindulged and underdisciplined at home. There may be some serious issues such as physical, emotional, or sexual abuse that are causing the misbehavior at church. It's also possible that there is some kind of trauma in the home such as the terminal illness of a family member, an impending divorce, or job loss. All of these should be considered if a particular student seems to be a regular violator of the rules. Don't just assume that he is a "bad" kid, but get to know him and his personal situation. You may gain some insight into why he is always in trouble. It may be a way of getting attention in the hopes that the other issues might be addressed in some way.

There are a number of physical problems that may cause students to become disciplinary problems. An increasing number of students are being identified as ADD or ADHD. You should learn all you can about this problem so you know how best to work with the student. Some students simply have a poor diet, and either the excess sugar has them hyper or they are lethargic and don't want to participate. Others suffer from a lack of sleep or excessive TV viewing.

The last area to consider in the way of discipline issues has to do with problems with groups. It is not always individual students who disrupt your meetings but groups of students. Usually these are part of a particular gang or clique. The solution is to break up the seating arrangement so the violators are not seated next to each other or to be sure that adult sponsors sit in the middle of the group.

Guidelines for Establishing Discipline

The following suggestions will help you in establishing discipline within your group. Most of these are self-explanatory. Don't let the simplicity of the guideline keep you from implementing it. These are tried and true over years of youth work and classroom experience. Keep in mind the age group and background of the students you primarily work with as some guidelines work better with specific age groups than others. Some are not appropriate for all age groups.

- Accentuate the positive.
- Expect the best.
- Allow youth input on making the rules.
- State the rules positively.
- Keep rules to a minimum; make them reasonable.
- Be specific with rules; explain them, don't assume.
- Be specific about the punishment for breaking the rules.
- Make sure the rules are known ahead of time.
- Make sure the punishment is worse than the offense.
- Warn once and only once.
- Never threaten with what you cannot or will not do.
- Build self-esteem; don't tear it down.
- Separate offender from the offense.
- Visualize potential.
- Start off with control.
- Enforcement of discipline must be consistent.
- Don't make a bigger deal of an issue than it warrants.
- Discipline privately if possible.
- Don't be afraid of losing your popularity.
- Do involve parents in ongoing problems.
- Do practice compassion and understanding; be transparent.

- Make the punishment a natural consequence of the misbehavior.
- Increase the punishment with the number of offenses.
- Never discipline in anger.
- Always back authority.
- Don't be afraid to admit your mistakes and apologize.

Specific Disciplinary Measures

Now that you are convinced about the importance of maintaining discipline within the youth group and classroom, you probably want some specific measures that you can implement that will help you maintain discipline. The following list is given to help you with that choice. When choosing a specific disciplinary measure, make sure that you take into account the age of the student and the severity of the infraction. Always try to match the punishment with the offense. In other words, try to make the punishment a natural consequence of the offense. Look over the list and choose the ones you feel the most comfortable using and which you believe will be the most effective with your students. Above all, don't be afraid to take action! "Unruly students will never get the lessons you are trying to teach, anyway, until they first learn to manage their behavior in your ministry setting. Don't allow one student's behavior to ruin a meeting for others."[10]

Unruly students will never get the lessons you are trying to teach, anyway, until they first learn to manage their behavior in your ministry setting. Don't allow one student's behavior to ruin a meeting for others.
—Doug Fields

I would caution you about choosing any kind of punishment that might be misconstrued as abuse. Never, ever, ever under any circumstances should you physically strike a student. You may have to break up a fight and restrain a student, but you should never hit or strike a student under any circumstances. Should you ever strike or hit a student, you open yourself and the church up to a lawsuit. I would also caution you against using any type of reprimand that might humiliate a student.

- Draw the individual aside (eye, name, gesture, touch)
- Remove a privilege
- Work it off
- Ask a question
- Be a name-dropper

- Sit next to the disturber
- Spend time out of the classroom with them
- Pause until quiet is restored
- Talk with parents; make parents sit with them
- Natural consequences of inappropriate actions
- Ask the offender what seems to be the problem
- Pray with teens when disciplining them
- Let them explain what they did wrong and why it was wrong
- Public apologies
- Allow them some options as to what punishment should be taken
- Group decision
- Grounded from an activity
- Recognize individual problems; it isn't usually the whole group
- Isolate a student
- Utilization method; give a specific teen a job to do
- Move around the room while teaching
- Follow up in the home
- Encourage and affirm teens whenever possible
- Set standards—enforce standards—anticipate problems
- Compensate for the disciplinary affair with sincere, positive attention. Problem youths only hear from adults when something goes wrong.

Qualities of a Good Disciplinarian

It is not enough just to have guidelines implemented and specific disciplinary measures in mind in order to maintain discipline. You as the leader must set the tone by your own actions and attitudes. The way you live your life in front of your students will greatly influence the effectiveness of your strategy. Sometimes it is a matter of personal characteristics. Other times it is a specific behavior that you demonstrate which will either reinforce good behavior from your students or give them a reason to rebel.

It should be obvious that you must practice what you preach. In other words, you need to be a model of someone who follows the rules and respects authority. This applies to everything from whether or not you obey the speed limit to your attitude towards the senior minister and other members of the staff.

Don't be afraid to admit it when you are wrong. Sometimes this means going to a specific individual, other times it means admitting your mistake to the whole group. While this is a very humbling thing to do, you will be amazed at how much weight it carries with your students. Their respect and estimation of you will soar if they see you willing to admit your mistakes.

You need to be consistent and impartial in your disciplinary measures. Unenforced law becomes no law at all. You cannot punish someone for an infraction of the rules one day

Unenforced law becomes no law at all.

and ignore it the next. You must also enforce the rules consistently as it applies to students. Don't come down hard on the regular troublemaker for something that you ignore in one of your favorite or leadership students.

It is not wise to have too many rules. Keep your rules to a minimum. Think about a typical situation and figure out what you can overlook or dismiss through a sense of humor. Be firm but merciful. It helps to think back to when you were a teen. Overall try to keep a positive and patient attitude.

The more you know about your students individually and corporately, the easier it is to deal with them when there are discipline issues. If you have visited them in their homes and spent time with them after school sharing a Coke or watching them in some kind of event, you will earn the right to be heard. They will be able to receive your correction much more easily because they know you care about them through your personal interest in their lives and activities.

Above all, don't be afraid of trouble or confrontation. Don't allow discipline to distance you and your teens. Too many rookie youth ministers make the mistake of overlooking discipline issues early in their ministry because they want so much to be liked and to have a "successful" program. Then later on, when the problem is out of hand and they try to correct it, it is either too late or it has escalated way beyond what it would have been if he had dealt with it when it first occurred. They are afraid if they make students "toe the line" that they will get mad and drop out of the youth program. Understand this, you are not called to be "liked" but to be a pastor and prophet to the young people in your charge.

Do not try to "crush" a problem to prove your power. This will only have a negative outcome. Either your students will see you as overly harsh and uncaring and reject you, or they will see it as a challenge and resist your efforts at discipline even more strenuously. You discipline a student for his benefit, not your own. Your goal is to instill values and correct behavior, not to build up your own self-esteem.

Discipline is like a root canal. It isn't fun, but it is good for you. Both are simple but decisive procedures that keep decay from destroying a whole structure, whether it be a tooth, a person, or an entire ministry. Once done, the weak and painful is restored to a state of strength and usefulness.[11]

Time for Reflection

1. How does this chapter change your understanding of discipline?
2. Does your own example encourage good behavior in your students or does it contribute to the discipline problem?
3. Are you afraid to discipline out of fear you will not be liked? What can you do to change this?

SUGGESTED READING LIST

Christie, Les. *When You Have to Draw the Line*. Wheaton, IL: Victor Books, 1988.

Fields, Doug. *Purpose Driven Youth Ministry*. Grand Rapids: Zondervan, 1998, pp. 327-343.

NOTES ON CHAPTER ELEVEN

1. Brian Giebler, "Discipline in the Youth Program," in *Methods for Youth Ministry*, ed. by David Roadcup (Cincinnati: Standard, 1986), p. 73.

2. Doug Fields, *Purpose Driven Youth Ministry* (Grand Rapids: Zondervan, 1998), p. 328.

3. Les Christie, *When You Have to Draw the Line* (Wheaton, IL: Victor Books, 1988), p. 37.

4. See Anthony Campolo, *Growing Up in America* (Grand Rapids: Zondervan, 1989), pp. 69-78.

5. Anthony Campolo, "The Youth Culture in Sociological Perspective," in *The Complete Book of Youth Ministry*, ed. by Warren S. Benson and Mark H. Senter III (Chicago: Moody, 1987), p. 41.

6. William F. Arndt and F. Wilbur Gingrich, *A Greek-English Lexicon of the New Testament and Other Early Christian Literature* (Chicago: The University of Chicago Press, 1957), pp. 608-609.

7. Joseph Henry Thayer, *Greek-English Lexicon of the New Testament* (Grand Rapids: Zondervan, 1975), p. 473.

8. Giebler, "Discipline," p. 75.

9. Ibid.

10. Fields, *Purpose Driven*, p. 339.

11. Ibid., p. 343.

Chapter 12

Recruitment, Retention, and Retiring of Volunteer Help

Dr. Gary B. Zustiak

"The staff does not exist for the youth pastor. The youth pastor exists for the staff." —*Dewey Bertolini*[1]

"The diversity of our students, the demands of leadership, and the need for quality one-on-one ministry forces us to build a team of associates who will lead the youth ministry with us."
—*Paul Borthwick*[2]

"A broad ministry can only stand on a broad foundation of volunteers."
—*Barry St. Clair*[3]

Why the Need to Recruit Volunteer Youth Workers?

There are a number of reasons why it is necessary for the youth minister to recruit a team of volunteer youth workers, not the least of which is the simple fact that it is impossible to do the job alone. Moses once tried to carry the weight of leadership alone, and he was advised by his father-in-law that this was not a good idea because he would only end up wearing himself out (Exod 18:13-26). Although Moses took Jethro's advice at first, he later slipped back into a solo leadership style. The result of this was that Moses ended up in despair and crying out to God for someone to help carry the burden of leadership because it was too heavy for him (Num. 11:10-17).

Youth ministry leadership in the local church is not a one-man show.

The long-term effectiveness of youth ministry depends on the ability of the youth minister to develop a group of committed adult volunteers who are capable teachers, counselors, and disciplers. While the professional youth worker is drawn to youth ministry by his or her love for young people and his desire to serve them, his key task is to develop adults, who will in turn work with youth.[4]

It should be a crime not to utilize a volunteer staff because the blessings of a volunteer staff flow both ways. The youth minister benefits from the gifts, abilities, and experience of the staff. It multiplies the effectiveness of his outreach a hundredfold. Many people are willing to help on a volunteer basis because they want the feeling, which their regular jobs do not give, of using their skills to make a lasting difference in the world and to feel appreciated.

The long-term effectiveness of youth ministry depends on the ability of the youth minister to develop a group of committed adult volunteers.

One-leader youth programs are self-limiting. They are limited in the number of people they can reach, the breadth of people they can reach, and the depth of individual ministry they can provide. Even youth programs with many workers are actually one-man bands when the volunteers function as chaperons and the youth minister carries out all the significant jobs. In a healthy church youth program, young people are able to look to a variety of volunteer adult leaders as role models, counselors, and teachers.[5]

A youth minister must ask himself a very serious question: "What are you going to leave behind when you leave?" If you do everything yourself, then when you leave the program collapses. If you train a staff of volunteer leaders, then when you leave, the program continues because you leave behind a staff who understands your philosophy of ministry and knows how to implement the programs that will carry it through. When you recruit and train volunteer youth workers you are leaving behind a legacy.

When the youth minister tries to carry out the responsibilities of the youth program all by himself, he always ends up "overcommitted, overworked, overwhelmed, and over a barrel."[6] When it is just one person trying to do all the work, there is always that nagging feeling, "I could and should have done a little bit more." The guilt can eat you alive. The effectiveness of the youth program is hindered if the youth minister tries to do everything himself. Most educators recommend one adult to every 6-12 people for optimum learning.

Veteran youth worker, Les Christie, has said "the long-term effectiveness of youth ministry depends on the ability of the youth worker to develop a team of committed adult volunteers."[7] Both the quality and the quantity of the youth program is in direct proportion

The purpose of youth ministry is not to entertain—it is to raise up a new generation of leaders who are mature and knowledgeable in the faith.

to the youth minister's ability to recruit and utilize a staff of volunteers. One of the reasons for this is that effective youth ministry is built primarily upon relationships. It is impossible for just one person to develop and maintain a large number of quality relationships. A number of leaders are needed to accomplish this goal. Programs will attract teens, but it is relationships that will keep them. Relationships, not programs, mold lives. Programs merely provide the framework for ministry to take place.

For too long youth ministry has been the butt of jokes in leadership circles. Youth ministers have more than once been referred to as the "balloons and Kool-aid brigade." The reason for this is that in the early years of youth ministry, the program focus was more on entertainment than serious discipleship. If youth ministry is ever going to get a serious hearing in the church, it will have to overcome its past. The purpose of youth ministry is not to entertain—it is to raise up a new generation of leaders who are mature and knowledgeable in the faith (Col 1:28; Eph 4:12-13; 2 Tim 2:2).

Some things in life should never be done alone because it isn't safe. When I was in high school, I was a member of the gymnastics team. I loved jumping on the trampoline and working out on the still rings. As much as I loved working out on these, I didn't get to spend as much time on them as I would have liked because in order to work them, I had to have a partner. Our coach had a strict rule: you never worked the apparatus without a "spot"—a person who was there to catch you if you fell.

Weight lifting would come under the same category, as would swimming and rock climbing. I'm sure you can think of some other examples. Fun as they are to experience, they are dangerous to do alone. So it is with youth ministry. It is dangerous to your own emotional, physical, and spiritual health to do alone for the long haul. Yes, you may be able to do it on your own for a year or two without any problems, but eventually something begins to break down as the years accumulate. The only way to safely avoid this is to develop a volunteer team to whom you can delegate responsibilities and duties.

A multiple youth staff is able to take advantage of the phenomenon called "synergy." Synergy is the term that is used to describe the observation that two people working together are able to get more done than two people working alone. There is something about working together that inspires and motivates people to do more than they would on their own. The whole is greater than the sum of its parts.

Not all teens are created equal. This is not a bad thing—simply an observation. Some teens are gifted scholastically, others artistically or athletically. There are teens who are shy while others are outgoing. Some are interested in computers while others have a passion for skateboarding. Because of this, teens need a variety of models and personalities working with them so they can find someone with whom they can identify and feel comfortable. This simple fact demands a volunteer staff because one person cannot possibly fulfill all these needs. Using volunteers gives Christian adults an opportunity to use the spiritual gifts that they have been given (Eph. 4:11-16; Rom. 12:3-21; 1 Cor. 12).

The Gerber corporation had for years this slogan and motto: "Babies are our business—our *only* business." KFC has a similar one that says, "We do *chicken* right!" What each of these businesses is saying is that by focusing in on just one product, they are able to provide a superior service. The same is true in ministry. When one person tries to do everything, he loses his distinctiveness. If a youth minister is gifted in evangelism, but has to spend most of his time doing administrative duties, then the very thing he is best at suffers. He has little time or energy left for doing what he is best at doing. The way to avoid this unfortunate situation is to recruit a team of volunteer workers and assign them responsibilities according to their gifts and experience.

When one person tries to do everything, he loses his distinctiveness.

> Understaffed youth ministries are often overburdened, stressed, and too tired for new vision. They fall into maintenance mode and stagnate. That is why it is so important for youth workers to start their ministries right by finding good leaders and learning to become a leader of leaders.[8]

Why Are Volunteers Hard to Find?

The commodity of the new millennium is time. Time is what most people and families value the most—not money or possessions. Because most people earn enough money to live comfortably, the accumulation of things is not what they desire most but more time. Time to spend pursuing their hobbies and interests. Time with family. Because of this, people are not as willing to volunteer their time as they once were. This does not mean that they won't, only that you have to convince them that giving you their time is going to be worthwhile.

Some are simply afraid. They are afraid of a youth culture they don't understand. Tattoos, body piercing, and brightly colored hair totally baffles them. They wonder if they will be accepted by the teens and liked. Others fear that volunteering to work in the youth department is something like imprisonment—once you're in you can't get out.

The lack of proper training keeps some people from volunteering. This is a legitimate concern. No one wants to take on a job without proper training and supervision. The failure and high dropout rate of many volunteers may be directly tied to this issue. No one wants to be seen as a failure, so rather than volunteer and take the chance, many choose to keep quiet when the youth minister asks for volunteers.

I have observed three different methods used to train volunteers. The most common one is the "sink or swim" method. This is where the volunteer is immediately given a class to teach or small group to disciple without any orientation or training. A resource or curriculum book is placed in his hands, the youth minister slaps him on the back and says, "Thanks for your help!" The new recruit is then thrown to the lions and left to his own devices and resources. Surely there is a better way!

The second method of training is the "cognitive-instructional" method. This is where the youth minister sets aside a Saturday morning or Sunday evening and lectures to the volunteers about creative teaching methods, characteristics of youth culture, how to handle discipline problems, and shares his philosophy of youth ministry. He may provide them with some youth resources taken from the church library or provide them with the selected teaching curriculum. This is not a bad method. It is certainly better than the sink-or-swim method. Much good information is disseminated at such a training event. This method is great for the theoretical, but what it lacks is the practical application.

By far the most superior way of training volunteers is by the "hands-on" method. This is where the new volunteer is given some preliminary instructional training but is then placed with a veteran youth worker and the new volunteer "shadows" them for a short period of time. They assist the veteran youth worker in the classroom responsibilities. They start out with being responsible for the easier tasks and then are given more difficult ones as their experience and confidence grows. The experienced teacher shares insights and guidance as they work together teaching and discipling the young people.

Why Are Youth Ministers Hesitant to Use Volunteers?

Not only are people hesitant to volunteer their time, but many youth ministers are often reluctant to recruit volunteers. Rookie youth ministers are often insecure about including other adults to work with the youth. What happens if the teens like the volunteers more than the paid staff? Some youth ministers see themselves as the "trained professional" and don't believe that volunteers can do the job as well or have as much to offer. They are proud and think they know it all and will be able to solve every problem that comes up in the youth group.

Other youth ministers are simply nearsighted and only see the daily problems and not the future possibilities. Yes, it takes more time to do a task when you are training someone and have to explain everything. But that is only during the training period. When they have been properly instructed, you can delegate many responsibilities to trustworthy volunteers who will do as good a job as, if not better than, you. This totally frees you up to spend your time elsewhere in areas that demand your expertise.

Unfortunately, volunteer recruitment is a never-ending process. Les Christie, in his book *Unsung Heroes,* estimates that there is a 30% turnover in volunteers each year.[9] The 30% turnover rate can be discouraging after awhile, and so some youth ministers simply give up. They think it is easier to try to do it alone than to constantly be on the lookout for new recruits and to have to take the time to train them. However what this statistic should mean is that the youth minister must always be on the lookout for bright new prospects who have what it takes to work with youth and that he must give a significant portion of his time over to training the new recruits.

Even when a youth minister is blessed with a number of excellent volunteers, he may not know how to delegate so this wonderful resource goes untapped except for chauffeuring teens to events and breaking up couples in the dark corners of the church. Dewey Bertolini suggests the following guidelines when delegating responsibilities to your volunteer staff:[10]

- Delegate anything that someone else can do. The youth minister's time should be devoted to the projects he does best.
- Delegate only to willing individuals. Find someone with a heart for the responsibility in question.
- Create the recognition of a team ministry. The motive of our delegation must never be perceived as personal laziness.
- Periodically check in with the people to whom tasks have been delegated. Constantly offer encouragement, advice, and support.
- Praise them along the way. Constantly remind the staff of their invaluable contribution to the overall goal of the youth ministry.

I would add to these guidelines, "Delegate—but don't dump." When you delegate something, it is a serious task or responsibility that needs attention. You may even like doing it but realize that your time would be better served elsewhere, so you allow another trusted adult to carry out the responsibility. When you "dump" on a volunteer, you simply pass off undesirable chores that no one likes doing, e.g., cleaning up the bathroom after the junior high lock-in.

Delegate— but don't dump.

Characteristics of Great Volunteers

When you are recruiting a volunteer staff, there are some specific personality types you want to have as a part of your team, especially from a programming perspective. First, you want to recruit some adults who have good people skills. Generally these people are outgoing, people persons who are good at building relationships. You also want some people who are adept at technical skills. These are organizational people—people who love making lists and setting up flow charts. Last of all you need some people on your team who are conceptually skilled. These people are dreamers, visionaries, and brainstormers. They come up with new ideas or ways to improve existing programs. You need all three personality types in order to have a balanced volunteer youth staff.

Any person working with young people in a teaching or discipling capacity must have an authentic personal walk of faith. The secret of a good teacher is in what he *is*, not in what he *says*. It is a fact of life, you cannot give away that which you yourself do not possess. How can a sponsor instill a passion for holiness in the lives of young people if that passion does not first exist in him? A sponsor must have the ability to model the behavior you desire in your teens. It has been said many times, "More is caught, than is taught."

The secret of a good teacher is in what he is, not in what he says.

You want people on your volunteer staff who have a sincere love of adolescents. They enjoy being around young people and have a desire to help them in making the major decisions about their life. You don't want people who feel "guilted" into volunteering, or who really don't enjoy being around teens. They will be miserable, and so will the teens who are placed under their care.

Teachability is an essential characteristic that you want in a sponsor (like Apollos in Acts 18:26). You don't want a staff who think they "know it all" or who are not open to new ideas and new ways of doing things. An eagerness and openness to learn is always a good sign in a volunteer.

You also need people who are flexible and adaptable. You know how the saying goes, "The best laid plans of mice and men oft go astray." So it is with youth work. The bus may break down on the way to camp, and you have to figure out some alternative way to transport all the teens and their luggage to the camp site. You might be planning on fifty teens showing up for a party and end up with five. Do you have people who can shift gears and come up with an alternate plan? And can they do this and remain calm and collected?

The adults who end up having the greatest impact on the lives of teens are those who are not afraid to be transparent and honest about the struggles in their own lives. This does not mean that they parade all their dirty laundry to the entire group at youth meeting, but when it is appropriate they share personal struggles and bits of their spiritual pilgrimage to the young people in their small group or class. This teaches young people that you don't have to be perfect in order to be a Christian, and it gives them hope if they struggle in a similar area. Young people desire the company of adults who are open and relational.

It doesn't matter what kind of gifts or strengths a volunteer may have if they are unreliable and undependable. I realize they are not getting paid to work with the young people, but when significant responsibilities such as discipling and teaching are delegated to them, the program and the young people suffer when the volunteer doesn't show up or fails to adequately prepare.

Willingness to help is one thing, being available to help is another. Volunteers must think through their commitment to the youth program before volunteering their services. An adult who wants to make a difference in the life of a young person must realize this will not take place in the classroom setting alone. Time must be invested outside the classroom. The sponsor should visit the young people in their homes, attend their ball games and other school activities, and be available for counseling and supported when needed. All of this takes time.

Reasons Why People Volunteer to Work With Youth

I wish I could say that everyone who volunteers to work with youth in the church does so for the right reasons. Unfortunately, that is just not so. There are many unhealthy reasons why people volunteer. The first and most common reason is that some simply want to extend their own adolescence. Either they loved being a jock or cheerleader and a member of the "in-crowd" and don't want to give that up, or they never were a part of the "in" group and are hoping to extend their adolescence so they can make up for what they have missed.

Others want a chance to work with the youth because they are on a particular crusade and see this as an opportunity to advance their agenda. Unfortunately their agenda usually has something to do with a particular aspect of youth culture they don't like. They are against body piercing, tattoos, brightly colored hair, etc. and want to make sure they get the chance to get on their soapbox in front of the teens and make their displeasure known.

Some look at youth work as sort of a "lonely hearts club." They use volunteering with the youth as a chance to meet someone who might become their soul mate. When they are at youth activities, they usually spend more time hanging out and talking to other volunteers looking for a potential partner than developing relationships with youth.

For others volunteering to work with the youth is a chance to build a personal empire. These are usually charismatic personalities who naturally draw a lot of young people to them. They glory in the attention and adulation they receive from the young people. These people are involved in the youth program for what they can get from youth, not for what they can give.

The last negative reason why people volunteer to work with the youth is that some are simply guilt-ridden, or when asked to help out with the youth, they just can't say, "No." They know someone *needs* to work with the youth and that it is very *important* to do so, but it really is not their passion. But, they volunteer because they were asked and feel guilty if they refuse.

The good news is that most volunteer youth workers get involved in the youth program for healthy or correct reasons. The first and most obvious reason to be involved in the youth program is that the adult has a genuine love for kids. They love their enthusiasm, boundless energy, optimism, and potential. Because they love teens, they volunteer their time to ensure that teens are being taught the important tenets of the faith and make themselves available for counseling and direction. They have a servant's heart and are willing to work wherever needed.

Some volunteer because an adult sponsor made a difference in their life when they were growing up, and they are simply trying to return the favor. I call these people "grateful debtors" (not to be confused with The Grateful Dead!). Gratitude is an acceptable motivation for getting involved in the lives of teens. These people think back to what was helpful for them growing up and simply try to duplicate that in their own ministry.

The opposite of the grateful debtor is the "deprived provider." This is the adult who struggled through the teen years and needed a significant adult in his life to help him sort through the trials of adolescence—but no one was there. They know how much they needed that guidance and discipling relationship, so they volunteer to work with youth to make sure that no one else ever has to go through life longing for an adult mentor but not finding one.

The Volunteer Recruitment Process

While it is essential that you recruit a great staff of volunteer sponsors, you do not want to make the mistake of going about trying to recruit them the wrong way. Standing in front of the church and making a mass appeal for volunteers and trying to play on people's emotions will not bring you the results you truly desire. Such tactics will often blow up in your face. The problem with making a mass appeal is that you have no way to screen the volunteers. You are obligated to take anyone who responds whether they would be desirable candidates to work with the youth program or not.

A better approach is to target key people you think would make great volunteers and go to them directly with your challenge. Your challenge is for them to observe the youth program for a while in order to get a feel for what takes place and what is required of volunteers. Then you enlist them in a training program where you share your philosophy of youth ministry and give a clear description of what is required of youth sponsors. Only after they have completed the training do you offer them the option of joining the volunteer staff. If they respond positively to the challenge, then you place them in a mentoring relationship with a veteran volunteer who "teaches them the ropes."

A good way to compile a list of potential volunteers is to simply ask the youth who are involved in your program to write down the names of people in the congregation whom they admire or whom they would like to have working with them. When you meet with the potential worker and announce that he has been personally selected by members of the youth group to lead and encourage them, it goes a long way in promoting confidence and in securing a positive response.

Above all, you must have high standards for your volunteers. When you are short on help, you will be tempted to compromise your standards for volunteers. Do not give in! While you might find some temporary relief, they will cause you more problems in the long run. "Better to have a few qualified staff people than many unqualified ones."[11] Young people deserve the best and should not have to work with negative models.

Better to have a few qualified staff people than many unqualified ones.

When you do recruit some new volunteers, be sure that you do use them. After they have been properly trained and mentored, give them a specific responsibility that you would like them to fulfill. Provide them with opportunities to build relationships with the young people. Keep them plugged in and focused. Match their abilities and talents with the job you want them to do.

Respect their time. It's okay to ask for their time, but don't abuse it. Avoid involving them in long, unnecessary meetings or projects. Remember, they have a full time job and a family on top of their volunteer duties. Be sure to give them plenty of advance warning about major events you need them to attend, and don't be changing the youth schedule unnecessarily. They may have arranged their job schedules just so they could help with an event only to have you change it at the last minute.

Once they are a part of the team, do not neglect or abandon them. Set a vision for youth ministry, communicate that vision to them, and clearly point out how they are a part of it and what their specific responsibilities are. Keep them informed about youth culture and what is happening with the individual members of the youth group.

Retaining Your Volunteer Staff

After you have gone to all of the trouble to recruit and train your volunteer staff, you want to do all that you can to retain them. While your volunteers enjoy their time spent working with the young people, realize that volunteers need fellowship time with their own age group. Be careful not to schedule your volunteers so tightly that they are not able to attend a Bible study or small group with their peers.

People stick with a ministry if they feel that they are not alone in it.

People stick with a ministry if they feel they are not alone in it. This means that you need to keep your volunteer staff updated on all your plans and events. It also means that you do periodic checkups to see if they are having any particular problems or are in need of any specific resources. Do not allow them to feel abandoned but a valuable part of a team.

Volunteers will continue to serve when it's obvious what they are doing is worthwhile. This means you may need to point out individual and private success stories they have helped to bring to fruition. If they have been doing evangelistic work with a particular young person, they should be the ones to pray with them and baptize them into Christ.

People are motivated to stay when they have the proper resources needed to do the job. Resources can mean anything from providing study curriculum and covering their expenses on staff retreats and youth events to paying their tuition for educational seminars and conventions.

Your volunteer staff will stay and grow when they know they are genuinely appreciated. One way to show this is to spend personal and social time with your sponsors. Send them personal notes, e-mails, and phone calls. Organize a special volunteer recognition day. Highlight a particular volunteer's contributions in your monthly newsletter. There are a number of creative gifts you can give your sponsor to show your appreciation.[12]

Deciding to "Retire" a Volunteer

It is inevitable that at some point in your ministry you will make a mistake and recruit the wrong person for the wrong ministry or the wrong age group. Or maybe the volunteer was the right person for the right job for a period of time, but something changed causing him to become unhappy and constantly complaining or criticizing you. When that happens, they should be relieved of that responsibility and given the opportunity to serve somewhere else.

Never keep a volunteer in a position just because they were assigned that responsibility at some point in the past. The thought of relieving a volunteer of a responsibility may seem frightening to you, but sometimes you just have to bite the bullet and do what the situation calls for. Remember the words of Howard Hendricks who said, "The test of an executive is how well you can fire. Anyone can hire."

Firing must come as a last resort after every effort has been made to salvage the volunteer. If someone isn't working out in the job he was recruited to do, remember, the person isn't wrong, the job is wrong for the person. Transferring a person from one area of responsibility to another isn't quite the same as firing outright, and doesn't have the same devastating psychological effect. Our job is to redeem people, but sometimes for the benefit of the overall program, certain people must be asked to leave the program. There is always the possibility that the volunteer is actually hoping you will relieve him of the responsibility because he is unhappy with it, but just doesn't know how to get out of it.

If someone isn't working out in the job he was recruited to do, remember, the person isn't wrong, the job is wrong for the person.

Realize that firing a volunteer may make you unpopular with the youth group or congregation. Sometimes a volunteer is very likable as a person, even if they are very unreliable as a sponsor. Others don't see the dropped responsibilities or poor performance—they only see a "nice guy." They may not understand your reasons or motives for letting him go. When this happens, it is best that you just "take the heat" and not aggravate the situation further by trying to explain your reasons. It won't make any difference with most people anyway, and you run the risk of further embarrassing the sponsor.

Reducing the Risk

Twenty years ago, this would not have been an issue. It wouldn't even have entered into the minds of youth workers. Now it cannot be ignored. Many church insurance policies will not even offer coverage to the church and staff if this issue is not properly addressed. What am I referring to? Doing a background check to see if any volunteers have any arrests or convictions in the area of child molesting. This issue cannot be ignored, especially in light of the large number of scandals concerning priests in the Catholic church who are being sued because of past sexual molestation.

Every person who is going to have contact with young people in the church, from the nursery on up through high school, must fill out an application and have a background check run—no exceptions. Many who have worked in the church for years may balk at the idea and some may even be offended. That is why it is important that you do the proper groundwork before implementing the screening process. Educating the board on the need for having a screening process and monitoring system in place is where you begin. Don't approach it from the standpoint that you don't trust your helpers, but from the standpoint that you want to protect all of the church's children. You must place the children's welfare ahead of anyone's feelings. If any volunteer or staff member will not support the screening and monitoring process, then he must not be allowed to work with the young people. Should you violate this rule and a young person ends up molested, you, the board, and the entire church may be liable.

In order to properly protect your young people and the church, you must implement a four-step process. The first is a worker selection or screening process. Every volunteer and staff member fills out a form, and background checks are run to see if there are any prior convictions for child molestation. If the volunteer has worked in any other churches, all the references must be called and verified. A record of the background check and reference follow-up must be kept by the church.

After all volunteers and staff have been approved, then a monitoring system must be set in place. It is best if all classes could be team taught, so that no teacher is ever left alone with the young people. But because most churches simply don't have that many volunteers, a monitoring system must be set in place. All classrooms must have windows in the doors or walls so that a roving monitor can see the activity taking place in the classroom. If for some reason a child is to be alone with a staff member, a phone call should be made and parent's approval secured. A written permission form should be filled out if this is to take place on a regular basis (such as providing transportation home after a youth activity). A written policy of what is considered acceptable and unacceptable behavior should be given to all the youth staff.

Someone in the church must be appointed as the official reporter for the church. This person is trained concerning what to do if anything suspicious is reported. They know what agency to call and how to properly report the facts surrounding any suspicious incident. All members of the volunteer team and staff must be familiar with this reporting process. All volunteers and staff members need to be familiar with the legal obligations with respect to the reporting of any suspicious activity to the authorities.

The church must also know how to respond if any accusations are made against a particular teacher or worker. This would include an explanation of the church's background-check policy and the monitoring system. The proper maintenance of all records with respect to background checks and the monitoring system needs to be in place.

While all of this may seem like a huge hassle, if you ever have to give an account for a volunteer's actions, you will be more than happy you followed the proper procedure. Better safe than sorry could easily be changed to better safe than sued in this situation. Besides, when it comes to the safety of the young people entrusted to you, a matter of inconvenience is a small price to pay.

Application for Children/Youth Work
First Christian Church
Anywhere, USA

CONFIDENTIAL

This application is to be completed by all applicants for any position (volunteer or compensated) involving the supervision or custody of minors. It is being used to help the church provide a safe and secure environment for those children and youth who participate in our programs and use our facilities.

Date:_____   Male _____   Female _____

Name in full:_____

Age :_____ Birthday: _____   Social Security Number: _____

Home phone: (_____) ____-_____ Work phone: (_____) ____-_____

Present address:_____

City: _____ Zip: _____

Have you ever been convicted of child abuse or crime involving actual or attempted sexual molestation of a minor?   Yes _____   No _____
If yes, please explain:

Were you a victim of abuse or molestation while a minor?   Yes _____ No ____

Note: If you prefer, you may refuse to answer the previous two questions, or you may discuss your answer in confidence with the senior minister rather than answering it on this form. Answering yes, or leaving the questions unanswered, will not automatically disqualify an applicant for children or youth work.

Name and address of church of which you are a member:

_____

_____

How long have you been a member? _____

List names and addresses of other churches you have regularly attended during the past five years:

_____

_____

_____

List all previous church work involving youth, e.g., Sunday School teacher, youth sponsor, etc., and the church where this work was performed:

_____

_____

_____

List any talents, training, education or other factors that have prepared you for children/youth work: _____

_____

_____

Personal references:

Name: _____   Name: _____

Address:_____   Address: _____

_____   _____

Phone: _____   Phone: _____

Relationship to you:_____   Relationship to you:_____

_____   _____

How long has this person known you?   How long has this person known you?

_____   _____

Applicant's Statement: The information contained in this application is correct to the best of my knowledge. I authorize any references or churches listed in this application to give you any information they may have regarding my character and fitness for children/youth work. I release all such references from liability for any damage that may result from furnishing such evaluations to you, and I waive any right that I may have to inspect references provided on my behalf.

Should my application be accepted, I agree to be bound by the rules and policies set forth by First Christian Church and to refrain from any unlawful or unscriptural conduct in the performance of my services on behalf of the church.

I further state that I have carefully read the foregoing release and know the contents thereof and I sign this release as my own free act. This is a legally binding agreement which I have read and understand.

Applicant's Signature: _____   Date: _____

Witness:_____   Date: _____

First Christian Church
Anywhere, USA

Permission to Do Police Department Background Check

Name:_____

       First   Middle   Last

Address:_____

                   Street

_____

      City   State   Zip

Date of Birth:_____ Place of Birth:_____

Social Security: _____ Race:_____Sex:_____

I do hereby authorize the Department of Social Services, the National Child Abuse Registry and the Police Department to release any information in their files under the above name and description. This information is being used to assist First Christian Church in determining my eligibility to serve as a volunteer in their youth program.

I hereby release the staff, First Christian Church, and all others from any liability or damage which may result from furnishing the information requested above.

_____   _____
(Signature)   (Date)

_____   _____
(Witness Signature)   (Date)

1. Do you have a volunteer screening and monitoring system in place? If not, why not?
2. Do you fully utilize your volunteer staffs' potential? Have you matched their gifts, abilities, and experience with their assigned responsibilities and duties?
3. What are you doing to show appreciation for your volunteer staff?
4. Do you have written standards for your volunteer staff? Do you enforce and stick to your standards?

Suggested Reading List

Christie, Les. Unsung Heroes. Grand Rapids: Zondervan, 1987.

Fast, Erica. "Recruit or Die: 20 Ways to Build Your Team." GROUP (September/October, 2001).

Hansen, Cindy. "50 Ways to Thank Your Volunteers." GROUP (January/February, 1997).

"Volunteers." Youthworker (Winter 1986).

Notes on Chapter Twelve

1. Dewey Bertolini, *Back to the Heart of Youth Work* (Wheaton, IL: Victor Books, 1989), p. 115.

2. Paul Borthwick, *Organizing Your Youth Ministry* (Grand Rapids: Zondervan, 1988), p. 80.

3. Barry St. Clair, "How Can We Find and Support Volunteers?" in *Reaching a Generation for Christ,* ed. by Richard R. Dunn and Mark H. Senter III (Chicago: Moody, 1997), p. 263.

4. Dick Alexander, "Developing Adult Leaders" in *Methods for Youth Ministry,* ed. by David Roadcup (Cincinnati: Standard, 1986), p. 63.

5. Ibid., p. 63.

6. Les Christie, *Unsung Heroes* (Grand Rapids: Zondervan, 1987), p. 9.

7. Ibid., p. 10.

8. Doug Fields, *Purpose Driven Youth Ministry* (Grand Rapids: Zondervan, 1998), p. 271.

9. Ibid., p. 31.

10. Bertolini, *Back,* pp. 122-123.

11. Ibid., p. 118.

12. See Cindy Hansen, "50 Ways to Thank Your Volunteers," *GROUP* (January/February 1997).

Chapter 13

Avoiding and Recovering from Burnout in Youth Ministry

Dr. Gary B. Zustiak

"We learn in athletics a principle that continually frightens me. 'No one will ever remember how we begin; they will only remember how we end.'" — *Dewey Bertolini*[1]

"One of the greatest tragedies of burnout is that it strikes our most productive people." —*Myron Rush*[2]

"The best and the brightest among us are the most vulnerable to burnout: the dynamic, talented, charismatic, goal-oriented men and women who give 100% to any project they undertake." — *Ruth J. Luban*[3]

The Very Real Danger of Burnout in the Ministry

Let's face the facts: the relentless pressures of ministry can become a constant physical, mental, emotional, and spiritual drain on the system. Like long-distance runners, youth workers who finish strong have learned how to pace themselves along the way. Unfortunately, too many of our ranks run like sprinters while participating in a marathon. Tragically, their end can be predicted with alarming accuracy.[4]

Burnout is that deep-seated feeling that you will never again feel rested or your energy level replenished. It is a vague sense of being trapped. You feel drained emotionally, mentally, physically, and spiritually, with nothing to show for all the effort you have put forth. Burnout is when the personal rewards and satisfaction from work are dwarfed by the mountain of energy needed to get the job done.

The youth ministry "salvage yard" is full of run-down, rusted-out, and busted-up youth workers who may be guilty of only one thing; they neglected their own spiritual, physical, emotional, and mental needs. No one is immune to burnout. Those who are involved in the people-helping professions, e.g., medical, social, psychological, and ministerial, are especially prone to burnout. Even the great leaders and prophets of the Old Testament found themselves spent and ready to quit. Moses and Elijah both suffered from feeling overwhelmed with the tasks before them and were ready to quit. In fact, both of them were so depressed that they asked to die! (See Num. 11:15; 1 Kgs. 19:4.)

The youth ministry "salvage yard" is full of run-down, rusted-out, and busted-up youth workers who may be guilty of only one thing; they neglected their own spiritual, physical, emotional, and mental needs.

I have even heard it said by well-meaning preachers, "The devil doesn't take a day off, so why should I?" To which I would like to respond, "Since when did the devil become your role model?"

Jesus knew the dangers of burnout and took appropriate measures to protect himself and his ministry. In Luke 5:15-16 crowds of people come to Jesus in order to be healed. These are people with legitimate illnesses such as leprosy, lameness, blindness, and hemorrhaging. Jesus is their only hope. There is no one else or no place in the entire known world where they can go and receive legitimate help for their condition. And yet the text says that Jesus withdrew himself from the people and their needs in order to go and spend time in prayer. Jesus said, "No." Why did he say "no" to hurting people for whom he was their only hope? It certainly wasn't because he had no compassion. We know that Jesus felt compassion for the crowds and their needs.

Jesus kept his ultimate purpose ever before him, and he was aware of his own physical, emotional, and spiritual limitations. Jesus' purpose in coming to earth was not to heal the sick; it was to die on the cross for the sins of all mankind. He was to be the spotless Lamb of God. Jesus knew that continual giving took its emotional, physical, and spiritual toll. In order to protect himself from Satan's attacks and to remain spiritually strong, he limited the amount of giving of himself and balanced that with a time of prayer and spiritual refreshment. Every youth minister would do well to follow the model of Jesus. Sometimes the most spiritual thing you can do is to say "no"— even when it is a legitimate need. You must base your decisions on what is best for the long haul. If you want to finish strong, you must avoid burning out early.

Some Symptoms of Burnout

As the saying goes, "Forewarned is fore-armed." If you are aware of some of the signs of burnout, you may be able to catch yourself in this dangerous, downward spiral before it is too late. The following signs are not given in any order of priority but are simply listed as a kind of checklist. The more of these symptoms you find present in your life, the greater the possibility you are facing burnout.

Sometimes the most spiritual thing you can do is to say "no"—even when it is a legitimate need.

- **Procrastination.** This is when standard operating procedure becomes, "Put it off until tomorrow." Planning ahead gives way to crisis management.
- **Grouchitis.** Your family, spouse, close friends, colleagues, become sparring partners.
- **Mind fatigue.** You daydream too much, wake up tired in the mornings, feel listless, forget meetings, and take important meetings and responsibilities lightly.
- **A loss of vitality.** You have no energy or keen interest in what you are doing.
- **Disillusionment.** A feeling that what you are doing has lost its purpose or meaning.
- **Loss of motivation.** You can't get started or excited about anything.
- **Feeling unappreciated.** A feeling that others don't notice, don't care, or take for granted your efforts and ministry.
- **A feeling that no one cares.** No one cares about you and your feelings. Your needs are ignored while you are expected to continually give, give, and give.
- **Intolerance.** You have developed an intolerance for mistakes no matter how small. You cannot deal with problems or surprises.
- **Loss of empathy.** You have no tolerance for other's mistakes or personal problems. You have lost the capacity to cheerfully go the second mile. You become insensitive to the needs of others.
- **Inability to renew personal strengths.** Nothing you do refreshes or renews you. Hobbies or activities that once refreshed you only seem tiring.

- **High involvement with low satisfaction.** You find that you are busier than ever in Christian service, but accomplishing little and enjoying it less.
- **Somatic problems.** You find that you are beset with physical ailments that won't go away, e.g., migraines, ulcers, high blood pressure, colitis, insomnia, etc.
- **Loss of joy.** The joy of the Lord has given way to a depression that you can't explain.
- **Loss of interest.** You spend fewer hours at previously favorite activities.
- **Sexual energies have waned.** You may find yourself so tired and uninterested in anything else that you have become completely impotent. This may scare you so much that you have failed to talk to anyone about it.
- **Dietary problems.** You find that you either begin to seriously gain or lose weight. You are either continuously snacking on junk food or may suffer from a total loss of appetite.
- **Artificial stimulants needed.** You find yourself more dependent upon stimulants and/or sedatives. Instead of 2 or 3 cups of coffee or Coke a day it is now 8, 10, or 12. More sugar is taken in. You can't sleep without a sedative.
- **Appearance.** When you no longer care about your physical appearance, it can be one of the signs of burnout. Watch for disheveled hair and rumpled clothes which are also dirty, wrinkled or ill-chosen. You may also find that you exhibit a poor skin color, develop a body slouch and facial ticks, etc.
- **Office arrangement.** Your office becomes disorganized or dirty. Bizarre arrangements of work space may be an indication that your personal life is the same way.
- **Personal affairs.** Your once ordered life gives way to poor money management, apathetic or hostile socializing, and little or no daily planning.
- **Life-style.** You develop random and decreased work patterns, withdrawn and secretive behavior, clinging desperately to one or two friends, poor relationships with spouse/family, etc.
- **Emotional.** Apathy, constant worry, memory loss, one-track thinking, loss of creativity, paranoid thoughts, constant irritability, loss of humor or hostile humor, sporadic work efforts, lack of playfulness, excessive crying, hopelessness.

- **Spiritual.** Significant changes in moral behavior, drastic changes in theological statements, loss of prayer and meditational discipline, moral judgmentalism, loss of faith, cynicism about church and spiritual leaders, one-track preaching/teaching, loss of joy in ministry and faith.

Causes of Burnout

Before we examine the causes of real burnout, you should be aware of temporary burnout. This can happen immediately following an intense peak experience such as camp or CIY conference. For an entire week you are running on adrenaline and an emotional high. Your body is physically taxed to its limit. The result is that after this peak experience you will naturally undergo a period of physical, psychological, emotional, and spiritual letdown. When this happens, don't panic. Know that it is only temporary until your body can recover from the demands of the previous week.

Now that you are able to distinguish between temporary and real burnout, we must examine the causes of real burnout. Burnout often is the result of working at a job that has unlimited or increasing demands. Ministry is one of those kinds of jobs. No matter how hard you work or how many hours you put in, there is always more that could have been done. There is always one more person you could have visited, one more letter you could have written, one more chapter you could have read, one more person you could have counseled, etc. There is an unending amount of work to do. Unless you learn how to draw reasonable limits and expectations concerning your time and performance, you will end up burning out.

Closely related to the problem of working in a job with an unlimited amount of demands is allowing unrealistic expectations concerning your job performance or personal life to develop. You must not expect too much too soon. The goals you set should be attainable and realistic. Don't expect to have 100 teens coming to your youth meetings in just three months. Allow a reasonable amount of time to pass before you begin making any kind of serious evaluations about your performance. Know that some in the congregation may have unrealistic expectations for your personal life—you are to be the model of

Unless you learn how to draw reasonable limits and expectations concerning your time and performance, you will end up burning out.

perfection. The pressure of living in a "glass house" can easily take its toll on you and your family.

We are often victims of the mistaken belief that self-worth is a by-product of productivity or success. We think the harder we work and the more hours we work, the more valuable we are to the church and the kingdom. This is a form of the works/righteousness heresy. There is nothing you can do that will make you more worthy in God's sight. You are already worthy simply because you are you and have been created in God's image and redeemed by His Son. Ask yourself this question. "Do I feel driven or called?" If you answered "driven" then you are a victim of the works/righteousness syndrome. You are trying to earn God's approval by your performance.

Burnout is right around the corner when you fail to limit the number of obligations and tasks you are accountable for. There is a limited amount of responsibilities and duties that you can do and do well. Anything beyond that and the quality of all of them begins to suffer. You must set your priorities in order and then accept or reject tasks based upon your priorities. Do not end up majoring in the minors.

A major cause of burnout is the failure to delegate. Do not try to do everything yourself. The era of the Lone Ranger is dead. Learn to trust reliable people with any task and duty they can and desire to do that will lighten your load. Do not be threatened by their ability or success.

While ministry is primarily a spiritual calling, you cannot ignore your physical health. Allowing your body to deteriorate due to the lack of exercise or a poor diet can lead to a decreased sense of energy and vitality. Don't get into the habit of stuffing down junk-food all the time or ignoring the need for regular physical exercise.

Because ministry is about servanthood you may end up with little public affirmation for your work. You are expected to sacrifice and do without. There may be little expressed appreciation for all of the positive things you do.

Avoiding Burnout in the Ministry

A person who finds himself smack dab in the middle of a burnout may reach out for a false cure in a desperate attempt to stop the downward spiral. One false cure would be falling prey to the erroneous assumption that if you work at a "frantic pace" long enough you will eventually get all caught up and then be able to scale back to a slower, healthier pace. This will never happen. The only thing you will succeed in doing is burning out faster.

Others will try to deal with their impending burnout by involving themselves in excessive leisure. They realize (too late) that their life has been consumed with work issues and that there has been no personal or down time. They try to compensate for their lost time by indulging themselves with excessive involvement in their favorite recreational activities. This only makes matters worse because when they get back to the office all the pressures and demands are still there, and now they have less time to complete their assigned duties and responsibilities.

Not knowing how to deal with the pain and pressure that leads to burnout, some will fall victim to alcohol abuse or turn to drugs. They only know they want the pain to stop and, in their desperation, turn to alcohol or prescription drugs. They may have tried other possible solutions and failed. This is their last resort. This further complicates their life because now they run the risk of developing a physical addiction or having to deal with the guilt and shame if their secret becomes known.

The best way to deal with burnout is to nip it in the bud. Prevention is much easier than recovery. One of the first things you must do is learn the art of self-awareness. You must learn how to monitor yourself and be able to take appropriate measures when you become aware of trouble signs starting to pop up in your life. Clean up your calendar. Rid yourself of unnecessary meetings. Give up responsibilities that are not absolutely essential to your ministry and program.

Closely tied to the ability to monitor yourself is the skill of learning the difference between expectation and reality.

Closely tied to the ability to monitor yourself is the skill of learning the difference between expectation and reality. It is not wrong to dream big dreams. Every youth minister should have vision. But when we allow our dreams or the expectations of others to overshadow reason, we end up feeling like a loser because we haven't "measured up."

A wise youth minister knows the value of seeking continual renewal in his life. Not only is renewal helpful in preventing burnout, but it is essential for maintaining a vibrant spiritual life. Dewey Bertolini has observed: "To attempt to lead a person spiritually while at the same time neglecting your own spiritual life would be a travesty. Any leader who fails to take nourishment daily from the Word of God will most certainly degenerate into a voice from a vacuum."[5] The practice of the spiritual disciplines is a must for the youth minister if he expects to experience continual renewal. The disciplines must be not be practiced out of guilt but should flow out of a genuine desire to know and experience God. I have found Richard Foster's classic, *The Celebration of Discipline*, and John Ortberg's, *The Life You've Always Wanted*, to be most helpful in this area.

> *"To attempt to lead a person spiritually while at the same time neglecting your own spiritual life would be a travesty. Any leader who fails to take nourishment daily from the Word of God will most certainly degenerate into a voice from a vacuum."*
> *—Dewey Bertolini*

Something that may not seem like much, but still yields positive results, is training yourself to get into the habit of noticing and nurturing the unspectacular good things that happen to you. Maybe it is being thankful for seeing a beautiful sunrise as you jog in the morning or the sweet smell of honeysuckle in the evening breeze as you sit on the porch and read the paper.

The youth minister who is going to be around for the long haul is one who has learned how to properly pace himself. Pacing has to do with understanding your peak energy times and wisely planning your calendar so that you allow yourself some "down time" or periods of low demand after a period of intense programming. For example, you do not want to follow three weeks of camp with a week of VBS. You need to plan for a couple of "buffer weeks" in between the rigors of the camping schedule and the demands of a VBS program.

Learn what your natural and spiritual gifts are and plan for your main responsibilities to fall in line with those gifts. Delegate to others areas where you are not gifted or knowledgeable.

> We cannot possibly be anyone other than who we are. While we must certainly seek to correct our character deficiencies, we must learn to accept our unchangeable characteristics. We all differ in terms of our gifts, talents, backgrounds, burdens, personalities, etc. The wise and fulfilled servant of Christ understands these differences and learns to minister accordingly.[6]

Recognize your limitations and learn to say, "No!" There will be lots of invitations that come your way. Most of them are worthy causes or ministries. But, you cannot be involved in all of them and maintain a healthy balance in your ministry. Be careful not to become overcommitted to programs.

Provide time and money for relaxation. Every person is unique in that something different relaxes and refreshes you. Some of my fellow staff members love to play golf and find it relaxing to hit the ball around. Others go nuts playing golf because they end up super frustrated with their lack of ability to properly hit the ball. My friend Chuck loved to go fishing. He could sit in the boat for hours and didn't care if he caught a fish or not. It was worth it just to sit in the boat and feel the gentle rocking from side to side. When I was in graduate school, I joined a Tae Kwon Do school. I took out my weekly frustrations by kicking the snot out of the workout bag. It is not important what you end up doing as much as it is that you recognize the need to find something that you enjoy that energizes you. Learn to relax without guilt.

Set priorities for your work time and limit the number of responsibilities that you take on. Have your priorities set in writing! You will find that you honor your priorities a lot more if you take the time to put them in writing.

Recovering from Burnout

If you think you're burning out, seek help. The place to start is to admit that you are in serious trouble and you need the insight of a professional counselor. Develop a support system of people you can confide in and pray with. These need to be people whom you can trust and who will keep you accountable concerning your priorities and your schedule.

Set aside time for worship and spiritual renewal. Schedule regular sabbaths into your schedule. These sabbaths can be of varying lengths and differing content. You might schedule two hours each week just to go to a matinee by yourself. One day a month you might set aside to travel to a park or lake and spend the *Pull back from activities but not from people.* entire day reading great theological classics. Once a year you might plan for a three-day sabbath where you stay at a spiritual retreat center and focus on prayer, meditation, worship, and listening to the voice of God.

Don't withdraw. Because being overly invested in the lives and problems of others contributed towards your burnout, you will be tempted to refrain from any social contact. But this is the worst thing you can do. Pull back from *activities* but not from *people.* It is the caring touch and interaction of a supportive group of friends that will bring back the joy of living and service once again.

Don't deny or bottle up your feelings. Let your frustrations and anger out. If you can't afford a professional counselor, find a trusted friend you can confide in. If this is not a possibility, at least write your feelings down in a journal. Pray out loud expressing your pain and heartache to God.

Diminish intensity in your life, at least until you have recovered emotionally, spiritually, and physically. Change what circumstances you can. Because you are in a paid staff position, you must put in a minimum number of hours and perform certain duties.

Determine your biological time clock. There are certain times of the day that you feel more energized than others. Use these times for high priority tasks and use your "slow" periods for less demanding tasks such as running errands, answering phone calls, or reading a book.

Make a clear transition from work to home. One of the problems with being involved in ministry is that it is all too easy to take your work home with you. You fill your briefcase with unfinished tasks from the office, and you try to work on them while you watch TV or play with your kids. This just doesn't cut it! You need to leave your work at the office. Your family deserves all of you, and you need all of your family. Having a particular ritual that you go through can help to make that transition from work to home more clear. For instance, you might stop off at the local Starbucks and have a cup of your favorite blend and read the latest edition of *USA Today* before going home. Another possibility is that you join the local YMCA and play a game or two of racquetball before you call it a day.

Quit listening to the trumpet blasts of others shouting their victories. Nothing can be more discouraging than comparing yourself to others and feeling like you come up short. Paul wrote in 2 Corinthians 10:12, "When they measure themselves by themselves and compare themselves with themselves, they are not wise." The measure of your success is not found in comparing your accomplishments or talents to others, but in your faithful stewardship of what God has given you.

Don't expect too much too soon. Don't expect things to be what they were before. The goal in overcoming burnout is to correct old, bad habits and learn some new, good ones. It means changes in the way you think, act, and do.

After burnout recovery has been completed, you will live your life differently. That doesn't mean you will no longer be the goal-oriented, productive, positive, high achiever you were before. You will have the potential to accomplish even greater things than before without fear of burning yourself out. But the way you accomplish them will be dramatically altered. The way you live your life and spend your time will be drastically different.[7]

If you are not sure how close to burnout you are and would like some kind of assessment tool, there are a number of self-scoring burnout tests available on the web. One site I would recommend is: **http://www.friedsocialworker.com/selfassessment.htm**. There are others also, but this will get you started. Along with the self-assessment tests are some practical suggestions on how to recover from burnout.

Time for Reflection

1. Are there any signs of burnout present in your life? Can you identify them?
2. What do you do that restores and renews your energy?
3. Do you have your priorities set in writing and do you make your decisions based on your priorities?
4. Can you say, "No?" If not, what keeps you from being able to say no?

SUGGESTED READING LIST

Faulkner, Brooks R. *Burnout in Ministry: How to Recognize It. How to Avoid It.* Nashville: Broadman, 1981.

Feldmeyer, Dean. *Beating Burnout in Youth Ministry.* Loveland, CO: Group, 1989.

Rush, Myron, *Burnout: Practical Help for Lives Out of Balance.* Wheaton, IL: Victor Books, 1987.

Notes on Chapter Thirteen

1. Dewey Bertolini, *Back to the Heart of Youth Work* (Wheaton, IL: Victor Books, 1989), p. 28.

2. Myron Rush, *Burnout: Practical Help for Lives Out of Balance* (Wheaton, IL: Victor Books, 1987), p. 14.

3. Ruth J. Luban, "Break the Burnout Cycle," **http://www.choicepoints.com/probfrm.html#stats.**

4. Bertolini, *Back,* p. 170.

5. Ibid., p. 19.

6. Ibid., p. 176

7. Rush, *Burnout,* p. 76.

Chapter 14

Using Retreats for Spiritual Formation and Change

Dr. Gary B. Zustiak

The Place of Spiritual Retreats in Scripture

The use of retreats for spiritual formation and change has a rich history in the Scriptures both for groups and individuals. In Exodus 5:3 Moses requests that the nation of Israel be allowed to participate in a three-day retreat into the desert in order to sacrifice and worship God. After his confrontation with the priests of Baal on Mt. Carmel, Elijah runs into the desert in search of rest and renewal and encounters God in the still small voice after the wind, the earthquake, and the fire (1 Kings 19). Immediately after his baptism Jesus was led into the desert by the Spirit and spent forty days and nights in retreat. During this time he was tempted by Satan three times and ministered to by angels (Matthew 4). In Mark 6:30-32 after an exhausting day of ministry and meeting the needs of others, Jesus calls the apostles to "Come with me by yourselves to a quiet place and get some rest." The apostle Paul spent three years in the desert of Arabia preparing himself for the ministry that God had called him to. There are many other Scriptures that point out the value of the spiritual retreat, but these will suffice to make the point. "Penetration into the world will be very shallow unless it is preceded by a retreat for preparation. We have nothing to say until God first speaks to us."[4]

Not only does Scripture point out the value of a spiritual retreat, but the latest research in contemporary youth culture and spiritual formation also verifies the value of taking young people away from their normal routines to a quiet place where the single focus is to develop a spiritual awareness and sensitivity to God. In fact, some have gone so far as to suggest that all the weekly youth meetings and Sunday School classes that teens attend do very little to help the spiritual growth of young people when compared to the impact that a week-long camp or retreat has on a young person. Dr. John Perkins, founder of the Voice of Calvary Ministries, said, "I can do more with the kids in my ghetto in one weekend of camping than I can do in six months of contact work."[5] In fact, John Westerhoff states that seventy-five percent of the Campus Crusade for Christ staff of over 10,000 made first-time commitments at a camp or retreat.[6]

Campus Crusade for Christ says that 75 percent of their 10,000-plus personnel made a first-time commitment to Jesus Christ at a camp or retreat.

John Westerhoff is so convinced of the power of retreats that he has suggested we eliminate the Sunday School and spend the money on retreats!

> If we really wanted to be effective in Christian education, we would eliminate Sunday schools and use the money that we spent on them for camps and retreats. If you could get everyone in your church away for two weekend retreats a year, you would have more and better Christian education than a whole year's worth of one-hour Sunday school classes.[7]

You may think that sounds a little radical, but he is not the only one who has made that suggestion. Rick Lawrence, in *Group* magazine, said something very similar. *Then make them better!!*

> I'll be blunt: Youth talks and Bible studies have little impact on your kids' spiritual growth, and it's time to shift your ministry focus to retreat experiences. Why? Because the 1,000+ Christian kids we surveyed say retreats are the single most important catalyst in their spiritual growth. But youth talks and group Bible studies barely register a blip on kids' spiritual growth radar.
>
> . . . Almost one in five kids said "participating in spiritual retreats" was "the one thing that's helped me grow most as a Christian."[8]

What Is the Purpose of Holding a Retreat?

There is no "one" correct reason for holding a retreat. There are many biblical reasons for involving young people in time away from their normal routine. Some reasons are more pragmatic than others, but all of them are legit. Always have a goal or purpose in mind when planning a retreat. Your goal or purpose should be formed out of a desire to meet a particular need within your group. "The most elaborate or intricately programmed retreat cannot be effective if it does not meet the needs of the students."[9]

One useful purpose for holding a retreat is that it allows you to reach out to the fringe students. These are young people who show up occasionally for your regular programming, but who have not made any kind of commitment to Christ or to the church. It places them in a spiritually saturated environment without the distractions of home or school and challenges them to do some serious personal evaluation with respect to their spiritual needs and their relationship with Christ.

Similar to reaching out to the fringe students is the need to evangelize the unchurched. These are young people who have never been challenged with the claims of Christ or their own spiritual need. The opportunity to go off camping in the mountains or to a lake retreat center for a weekend may be just what it takes to get them to come along. Some of these young people will never set foot in a church because of a bad experience sometime before in their life or because of a negative family influence. This may be their only opportunity to hear the gospel.

Another reason for holding a retreat would be to help build youth group identity and community. Just because a number of teens all attend the same church and youth group does not mean that they have a sense of unity—or that they even like each other! Youth groups can be as fractured with cliques as any high school or junior high. Just getting together one night a week at youth group is not going to change all that. It is going to take some purposeful training and a good chunk of time to overcome any prejudices and favoritism that may exist. Think how many times Jesus had to take the apostles away by themselves and explain his teaching to them or settle some kind of dispute. Why should your youth group be any different?

Don't make the mistake of thinking that retreats are only for fixing problems. They can be used proactively as well. A retreat is the perfect setting for training on some particular aspect of Christian ministry or spiritual topic. There are a number of themes that you could choose that would serve as the focus for the weekend. It could be anything from understanding your spiritual gifts, pursuing holiness, stewardship, or worldwide missions to love, sex, and dating.

Whatever the purpose for your retreat, don't overschedule it so that the weekend is so full of teaching and exercises that the young people don't get some free time for simple rest and relaxation. That was one of Jesus' chief concerns for the apostles and why he called them to get away. Sometimes life and ministry is so demanding that it can wear you out. Young people today lead incredibly busy lives. It is amazing how many of them carry Daytimers or Palm Pilots just to keep their busy schedules straight.

Whatever the purpose for your retreat, don't overschedule it so that the weekend is so full of teaching and exercises that the young people don't get some free time for simple rest and relaxation.

They have school, band practice, sports, scouts, part-time job, church, family, and friends. They are one step from exhaustion. Provide times of refreshing, relaxation, and renewal.

Participation in a retreat provides opportunities for creating positive Christian memories. While this is not one of your main purposes in planning a retreat, it is a nice side benefit. The formation of positive Christian memories can come from any aspect of the retreat, from the van ride to the retreat center to the one-on-one counseling that takes place during free time in the afternoon. Some unplanned and unexpected events can even become treasured and "special" memories.

The first memories I have are from times spent with the youth group I ministered to in Idaho. After arriving at our getaway location, one of our teenagers Greg was so excited to be at the retreat that he ran and jumped off the porch of the retreat center without first checking out the other side. Had he done so, he would have seen that it was built on the side of a hill! He didn't look and fell nearly fifteen feet and severely sprained his ankle. This took place within the first ten minutes of arriving at the retreat. I hadn't even unloaded the van yet! It just so happens that this was the weekend before graduation and he ended up having to make his way across the stage on crutches to receive his diploma. The youth group stood and cheered as he hobbled across the stage when his name was called.

Another memory that comes to mind is the time we formed a small work crew to help prepare dorms for the incoming students at a local Bible college. My original plan was to spend two days washing windows, shampooing rugs, dusting, and any other light cleaning that might be needed to make the dorms ready for the new year. My work crew was made up of five students—one boy and four girls—plus myself.

When we arrived at the college, the president informed me that he had a change in plans for our work crew. He wanted us to paint the entire gym two colors and with oil-based paint. And we only had two days! He had already purchased all the paint and rented the scaffolding. I put the challenge to the students. I promised them if they worked their hearts out from 8:00–5:00 we would stay up doing fun things in the evening as late as they wanted, with the only stipulation they had to be up and ready to paint at 8:00.

They accepted the challenge. After the first day, what a mess! The crew had to go and stand out in the parking lot and wipe themselves off with rags soaked in paint thinner because they had gotten so much paint on them! But, after two full days of hot, sweaty work, we made our goal. We completely painted the walls of the gym—in two colors with oil-based paint.

Every time we would come back to visit the college, the teens who were a part of that work crew would walk into the gym, puff out their chests and say, "Yep—I painted this gym. This gym is mine. I even have my initials painted in that corner!" (I think some still have beige paint permanently stuck in their hair!)

On a more serious side, the block of time set aside for a retreat often opens up opportunities for counseling the teen from a troubled background. Even if you are aware of some problems in a particular teen's life, you may not be able to hook up after regular youth meetings or Sunday church. A teen is usually more willing to talk in a setting that is away from prying eyes and ears and when he is sure that you have more time to listen. This is a great reason to make sure that you plan into your schedule a sufficient amount of "free" time so that you can take advantage of such opportunities.

Retreats are a great way to prepare leaders for Christian service, both adult volunteer staff and student leaders. With all of the planning

A teen is usually more willing to talk in a setting that is away from prying eyes and ears and when he is sure that you have more time to listen.

and preparation that needs to be done for a retreat, this is a great opportunity to delegate many of the responsibilities to your leadership staff. This gives them real responsibility, and they will get to see immediate results for their effort. Involve your leadership staff in planning the schedule, the food menu, the theme, the location, teachers, recreation, decorations, worship, main speaker, and any special events. This lightens your load and allows them to use their gifts.

If you do not have a definite purpose in mind for planning your retreat, then discover your purpose by evaluating the needs of your group. This can be done by taking a formal survey of the group members, parents, and volunteer staff. You can also discover the needs of your group by simply being observant and listening to the conversations and discussions of your teens and volunteer staff. Certain topics and themes will dominate their conversations. Choose a topic that would be both biblical and relevant to your target group.

Advantages of Participating in a Retreat

One of the key advantages of participating in a retreat or week of camp/conference is that you are able to spend extended periods of time with your young people and staff. This serves to improve relationships in the group. The young people get to know one another better, and they get to know the volunteer staff on a more personal level. There is something about being in a more informal setting that breaks down barriers and enables people to open up and share about their life. This is something that you cannot program into a regular lesson time—it happens as a result of the setting and the extended time spent together.

Longer blocks of time make possible some activities that Sunday school and regular evening meetings just do not permit. Some of these are crucial to building community and a sense of identity. When students are forced to spend longer periods of time together, it is easier for them to break out of their own little cliques and groups and engage with others they may not usually associate with.

The passage of time (at least a week) between regular meetings of classes or youth groups causes a loss of impact and continuity. During a typical week, even if a young person does attend Sunday school and youth group, those only take up an hour or hour and a half at the most. The students have usually come from home, work, or some kind of school activity and immediately go back into a similar situation. They do not have time to let the point of a lesson sink in. The television, computer, and CD player get more overall time in a day than the youth minister, so it is no surprise that what he has to say loses its impact when looking at the amount of time these other distractions take up in the life of a teen.

This is not so on a weekend retreat or a week of camp. An entire morning or even the whole day can be given over to the emphasizing and teaching on a particular spiritual truth. There are no distractions of television, radio, or computer to compete for the teen's attention. Most teens do not have to be strong-armed into considering spiritual issues. All they need is the proper setting and motivation.

A sad, but nonetheless true fact concerning young people is that they are not as concerned about the "what" of an activity as much as they are concerned about the "who" of it. In other words, they want to know who's going before they commit themselves to attending. If the "right" people go, it really doesn't matter what the activity is, the kids will show up. The opposite is also true. You can have the coolest activity in the world planned and if the "in group" is not going to attend, you will have problems promoting it. The way this applies to the importance of retreats and camps is that if previously inactive young people can be encouraged to attend a lock-in or retreat, they will have enough time to gain some acceptance into the group and are more likely to return to subsequent activities.

A sad, but nonetheless true fact concerning young people is that they are not as concerned about the "what" of an activity as much as they are concerned about the "who" of it.

Planning the Retreat

When you first begin to do your initial planning, it is important that your volunteer staff and student leaders have ownership in the project. If they don't own it, they won't support it or attend. It will be doomed from the start. Allow them input on the kind of retreat you are planning, the date, and the site.

Make sure that you have a specific purpose in mind. Never do any kind of activity without a purpose. I tried to plan three retreats a year—each with a different focus and target group in mind. I would have a yearly evaluation and planning retreat where the youth and volunteer staff got together to evaluate the good, the bad, and the ugly of the previous year's program and to dream about what we wanted to change and add to the next year's program. Only members of the youth group were allowed to attend this retreat. I didn't want guests voting on study topics and activities that they would probably never attend.

It is always good to have one retreat that is service project oriented. You can do things such as minor construction at your local church camp, dorm room preparation for Bible colleges, general cleaning and minor repair at children's homes, helping with sidewalk VBS for inner city missions, building houses for the poor across the border in Mexico, etc. Many organizations such as Christ In Youth, Group, and Amor offer preprogrammed service projects that your group can join. These have the added benefit of having all the contacts, projects, and supplies taken care of for you. All you have to supply is the manpower. You should allow your teens to invite their friends on these kinds of retreats because many times the experience of being part of a group who is helping people in need can be more convincing of the truth of the gospel than the most carefully prepared lesson.

One retreat should be outreach focused. This is something like a winter ski trip, Six Flags outing, or summer beach trip. You encourage the members of your group to invite all of their friends to this activity. The idea is that you go and have a lot of fun and interactive time during the day and the evening concludes with a time of worship and a challenge. It is "church lite"—seeker-service type stuff. The idea is that you use the fun activity as a "hook" to meet new kids and as a way to present the gospel to kids who would probably never darken the door of a church. Caution: Do not make your guests feel trapped or manipulated. Be up front about the schedule and don't have "heavy" evening messages. Be content to plant seeds and make plans for careful follow up after the retreat.

You must plan well in advance of the scheduled event—at least 3-6 months if it is to be successful.

You must plan well in advance of the scheduled event—at least three to six months if it is to be successful. There are a number of key issues that you need to consider when choosing a date for the retreat. You need to look over the youth group schedule. You don't want to put too many high impact or expensive activities too close together. This runs the risk of diminishing the effect of the retreat or unnecessarily eliminating some teens because they are all tapped out financially.

You need to look at the church calendar also. The board may take a dim view of you heading off with the teens for a retreat the same weekend of the congregational meeting! You do not want them to think you are running competition with any key programs the church is doing. Plus, it is important for the teens to be involved in the life of the church. It would be wrong to remove them during a major church function.

Pay attention to the calendar and especially the holidays. Depending upon your church and community, the holidays can either be a great time for a retreat or a horrible one. If your congregation is made up of basically younger parents who all take off to grandma's for the holidays, then it would be foolish to plan something that same time period. On the other hand, if your students have time off from school, but nothing special is planned with their family, then this would be a great time to offer them an exciting alternative.

It would be event suicide for a youth minister to plan a major activity without first consulting the school calendar. If you serve in a large metropolitan area, you may have students who attend your church who come from twelve different schools. It is a huge task trying to keep track of all the major events with that many schools, but you need to make sure that you get copies of the activities calendars from all the schools before you even think about scheduling an event. Consider it a hazard of the trade.

Most areas have some regular events that occur at about the same time every year. The local Bible college will have its annual weekend recruitment push and some kind of an event for junior highers. You should support these events and not schedule a program that ends up competing with theirs. If any kind of training seminar sponsored by Group or Youth Specialties comes to your area on a regular basis, you definitely want your adult leadership to be able to take advantage of such an opportunity.

It may be impossible to avoid all scheduling conflicts when you consider all of the different schools, church events, community activities, and sporting events you have to take into consideration. The least you can do is avoid scheduling conflicts with major events like homecoming, prom, and graduation.

Part of smart planning is trying to anticipate problem areas. You always want to have a "plan B" in store for every major aspect of your retreat or camp. Weather is always a factor that can wreak havoc with a weekend retreat. If all of your activ-

Part of smart planning is trying to anticipate problem areas.

ities are scheduled for outdoors, do you have a large enough meeting area, where they could still take place indoors? If you don't, it can be a long weekend with everyone just sitting in their cabins! What happens if you have planned a ski retreat for six months and there is no snow? Have an alternate plan ready.

Transportation problems is another factor you must plan for. If your church owns a bus, it *will* break down. If you have a caravan of vehicles, one is destined to overheat or blow a tire. If it is possible, it would be great to have a mechanic with his tools along as one of the adult staff if your church is fortunate enough to have him as a member of the congregation. A cell phone is a must. You don't want to be stranded out in the middle of nowhere.

While you hope and pray you don't have any medical emergencies, you cannot ignore the possibility in your planning. Having every young person sign a medical release form is a must. You need to do some advance research and find out where the nearest medical facility is located and provide maps and phone numbers to all of your adult staff. If you have a nurse in the congregation who is willing to help out as a sponsor, you are doubly blessed.

Find out what your church liability and medical insurance covers and what it doesn't. Don't assume anything! I remember asking our financial secretary if our church policy covered a roller skating party. He assured me it did. I was ministering in a small resort town at the time and the nearest roller rink was 50 miles away. We had 75 young people signed up for this event. I had over 20 volunteer drivers signed up to help. I wanted to be sure we would be covered. That was the reason I had asked about the insurance.

On the return trip home it started to snow. One of our volunteer drivers was involved in a car accident. Fortunately no one was hurt, but the car was totaled—and they had just purchased it two weeks previously. I figured the church insurance would replace their vehicle since it happened during a church-sponsored event. To my dismay I was later informed that the church insurance policy didn't cover personal vehicles. The only thing it would have covered was some basic medical if a teen got hurt skating and even then it would only pay *after* the teen's family medical program had paid. This meant the family was out a personal vehicle and I felt responsible. From then on I would warn the volunteers that they drove at their own risk and the church would not be responsible for any damages that might happen to their personal vehicles. I made sure volunteers had appropriate personal insurance.

Cost is always going to be a factor that you must take into consideration when planning a retreat. The only way to accurately predict how much the event will cost is to make up a detailed budget. Once you have your total, then you can decide how you are going to pay for it, either by having the church subsidize some of it, involving the youth in fund raisers, or passing the total cost along to the participants. When figuring the budget, be sure to include the cost of:

- Speakers
- Worship band
- Rental for the retreat facility
- Transportation costs
- Food and utensils
- Publicity
- Materials for games and special events
- Banners or decorations
- Sound system and lighting

Discipline problems are always an issue whenever you gather a group of teens together—especially if you have a lot of unchurched kids in attendance. One of the things you can do in the way of prevention is to write out the rules for the retreat—along with the punishment for breaking the rules. Have the teens sign an agreement to the rules before they leave. Provide a copy of the signed rules to the parents, also. Try to keep the rules to a minimum. Be sure you enforce the rules consistently and fairly.

Misbehavior and discipline problems are times to teach teens that there are consequences for their actions, that their behavior does not take place in a vacuum, and that what they do affects the feelings and relationships of others. Most deviant behavior is only a surface indication of a deeper struggle. It takes patience, time, and good listening and problem-solving skills to get to the deeper issues.[10]

Be sure that you have adequate staff for the number of participants involved. Think through the various responsibilities that must be covered and recruit and assign duties appropriately. You will need: teachers, guest speaker, recreational director, worship leader, cooks, cabin moms and dads, nurse, mechanic, and drivers.

Choosing the proper site is very important as the setting can either make or break a retreat. Be sure to personally visit the site before the retreat. Don't trust brochures or others' evaluations and recommendations! Select a site on the basis of your retreat objective. Carefully think through the maximum distance you would expect the

Be sure to personally visit the site before the retreat. Don't trust brochures or other's evaluations and recommendations!

group to travel. Be sure you are familiar with all the agreement stipulations of the rental contract. For example, if you reserve rooms for 50 and only 35 show up, are you responsible for the 15 unused rooms? Do you have to use the camp's cooking staff or can you bring your own crew and cook your own meals? Don't sign any agreements until you have carefully read the entire document.

Good promotion will help with the success of a retreat. Use every available means to get the word out. Have students design posters using their computers and a desktop publishing program. Put together some creative skits to be used as announcements. Place key information about the retreat in the church bulletin and newsletter. Be sure to include it on your web site and send out mass e-mail invitations with a link to the appropriate spot on the web where all of the pertinent information can be found. It is helpful if you are able to have some pictures of the retreat center on the web site to whet their appetite. Follow up with a phone call the week before the sign-up deadline. When sending the information out, be specific in communicating the purpose of the event. Highlight the registration deadline and late fee.

Here is a check-list of some of the basic fundamentals that are needed for a successful retreat:

- Van drivers
- Sponsors
- Teachers
- Cooks
- Extension cords
- Electrical adapters
- Video projector
- Screen
- Laptop computer
- Digital camera
- 35 mm camera

- Film
- Sound system
- Worship band
- Medical release forms
- Nurse
- Matches
- Games/crowd-breakers
- First-aid kit
- Communion cups and trays
- Extra Bibles
- Communion juice and bread

- Recreational supplies
- CD player
- Praise CDs
- Snack food

- Drinks
- Paper cups and plates
- Eating utensils

When you work out your final schedule, be sure to pace the program realistically. You don't want to run at full steam from Friday night until Saturday afternoon and then fizzle out only to see boredom and disinterest take over on Sunday. If you save up all the "good stuff" until late Saturday night you run the risk of losing the interest of the group by Saturday breakfast. Scheduling a speaker late Friday night and right after Saturday breakfast—giving the impression that the whole weekend will be spent in meetings may turn kids off. Crowding meetings within five minutes of meal times, leaving no time for washing up or interaction is just too tight. It needs to be more relaxed. Don't overschedule, filling up every 30-minute period with an activity, leaving no opportunity for one-on-one relationships and counseling.[11]

You have not finished your planning until you have come up with a way to educate your teens and adult staff about the dangers of the "let-down" after camp or retreat. It is inevitable that after the peak experiences that naturally come as a part of the retreat encounter, these will be followed by some down times. When you first come down from the mountain, Satan is most likely to attack. Being aware of this possibility is half the battle. Preparing your students and adult staff for this can help them to become victorious. Be honest with yourself about your energy limits and that the end of the retreat is a vulnerable time.

Time for Reflection

1. How have camps and retreats influenced your own spiritual pilgrimage? In what ways can you duplicate that in the lives of your teens?
2. What are some different possibilities for a service retreat that you could do in your area?
3. If retreats and camps have the greatest impact on the spiritual development of teens, why don't you make more of them available to your teens?

Suggested Reading List

Cannon, Chris. *Great Retreats for Youth Groups*. Grand Rapids: Zondervan, 1994.

Reichter, Arlo. *The Group Retreat Book*. Loveland, CO: Group, 1983.

Notes on Chapter Fourteen

1. Paul Borthwick, *Organizing Your Youth Ministry* (Grand Rapids: Zondervan, 1988), p. 148.
2. Jayne Price and Richard Price, "Effective Youth Retreats," in *The Complete Book of Youth Ministry*, ed. by Warren S. Benson and Mark H. Senter III (Chicago: Moody, 1987), p. 355.
3. David Wheeler, "Camping and Retreats," in *Ministering to Youth*, ed. by David Roadcup (Cincinnati: Standard, 1980), pp. 175-176.
4. Wheeler, "Camping," p. 176.
5. John Perkins quoted in Chris Cannon, *Great Retreats for Youth Groups* (Grand Rapids: Zondervan, 1994), p. 9.
6. Jim Burns, *The Youth Builder* (Eugene, OR: Harvest House, 1988), p. 92.
7. John Westerhoff quoted in Burns, *Youth*, p. 91.
8. Rick Lawrence, "What Really Impacts Kids' Spiritual Growth," *GROUP Magazine* (February 1995), **http://www.groupmag.com/articles/details.asp?ID=1960**
9. Price and Price, "Effective," p. 356.
10. Ibid., p. 363.
11. Adapted from John Pearson, "Weekend Retreats," in *The Youth Leader's Source Book*, ed. by Gary Dausey (Grand Rapids: Zondervan, 1983), p. 216.

"For those God foreknew he also pre-
destined to be conformed to the likeness of his Son, that he might be the
firstborn among many brothers."
—*Paul*

"For even the Son of Man did not come
to be served, but to serve, and to give
his life as a ransom for many."
—*Jesus*

"Whether we are young or old, our first
reactions are normally selfish."
—*Gene Getz*[1]

Chapter 15
Youth and Service

John Mouton

Self-Absorption and Today's Youth

It was the best of food; it was the worst of food. I sat in the dim light of the naked, generator-powered bulb and ate a meal that, under other circumstances or better illumination, might not have been much to write home about. But this was a meal seasoned by hunger. It had been a long day filled with bad roads, river crossings, and the sights, sounds, and smells of a foreign land, but not much food. So I was wolfing down my food and thinking, "I wonder what this would taste like if I was actually chewing it," when I heard a commotion from the other side of the room. It seems that a guy named Tom, (not his real name), was upset about the food. Specifically he was incensed that no one had bothered to ask him what he wanted on his sandwich before it was prepared. The girl who made the sandwiches got upset and things degenerated from there.

All the time this was going on there were little eyes watching us through holes in the concrete block walls. Since we had arrived after dark, we hadn't seen the small bodies with distended bellies that the eyes belonged to. It was not until the next day, when we saw the children eating the moldy bread we had discarded, that we all realized the scene Tom had caused the night before had been played out in front of children who were starving.

What followed was a time of real soul-searching for all of us. Coming face to face with people in great need made us painfully aware of our own self-centeredness.

Coming face to face with people in great need made us painfully aware of our own self-centeredness.

I had an advantage over Tom in the food department. In addition to being famished that night, I had been raised by a father who made it his mission in life to make me eat things I didn't like. (This left me with taste buds that have almost no discretion.) So eating things that are different wasn't a problem for me. It was all those other times, when I was tempted to get the best places to sit, ride, or sleep for myself, that I realized that when push came to shove, I was more interested in looking out for my own interests than the interests of others.

This is, in fact, a problem that mankind has struggled with since the days of Adam and Eve. It is a struggle that is critical to our relationship with God. And it is a struggle that has been made even more difficult for the young people we work with by the society in which we live.

In their book, *Hollow Kids: Recapturing the Soul of a Generation Lost to the Self-Esteem Myth*, Laura L. Smith, Ph.D. and Charles H. Elliott, Ph.D. advance the premise that

> There are a significant number of children and teens today that have lost touch with the value of contributing to the community, of what we used to call making a difference in the world. Who instead focus on instant gratification, frantically searching for pleasure through materialism, reckless adventure, or drugs and alcohol.[2]

They point to "an alarming rise in depression, anxiety, and violence among our youth. More kids are in jail than ever before and rates of violent behavior have skyrocketed. So have dangerous eating disorders. Kids today are 10 times more likely to be depressed than they were a generation ago. Suicide rates among teens have tripled."[3]

In trying to identify a cause for this trend, Smith and Elliott admit that there is not one simple answer. They do, however, conclude from their study that a component of every problem mentioned above is "something called self-absorption. Self-absorption is just what it sounds like, always thinking about me, me, me."[4]

And why are kids today so self-absorbed? They suggest that it stems from the "self-esteem movement"[5] that began in the late '50s and exploded in the '80s. It has ". . . infiltrated our culture and offered a panacea to cure all of society's ills. Everyone, especially our kids should feel good, all the time. This message fundamentally changed the way we educated our kids and even the way we parented."[6]

If our goal is to be conformed to the likeness of God's Son and to help others do the same, and if God's Son came to serve not be served, then a generation predisposed to self-centeredness, that has been taught to think more highly of themselves, will certainly present a challenge to today's youth workers.

Jesus also faced the challenge of working with people who were so caught up in themselves that they failed to think of others. His example provides principles that should help us as we meet the challenge in our ministry to youth.

The Example of Servanthood

Our Lord, on the night he was betrayed, took two common elements and used them to teach his disciples, and us, a most important lesson. When we reflect on that night, we usually think about the wine and the loaf. It's tempting to overlook the basin and the towel.

Gathered at the Passover feast, the disciples were keenly aware that someone needed to wash the others' feet. The problem was that the only people who washed feet were the least. So there they sat, feet caked with dirt. It was such a sore point that they were not even going to talk about it. No one wanted to be considered the least. Then Jesus took a towel and a basin and redefined greatness.[7]

This was Jesus' final opportunity to make sure that his disciples understood his mission. It was his last chance to make sure that they would be prepared to carry on the mission after he left. And in that context he focused the eyes of his disciples on serving one another.

Here are three reasons to consider that same kind of focus for the young people you work with:

More than any other single way the grace of humility is worked into our lives through the Discipline of service.

1. Getting the focus off of ourselves and onto serving others is the best discipline for dealing with the "Me" problem.

   More than any other single way the grace of humility is worked into our lives through the Discipline of service. . . . Nothing *disciplines* the inordinate desires of the flesh like service, and nothing *transforms* the desires of the flesh like serving in hiddenness. The flesh whines against service but screams against hidden service. It strains and pulls for honor and recognition. It will devise subtle, religiously acceptable means to call attention to the service rendered. . . . The flesh must learn the painful lesson that it has no rights of its own. It is the work of hidden service that will accomplish this self-abasement."[8]

2. Getting kids involved in service helps them see that God can use them to complete his mission. This will fuel their passion like nothing else.
3. Because Jesus told us to.

Years ago, when my dad was teaching me to fly an airplane, he insisted that I use a memorized checklist before every takeoff. For that simple airplane, the word CIGARS was used to form the acrostic:

C– Controls
I – Instruments
G– Gasoline
A– Air trim
R– Run up
S– Seatbelts

It was important to go through this before every flight because of how critical these items are for the safety of the people on board.

May I suggest a "checklist" for us to use in the even more important task of training up young people. With apologies to "Old MacDonald" we'll use the letters E. I. E. I. O. to make it easier to remember.

Example

Having lived out servanthood before his disciples, Jesus took one last opportunity to give them an example. "So he got up from the meal, took off his outer clothing, and wrapped a towel around his waist. After that, he poured water in a basin *Service should be a lifestyle, not a project.* and began to wash his disciples' feet, drying them with the towel that was wrapped around him" (John 13:4).

Service should be a lifestyle, not a project. Youth leaders who would help others serve as Jesus did must first model servanthood in their own lives.

Unfortunately, serving others comes about as naturally to us as it does to the young people we work with. (By the way, the "Tom" in the food story was a Youth Minister.) In addition to the problems of our selfish nature and the influence of our society, we can be influenced by standards of success in youth ministry that favor attributes like charisma, drive, and the ability to delegate over humility, compassion, and a servant's heart. The result can be ministers who desire to resemble CEOs more than compassionate servants.

Henri J.M. Nouwen describes the problem like this: "The tragedy of Christian ministry is that many who are in great need, many who seek an attentive ear, a word of support, a forgiving embrace, a firm hand, a tender smile, or even a stuttering confession of inability to do more, often find their ministers distant men who do not want to burn their fingers."[9]

Jesus said, "If anyone would come after me, he must deny himself and take up his cross and follow me"(Matthew 16:24). In spite of what the self-esteem movement has told us, self is the problem and not the solution. We must deny—not embrace—self if we want to follow Jesus. And it's not a final step for the spiritual elite; it is the prerequisite to genuine discipleship.

In the midst of writing this chapter, I made a trip to Tulsa, Oklahoma, where I was to catch a flight to a youth conference in India. While there I received an emergency phone call. My son had been involved in an accident and was being "life-flighted" to Joplin, Missouri. I was told that he was in very critical condition, and that my wife and I should get there as quickly as we could.

On that trip from Tulsa to Joplin, I remember the temptation to bargain with God for the life of my son. I was immediately convicted about the possibility that I had anything in my life with which to barter. How could Jesus be Lord of my life if there were things I had held back?

If we would model servanthood, perhaps we should continue to ask that and a few other related questions:

- Have I followed Christ's example by being completely submissive to the Heavenly Father? Is there anyplace I wouldn't go? Anything I wouldn't do? Anything I wouldn't eat? Any risk I wouldn't take?
- Will God's leading in my life always involve greater pay, increased comfort, and more security?

- Am I growing in my love for God and in awareness and compassion for those in need, both around me and around the world?

Instruction

Jesus did more than just model servanthood, He taught about it often. Our students need to be prepared spiritually or we run the risk of serving for all the wrong reasons.

I still remember how painful it was to hear how a group of inner-city homeless in Chicago felt about a church youth group from the suburbs that came in once a month for what they called their "bum run." The people were made to feel like nothing more than a project to help the group members feel good about themselves.

The people were made to feel like nothing more than a project to help the group members feel good about themselves.

In his book, *A National Survey: What I Wish My Youth Minister Knew about Youth Ministry*, Mike Nappa shares the following quotes from teenagers about their experiences in service projects:

- "I feel happy and proud of myself because I helped somebody else instead of myself."[10]
- "Usually I feel good about myself. I've become tighter with the group, more connected with them—and we've accomplished something."[11]
- "After a service project, I get a good feeling, a sense of accomplishment. Especially this year because I've never done anything like this before where you actually help build stuff."[12]

It is true that serving blesses the server. And yes, young people get excited about the fact that God can use them to do something significant with their lives. There is no doubt that serving with a team can result in wonderful bonds of friendship being formed. These are all true and can be considered for the purposes of recruitment and planning . . . they just can't be the primary motivation for our service. *They must be seen as by-products, not the end product.* Our goal must be the same as Christ's, revealed in Romans 15:8-9: "For I tell you that Christ became a servant to the Jews on behalf of God's truth, to confirm the promises made to the patriarchs so that the Gentiles may glorify God for his mercy. . . ."

Here are a few suggestions for helping us see service through God's eyes:

1. Give a scriptural basis from which to understand service. Study and teach on the examples from the life of Christ. Teach on passages like Philippians 2:1-11 and Matthew 25:31-46.
2. Help students understand the need to see service in the context of community and hospitality. The needy should be seen as people to be loved and included rather than as projects.
3. Help create an awareness of the needs of others. Point out that "the least of these" can be all around us. Bring in guest speakers from local service agencies. Continually find creative ways to inform students about global needs.
4. Don't be afraid to talk to young people about sacrifice and suffering.

Experience

When Jesus had finished washing His disciple's feet, He said:

Now that I, your Lord and Teacher, have washed your feet, you also should wash one another's feet. I have set you an example that you should do as I have done for you. I tell you the truth, no servant is greater than his master, nor is a messenger greater than the one who sent him. Now that you know these things, you will be blessed *if you do them*" (John 13:14-17, emphasis added).

All the information in the world will be useless, boring, and quickly forgotten if you don't put it into practice. Even a great example is powerless unless the observers are challenged and given an opportunity to "do."

Fortunately, young people enthusiastically embrace opportunities to put their faith into action by serving others. And those acts of service, if properly led, can be a most powerful tool in helping young people develop the heart and mind of Christ.

All the information in the world will be useless, boring, and quickly forgotten if you don't put it into practice.

Here are some practical ways to improve your experience:

1. Start Small. Begin by taking your group to local nursing homes or soup kitchens. Reach out to international students or immigrants in your own community. Seek opportunities to reach out

to widows, the disadvantaged, and the elderly. And remember to always strive to serve in the context of fellowship and hospitality by connecting people to the church.

2. Expose them to a variety of types of service. This will provide opportunities for people with different gifts, interests, and abilities to "connect."

3. Choose projects within the realm of your group's abilities. You don't want to have to listen to things like "Remember the time we had the Jr. High boys dust Mrs. Johnson's heirloom china and crystal collection!"

4. As a leader, you must show that you are willing to do any job you ask the team to do. At the same time, you must not spend so much time at the "task" that you neglect your responsibilities to motivate, coordinate, oversee, and provide quality control.

5. Help your students visualize the finished product.

6. Give each student a small, specific job. Make sure they understand what you want them to do. Check on them periodically.

7. Know who works well together and who does not.

8. If possible, spend time with the host and make time for the students to do this as well.

9. Help students know how to use, maintain, and be responsible for their tools.

10. Don't allow horseplay or practical jokes.

11. Protect your students from danger.

12. Plan "Service Trips" that will involve a greater time commitment.

This will take a significant amount of planning and preparation. There are resources in the recommended reading list to help with the planning, but I would encourage getting involved with an organization that provides service opportunities, especially if this is your first attempt.

At Christ In Youth we have found it helpful to separate trips into two broad categories: service trips and short-term mission trips. This is not to say that "missions" should ever be divorced from service, but rather to define experiences that have a different focus.

The focus of a service trip is a project or projects. (The focus of short-term mission trips will be discussed in the next chapter.) The objectives would include teaching servanthood while meeting the needs of others. Group dynamics can be enhanced and relationships within the group established and strengthened.

Service trips can include virtually everyone. Age restrictions can be lowered and new or even non-believers included. Group sizes can be fairly large, depending on logistics, and the application process can be made easy.

Before you decide to go with an organization, here are nine questions you should ask:

1. What type of work will we do?
2. What will we be expected to bring?
3. How does the organization's philosophy of ministry compare with ours?
4. Will our service be connected to a local church?
5. How many experienced staff members will be assigned to our group?
6. What requirements for participation does the organization set?
7. What training is required?
8. What is the organization's track record?
9. What will it cost us?

From a stewardship standpoint it should be noted that it is not necessary for service trip destinations to be far away. Often staying close to home just makes more sense.

Interpretation of the Experience

"When he had finished washing their feet, he put on his clothes and returned to his place. 'Do you understand what I have done for you?'" (John 13:12).

Even when experiences are preceded by great examples and preparation, it is always helpful to make sure that everyone understands what has happened. One of the best ways this is accomplished is by "debriefing." Even those who get involved in service for the wrong reasons can experience tremendous growth if given a little direction. Here are a few suggestions:

Even when experiences are preceded by great examples and preparation, it is always helpful to make sure that everyone understands what has happened.

1. Try to debrief as soon after the experience as possible. In the case of longer service trips, try to debrief daily.
2. Choose a location where people can speak freely with as few distractions as possible. You may want to include people outside your group (such as the people being served) in some of your

debrief, but you will also want to have a time that is for your group alone.

3. Facilitate discussion by asking open-ended questions like:
   - What did you do today and how did you feel about it?
   - What do you think God might be trying to teach you through this experience?
   - What were some of the preconceived ideas you had about the people we came to serve and in what ways, if any, have those ideas changed?
   - How has this experience affected the way you view the world?
   - How will this experience impact your life?

Ongoing Support and Encouragement

Shortly after he had washed their feet, Jesus told the disciples that although he was leaving them, he would not leave them as orphans. Jesus knew that they would continue to need help, and he promised to provide it through the person of the Counselor.

If serving is to be a lifestyle for us and for our students, ongoing support and encouragement will be absolutely essential. We can never have a "been there, done that" attitude when it comes to service. Our sinful nature and the influences of this world will necessitate that we remain vigilant and disciplined, relying on the power of the Spirit. And every time we are tempted to "throw in the towel," we remember Christ's example and take it up to serve.

Time for Reflection

1. What are some signs of self-absorption that you have seen in the young people you work with?
2. "Service should be a lifestyle, not a project." Do you agree with this statement? Why or why not?
3. What are some dangers of involving students in service projects? How can this be avoided?
4. What is the difference between service projects and mission trips? Why is this distinction important?
5. Why is "debriefing" an important task to do after a service project or mission trip? How should it be done?

SUGGESTED READING LIST

Burns, Ridge, with Noel Becchetti. *The Complete Student Missions Handbook.* Grand Rapids: Zondervan, 1990.

Campolo, Anthony. *Ideas for Social Action.* Grand Rapids: Zondervan, 1983.

Case, Steve, and Fred Cornforth. *Hands-On Service Ideas for Youth Groups.* Loveland, CO: Group, 1995.

Wilkes, C. Gene. *Jesus on Leadership.* Wheaton, IL: Tyndale, 1998.

NOTES ON CHAPTER FIFTEEN

1. Gene A. Getz, *Living for Others When You'd Rather Live for Yourself* (Ventura, CA: Regal, 1985), p. 179

2. Laura L. Smith, Ph.D., and Charles H. Elliott, Ph.D., from a Q. and A. regarding *Hollow Kids: Recapturing the Soul of a Generation Lost to the Self-Esteem Myth* (Prima Publishing, 2001 found at **www.hollowkids.com**).

3. Ibid.

4. Ibid.

5. Ibid.

6. Ibid.

7. Richard J. Foster, *Celebration of Discipline: The Path to Spiritual Growth* (New York: HarperCollins, 1978), p.126.

8. Ibid., p.130.

9. Henri J.M. Nouwen, *The Wounded Healer* (New York: Doubleday, 1979), p. 71.

10. Mike Nappa, *What I Wish My Youth Leader Knew about Youth Ministry* (Cincinnati: Standard, 1999), p. 147.

11. Ibid., p. 146.

12. Ibid., p. 150.

"All of history is moving toward one great goal, the white-hot worship of God and his Son among all the peoples of the earth. Missions is not that goal. It is the means. And for that reason it is the second greatest human activity in the world." —*John Piper*[1]

"I have discovered feelings of intentionality, mission, and purpose that cannot be generated at any summer camp or retreat. Short-term missions projects . . . have become the very essence of ministry to many youth groups."
—*Ridge Burns*[2]

Chapter 16

Short-Term Missions

John Mouton

Nothing you will do in youth ministry will cost more. Nothing you will do will involve greater risks. Yet nothing has the potential to be a more effective tool in discipling young people to be like Jesus than short-term missions.

More and more churches are coming to this conclusion, resulting in a fadlike popularity for short-term missions. It seems as if every youth group in the country is doing them. If you are a youth leader, you are probably already involved or are feeling the pressure to get involved because everyone else is.

If you are already participating in short-term missions, this chapter can help you examine your direction and improve your leadership skills. If, on the other hand, this is all new to you, our hope is that we can touch on a few basic principles that will help direct you and spark an interest that will lead you to further study and involvement.

Getting Involved for All the Wrong Reasons

Unfortunately, just because something is popular does not necessarily mean that it is good. The truth is, not all short-term missions are effective or helpful. Some missions have stopped receiving groups because their experiences have been so negative. Others have questioned whether or not short-term missions actually hinder the recruiting of long-term missionaries. They point to the fact that although short-term participation is at an all-time high, involvement in long-term missions is declining.[3]

The experience of others has shown participation in short-term missions to be highly effective. Groups like STEM (Short Term Evangelical Missions) Ministries have studied past trip participants and have found dramatic

Just because something is popular does not necessarily mean that it is good.

increases in a number of missions-related activities, including their financial support of missions and their desire to return to the mission field.[4] Still others point out that Jesus used a short-term mission type of experience when he took the disciples through Samaria and taught them about the extent of the harvest and his purpose on earth. It would seem that the problem is not the concept of short-term missions, but rather a poor understanding of their purpose.

Some, for example, see their primary objective as the change in the lives of the team members. Although change can and should take place, this shouldn't be seen as the end objective, but rather a means to our ultimate end of making disciples of the nations.

Others seek to accomplish some high-profile task without ever connecting with a local mission or church. These groups run the risk of giving those students a "been there, done that" attitude that fails to motivate them to consider the only type of missions that has proved to be truly effective, that is long-term.

If, however, your objective is to develop in people the global mind of God, incorporated in every aspect of their lives, and to recruit the next generation of missionaries, then you will have a long-term focus that achieves the other objectives along the way.

Definitions

As we begin to clarify our purpose, perhaps we should look at some basic definitions. We have found it helpful to distinguish between a short-term mission trip and what we described in the last chapter as a service trip. Obviously every mission trip involves service, and every service trip involves mission, but we have found that our trips can be more productive if we differentiate between these two basic types.

As mentioned in the last chapter, a service trip is centered on a project. The objectives would include teaching servanthood while meeting the needs of others. Group dynamics can be enhanced and relationships within the group established and strengthened.

A mission trip, on the other hand, is centered on missionaries. This is absolutely critical if your objective is what we believe it must be: to recruit long-term missionaries and to develop in young people the global perspective of God. You want team members exposed to someone about whom they can come to say, "Maybe God could use me to do what they're doing." You want them to experience something of what ministry in that context involves. You want them to get involved in people's lives so they can develop a burden for their spiritual needs and the understanding that God can use them to meet those needs.

You want team members exposed to someone about whom they can come to say, "Maybe God could use me to do what they're doing."

A service trip is the kind of experience that can include virtually everyone. Age restrictions can be lowered and new or even nonbelievers included. Group sizes can be fairly large, depending on logistics, and the application process can be made easy.

A mission trip, on the other hand, is not for everyone. Although we would like to take everyone, some are just not ready. Those who are not prepared spiritually, emotionally, and physically run the risk not only of failing to get from the experience what they should, but even of being a disruption to others on the trip and harming the reputation of Christ and the mission. Age restrictions need to be raised, group sizes kept smaller, and the application process made difficult enough to "weed out" those who are not properly motivated.

So how can you involve your students in short-term missions in a way that will have the maximum impact? Believe it or not, that same incredible mnemonic device (E.I.E.I.O.) we used for service can be used here.

Example

Bob Pierce, founder of World Vision International, comments: "A personal obedience to the missionary vision is a primary requisite for the young people's sponsor if he would instill this vision in the heart and minds of those under his guidance."[5]

Melissa was the kind of girl that every leader would like to have on their team. She had a great attitude, a servant's heart, and a sincere openness to anything that God might want to do in and through her. She recently wrote about the experience, and what she said gives insight into what brought her to that point.

I was sixteen when I went on my first mission trip to Samborondon, Ecuador, with Christ In Youth in 1995. I was a fairly new Christian from a non-Christian home with a fresh passion for getting involved in God's work. I had a youth minister whose enthusiasm for missions bled into mine and I anxiously waited for the day in which I would be able to participate in an overseas mission trip.[6]

"I had a youth minister whose enthusiasm for missions bled into mine."

Youth workers who want to see young people develop a passion for getting involved in God's work must model that passion themselves. Here are three activities that will stoke your own missions fire.

1. *Study*—Understanding that our God is a missionary God is a prerequisite to understanding His book. And understanding that His book is about missions from Genesis to Revelation will give us the perspective we need to study it intelligently. (John Piper's *Let The Nations Be Glad* is a good resource that helps illuminate God's plan.) Once we understand a little about missions, we come to understand that, for us, missions is not optional. C. Peter Wagner put it this way in his book *On the Crest of the Wave*.

> Some things in life are optional and some are not. Wearing shoes is optional. Eating is not. Driving a car is optional. But once you choose the option, driving on the right-hand side of the road (here in America) is not. Becoming a Christian is optional. But once you decide to ask Jesus Christ to take control of your life, involvement in world missions is no longer optional. I'm not saying these things are impossible. You can choose to go without eating, but if you do, you must take the consequences . . . You can choose to drive on the left but you will pay fines and cause accidents.[7]

Excellent!!

In addition to studying to better understand God's passion for spreading the good news of His Kingdom to every people, tongue, and nation, you should also study about missions history and the biographies of great missionaries. Learning about great heroes of the past like Jim Elliot, William Borden, Bruce Olson, Henry Martyn, and William Carey will not only fuel your passion, but will also help you begin to form your own philosophy of missions.

2. *Develop your own global awareness*—People in the United States tend to be some of the most ethnocentric people on the planet. In other words, if it's not happening here, it's not important. Buy an up-to-date map. Get a copy of *Operation World* and begin learning about and praying for the nations.

3. *Go yourself*—Like the man said when asked to describe what it's like to eat a hot Krispy Kreme donut, "sometimes you just have to experience things for yourself." Plus, it's always better to say, "follow me" than "you go." This will be a crucial step in the development of your own philosophy of how to reach the nations with the gospel. Not to mention the fact that your church will be more willing to let students go on a trip when they see that you have returned alive and transformed.

Instruction

Now it is important that you begin to teach your students some of what you have been learning. Here are some ways you can begin to make that happen:

1. Create a missions environment by having "missions stuff" around. This could include things you brought back from your own trip or items borrowed from missionaries your church supports.
2. Provide reading and video resources.
3. Arrange live exchanges with missionaries on the field.
4. Correspond with missionaries.
5. Minister to international students in your own area.
6. Pray for specific missions.
7. Arrange for special events and projects.
8. Sponsor a child.
9. Show missions related videos. (A couple of great examples are *The Harvest* from Venture Media Productions, 1-800-729-4351, and *Beyond the Gates of Splendor* from Bearing Fruit Communications, information available at **www.beyondthegatesthemovie.com**.)
10. Include missions in your lesson planning. Teach a series on missions, do a study on missions from the book of Acts, teach about mission heroes of the past, etc.

Experience

After you have instructed about the need to be sensitive to God's heart and obedient to his command, and have modeled that sensitivity and obedience in your own life, you're ready to help your students put into practice the things they've heard. In this way you avoid the trap of getting them "all dressed up" but giving them "no place to go."

One of your first decisions will be whether to organize a trip on your own or go with an organization. Here are some advantages that each has to offer:

Advantages of going on your own:
1. The freedom to select a specific mission
2. The freedom to set your own schedule
3. The ability to control aspects of the trip such as objectives and policies
4. Possible cost savings
5. Possibilities for extensive prefield orientation and posttrip follow-up

Advantage of going with an organization:
1. It may lend credibility to the trip with parents and church leaders, which may be especially important if your church is new to short-term missions.
2. You can benefit from their experience in areas like cultural considerations, policies, transportation, food, lodging, leadership, safety issues, etc.
3. You have access to good missionary contacts. (Not every missionary should host groups.)
4. You have more locations from which to choose. (You may have a young person in your group who has an interest in or feels a calling to a part of the world that you can't offer a trip to.)
5. You have more types of trips from which to choose. (For example, "specialty" trips such as medical missions.)
6. People grow more when "stretched" by going with people outside their own group. (This may be due to a number of reasons, including increased vulnerability, the freedom to escape predetermined roles, and the absence of group "baggage.")
7. Organizations can help screen out those who are not ready to go so that you don't have to be the "heavy."

8. The time commitment from you should be much less.
9. You can get involved even if your church or group is too small to go on your own.

As you weigh the advantages and make your decision, remember that if this is your group's first short-term mission experience, it needs to be a good one. You would be wise to do everything you can to stack the deck in your favor, including going with an organization.

It is also important to note that even if you run your own trip, you will probably have students that will benefit from going somewhere "on their own." Consider working with an organization to make that happen.

When it comes to choosing an organization, make sure you do your homework. Consider the following questions:

1. How well do you know them?
2. What is their theology?
3. Where do they go, and with whom do they work?
4. What are their objectives, and do they line up with yours?

Whether you go on your own, or with someone else, your next decision may be where to go. Here are a few suggestions to consider:

1. Seek the Spirit's leading.
2. Consider missions that your church supports.
3. Choose a missionary who is productive, relates well to youth, and believes in the value of investing in the lives of your team members.
4. Evaluate time requirements.
5. Consider expenses.
6. If going on your own, a set-up trip is a must.

Now that you have decided where to go, it becomes necessary to recruit. If you have already led by example and taught about missions, this part should be relatively easy. Here are a few suggestions:

1. Use testimonials from young people.
2. Provide written information about dates, cost, itinerary, etc.
3. Develop a timeline.
4. Address objections (waste of money, dangerous, can't afford it, etc.)
5. Require applications and/or interviews.
6. Require a deposit with the application.
7. Screen applicants—not everyone should go.

8. Publicize cutoff date and maximum numbers.
9. Encourage applicants without making it too easy.

Interpretation of the Experience

Helping students see what they saw and what you want them to see is a vital part of the experience. This one, often neglected step, can mean the difference between positive and negative long-term results.

We have found two components to be necessary:

1. *Journaling*—Team members should be asked to journal before, during, and after the trip. It really doesn't matter if they are the "journaling type," they need to record their thoughts to help them remember and process a flood of experiences that may overwhelm them at the time. It's a good idea to provide specific journaling time each day during the trip.

2. *Debrief* - Often overlooked because leaders are unsure about how to go about it, a good debrief can transform the way individuals and the group as a whole respond to the things that happen on a trip. Here are a few suggestions:

   + Find a place to meet that provides a safe, relaxed atmosphere.
   + Have a clearly defined purpose in mind. This will vary depending on the stage of the trip, but could include things like helping team members "unpack" what's happening, resolving conflict, and providing closure to the trip.
   + Be a facilitator. Be sure that you're not doing all of the talking but instead are "drawing out" discussion from the team members. Open-ended questions or questions that call for a sharing of feelings can be effective tools in getting people to open up. Here are some sample debrief questions:
     ◇ What did you do today and how did you feel about it?
     ◇ What were your expectations and how is the trip "measuring up"?
     ◇ What happened that was frustrating or difficult and how did you handle it?
     ◇ What do you think God is trying to teach you?
     ◇ What has this trip taught you about God's character?
     ◇ What has this trip taught you about yourself?
     ◇ Describe how someone you have met on this trip has impacted your life?

◇ What will be different about your life when you get home?

◇ Do you see yourself pursuing long-term crosscultural mission, and if not, what role do you see yourself playing in your obedience to the great commission?

✦ Provide closure. This doesn't mean that everything will always be resolved, but as a leader you will need to decide when it's time to move on.

Earl Davis, a Project Adventure trainer, uses a metaphor for debriefing that you may find helpful. In his metaphor, he asks you to think of a debriefing session as a fishing trip. "As a leader, your task is to find some issues in the lake and reel them in so the group can learn from them."[8]

He then suggests that you begin the debriefing by asking some open-ended questions like, How did you feel about this activity? He recommends, "Begin with a broad net—cast it out and see if there are any ripples on the surface."

Your task is then to cast your "hook" in the direction of the ripples to see if there is something there worth pursuing. For example, someone's response to the question about frustration or difficulties might be a ripple that indicates a broader, deeper problem. As you fish that area with follow-up questions, you may find out the issue even involves others who have been reluctant to speak up. In any case the key is to be observant enough to spot the ripples and perceptive enough to know which ones to go after.[9]

Ongoing Encouragement and Support

Don't make the mistake of thinking that the experience is over when the trip is over. Shortly after returning from a thirty-day trip to Southeast Asia, Jonathan began a note to those who had prayed for and supported him with these words:

I wish I was able to convey to you the impact this trip has had on me—but I still don't fully understand it myself! I am reminded of what Tiger Woods said after he won a professional golf tournament by the largest margin in history. He said that he probably wouldn't realize the full scope of what had just happened until a couple of years down the road. I feel the same way. I may not realize the full scope of what happened until several years down the road, and some of the results I may never see or know.[10]

The fact is, God will continue to work in the lives of short-termers long after they return home. Our job is to help them process what is happening in a way that will facilitate long-term growth and involvement in Kingdom work.

Reentry

One of the first things we can do is help them through the process of reentry. Factors like the personality of the participant, the nature of the trip, and the duration of the trip can all affect the issues that come up when one reenters his own culture. Here are some suggestions to help navigate this potentially problematic area:

1. Don't expect your family and friends to be as excited about your experience as you are. Try to remember how you felt before you had this experience firsthand. Don't be condescending. Do be patient.
2. Set realistic goals for implementing changes that you are committed to seeing take place.
3. Don't assume that you are now an expert on missions.
4. Prepare for ways to effectively share the experience you have had with others.
5. Ask God for wisdom as you reflect on your journal.
6. Pray for God's direction in your life.

Encouraging Continued Involvement

The young people who participate in short-term missions will be greatly affected by what they see and encounter. You do not want to make the mistake of only providing them with some new kind of experience or thrill. You want what they have experienced to have a life-changing effect that will last a lifetime. Consider the thoughts of Katie as she reflected on her trip to Ghana:

On the airplane coming home, I felt such a mix of feelings. I kept remembering how sweet it was to have five or six children trying to hold my hands at one time. I thought of those who had given their lives to Christ. I remembered the children who asked us when we would send them Bibles, because they wanted to read God's word for themselves. I remembered a woman begging me to take her baby with me when I left. I remembered praying with a crippled man, singing and dancing with fifty children in the church, hearing the sound of the drums as the people worshiped and danced, and Ebenezer running after our bus as we left.

I remembered when one of the leaders asked us if we would come back. He told of the great need and described how Jesus left the glories of heaven to come suffer, serve and die for us. I remembered crying as I listened to him speak of Jesus, and praying to be more willing to give everything for the sake of the gospel. —Katie, Ghana Medical Trip[11]

Hearts will be broken and eyes will be opened, but it is the continuing accountability, encouragement, resources, training, and exposure to networking opportunities that will make the difference on whether many follow through with commitments made when passions were stirred on a short-term mission trip.

Time for Reflection

1. How does involving your young people cost you a great deal, yet pay back great dividends?
2. In what ways can short-term missions be detrimental?
3. What is the difference between a service trip and a mission trip? What are the distinct advantages of each?
4. Why is follow-up so important after a mission trip? What kind of things should you do in the way of follow-up?

SUGGESTED READING LIST

Borthwick, Paul. *Youth and Missions.* Wheaton, IL: Victor Books, 1988.

Forward, David C. *The Essential Guide to the Short Term Mission Trip.* Chicago: Moody, 1998.

Murdoch, Lincoln P. *Launching the Great Go Mission.* Omaha: Step Up To Life Press, 1992.

Piper, John. *Let the Nations Be Glad.* Grand Rapids: Baker, 1993.

VanCise, Martha. *Successful Mission Teams: A Guide for Volunteers.* Birmingham, AL: New Hope Publishers, 1999.

Notes on Chapter Sixteen

1. John Piper, *Let the Nations Be Glad* (Grand Rapids: Baker Books, 1993), p. 15.

2. Ridge Burns, "How to Plan and Lead a Student Mission Trip," in *The Complete Book of Youth Ministry,* ed. by Warren S. Benson and Mark H. Senter III (Chicago: Moody, 1987), p. 397.

3. Ryan Shaw, "The Student World and Mission—How Are We Doing?" *Mission Frontiers* (September-October 2002).

4. *Is Short-Term Missions Really Worth the Time and Money,* 2nd printing, © 1991 by STEM Ministries, Inc. (Minneapolis, MN: STEM Ministries, 1993).

5. Bob Pierce, *Emphasizing Missions in the Local Church* (Grand Rapids: Zondervan, 1964), p. 81.

6. Melissa DeShayes, *Connection,* Christ In Youth (Summer 2002).

7. C. Peter Wagner, *On the Crest of the Wave* (Ventura, CA: Regal, 1983), p. 5.

8. Earl Davis, quoted in *QuickSilver,* © Project Adventure, Inc., ed. by Karl Rohnke and Steve Butler (Dubuque, IA: Kendall/Hunt Publishing Co., 1995), p. 34.

9. Rohnke and Butler. *Quicksilver.*

10. Jonathan Mouton, *Connection,* Christ In Youth (Summer 2001).

11. Katie, Ghana Medical Trip—personal conversation.

"In a society filled with dysfunctional homes; technology that promises instant and continual pseudo-intimacy through television, movies, and computer forums; and a youth culture that is increasingly isolated from significant intergenerational relationships, many students find themselves in defective, unsatisfying relationships. These students look for love but soon despair of discovering a friend's love that will touch them at their deeper, personal levels. In such a barren relational desert, a small group can be an oasis standing in stark contrast to the mirages that have promised but failed to deliver the relief and refreshment of interpersonal intimacy." —*Jana L. Sundene*[1]

"Kids need a place to talk, a safe place where they can say whatever is on their minds without fear of ridicule or retaliation. They need a place where they can ask any question and find answers, express any feeling and find acceptance, and share any secret and find trust." —*David R. Veerman*[2]

Chapter 17
Small Groups: the Nonnegotiable Factor in Youth Ministry

Kevin Greer

Let's just come right out and say it: *Your youth ministry will fade and die without the inclusion of small groups.* I'm not sure if anyone will say it as plainly as that, but it is time we acknowledged this blunt truth. The last thing we need is a youth ministry that treats all students as spectators of our incredible ability to put together a big program. Everyone knows the value of the big program is to attract students to the ministry or to the church and to create a thirst in them to want to know more. It is the role of small groups to connect and keep the students once they have arrived.

Why Small Groups?

What is so special about small groups? Why does a youth program need them? What exactly is it that small groups are trying to accomplish? What makes them so important in the context of youth ministry?

These are important questions and will be answered by looking at the various contributions that small groups make to the lives of students.

Your youth ministry will fade and die without the inclusion of small groups.

1. *Belonging.* Students are given opportunity to connect with others. There is strong need for "belonging" among teenagers and being a part of a small group, even if it is for only a short while, gives students the security of fitting in.

2. *Blending.* Small groups also allow for blending together students who might never have met one another. There can be a blending together of high school seniors with freshmen, dropouts with "A" students, or athletes with kids that could care less about sports of any kind. All too often we stick to what and who we know, never venturing out of our comfort zone. It's amazing how much more you can learn from people that are not just like you.

3. *Relational Intimacy.* We long to know and to be known. We want to feel like someone cares and that feeling can only come in a small group. A large congregation or crowd setting will usually feel impersonal.

4. *Learning and Life Application.* Through discussion and shared thoughts a group can give insights and personal application that an individual might never think about. "Small groups encourage the interactive exploration of ideas and options rather than the more traditional educational approach which is built upon a teacher-to-group handing down of information."[3]

5. *Support and Encouragement.* Upon learning that one of your group members is going through a difficult time, the group should seek ways to encourage and lend a hand. If a student is not in a small group, there is a good chance no one would know they are hurting.

6. *Accountability and Healthy Confrontation.* As a group gets to know one another they can discern when a friend needs to be confronted and pushed to get his/her life on track.

7. *Mentoring.* Adults leading small groups are given serious opportunities to do real ministry, rather than just straightening chairs, fixing snacks, or running tech stuff. They will have the opportunity to help shape lives. Teens need significant godly adults in their lives to steer them into the will of God.

8. *Prayer.* In a small group, a guy can share a need and receive prayer support from others. Needs will often remain unspoken when a teen is in a large group.

Small groups are not just one of the things a youth ministry should incorporate; they ought to be the foundation for the entire program.

One youth pastor recently touted small group ministry as "the most essential tool for discipleship in the youth ministry today." Because of their recognized contribution to personal lives and youth group growth, small groups have become the norm rather than the exception for the practice of Christian youth ministry.[4]

Small groups are not just one of the things a youth ministry should incorporate; they ought to be the foundation for the entire program.

It is the best possible use of adults for doing ministry and meets more individual needs than a large spectator program ever will. There are many ways to use small groups in your youth ministry and most programs will incorporate several different methods.

Different Kinds of Small Groups

Do not assume that all small groups are the same, for they are not. The stated purpose for each small group will greatly affect the dynamics of the group and the length of time that the members of the group are committed to staying together. We will list eight possible types of small groups your youth ministry could incorporate.

1. *Discipleship*—A group of four to six students of the same gender meeting with one or two adults over an entire school year with the purpose of spiritual growth and accountability. Discipleship groups are set apart from other small groups in two areas: mentoring and commitment. Students are asked to make a commitment to being there every week and to doing assignments. The adults are more than facilitators or teachers, they are mentors.

2. *Bible Studies*—These groups meet for the purpose of study and prayer. Their purpose, like a discipleship group, is growth and Christian maturity. The difference is that the group may only meet for six weeks, nine weeks, or thirteen weeks, depending on the length of the study. These groups usually don't call for as

strong a commitment to attendance either. They are often not limited in number. This is a very common model used for the traditional Sunday school or midweek youth Bible study. The leader's emphasis is not on mentoring his or her students, but on teaching a particular course of study.

The stated purpose for each small group will greatly affect the dynamics of the group and the length of time that the members of the group are committed to staying together.

3. *Discussion*—This group usually incorporates eight to twelve students with one leader for the purpose of life application and further learning. They are most often used in a Sunday morning Bible class or directly following a message at youth group or some other event. Discussion groups can be used in a variety of ways. An entire lesson could be discussion oriented, a message could be given with time for small groups to meet afterward to discuss and apply the message, or the teacher might break up his/her lesson with short discussion questions.

4. *Shepherding*—These "Care Groups" are set up for the purpose of shepherding the flock. Most often this is done by dividing the youth into groups by schools or geographical areas. One or two adults might be assigned to a group of twenty or more students with the intention to follow up when a student has missed youth group or to keep inviting them to attend upcoming events. Care groups don't necessarily meet together with any kind of regularity or with a deeper level of commitment. It is simply one leader making connections with his or her group of students. Often this is done with phone calls, cards, letters, visits, or with group meetings. The purpose is to care for those who have come into the church or youth program and to keep them from slipping through the cracks.

5. *Evangelistic Cell Groups*—The purpose is outreach. A group may begin with four students and multiply throughout the year to eight students and then to twelve or sixteen and so on. As the group grows the cells multiply forming other groups. The intention is for the cell to multiply and split every few months. The groups are short term and outreach driven.

6. *Short Term/Special Interest Groups*—A small group can be set up for the specific purpose of studying a topic. A group might focus on how to study the Bible, on leadership, or overcoming

sexual sin, etc., and the group would attract those interested in that topic.

7. *Leadership Team*—This group functions for the purpose of feedback, planning, and prayer. It is usually made up of a handful of dedicated students who meet monthly with the youth minister and other adult volunteers. They are asked for input into current and future events, studies, retreats, programs, etc. They are also expected to attend and lead at all youth ministry functions. Many times these students are given responsibilities for specific elements of the program.

8. *Support Groups*—Often counselors will suggest a need for a student to be a member of a group of peers struggling through some of the same issues. Many communities will offer support groups for teens struggling with alcohol, drugs, suicide, the breakup of the family, abuse, etc. Some churches may also be able to offer these kinds of groups.

Always understand the purpose behind each small group and keep the purpose at the forefront of that small group. *When the purpose is unclear it will be lost.* When a group tries to accomplish three, four, or five different purposes rather than focusing on the main reason they were put together, the results will be mediocre at best and there is a strong possibility that the group won't accomplish any of their objectives with excellence. Keep the purpose clear and simple and state it often.

Always understand the purpose behind each small group and keep the purpose at the forefront of that small group. When the purpose is unclear it will be lost.

When determining what kinds of small groups to implement in your youth ministry it would be wise to consider your team of adult volunteers. Do you have enough adults involved? Are they trained? Are they prepared when they teach or lead? Do they interact well with the students? Where are they in their walk with God? If we are to impact more than twelve to fifteen students, then we must recruit, train, and spend time with adult volunteers. Begin with involving them in simple discussion groups. For instance, you might be teaching a lesson and then break the students into small groups with one adult leader over each. Give the leader four discussion-oriented questions to lead the group through in a period of five minutes. This may not seem like much time, but to a new recruit it will seem very long if the discussion doesn't go well. Give them a chance to succeed at something small first. After that move them into other opportunities. Almost all of my discipleship group leaders were first recruited to lead discussion groups in Sunday morning Bible study or at youth group. Over time and through periodic training they became better and better at leading students and helping them grow in their relationship with Christ.

Effective Discussion Leading

Small group leaders must cultivate the ability to interact with students, to get them to talk about their life and their faith, and to create an open forum for sharing thoughts and ideas. Discussion leading comes naturally for some, while it takes sincere effort from others. Our goal as teachers is to lead the students into discipleship, that is, lead them into doing God's word. Students need to be actively involved in the lesson. The more they're involved, the more they will learn and retain. One of the best ways to involve students in the learning process is discussion. *Why bore students with another lecture when you can inspire, challenge, and encourage by having them be active participants in the lesson?* Discussion is also a great way of building group unity and friendships. If they talk together, work out differing opinions, and arrive at a common conclusion, it will have a unifying effect.

Discussion is an opportunity for each person to express his or her ideas. The students can give their opinions. We want them to be honest and real, not just spit out the answers they think the teacher wants to hear. An open discussion gives the student the very real impression that his thoughts

Why bore students with another lecture when you can inspire, challenge, and encourage by having them be active participants in the lesson?

are important and you want to know what they are. It's an opportunity to hear from more than just the teacher. It is amazing that you could talk to your youth group for months on commitment to Christ, and then a high school junior stands up at youth group one night, stammers through a three-minute testimony, and the entire group rallies together in a call to be more committed. It is vitally important that students talk with their peers about their Christian walk and receive encouragement from others who are in the trenches along side them.

The key ingredient in leading a discussion is the teacher. You are the leader, guide, moderator, and teacher as well as a member of the discussion. You are the one that keeps the discussion on the right track. When things get off on tangents, you have to know when to steer it back to the goal of your study. We were talking about cults one night at youth group and out of the blue Dan asks, "What do you think about capital punishment?" Hey, that's a great question, but it had nothing to do with what we were talking about. It must have been important to Dan though. The best response might be to tell him it is a great question and promise him that you'll talk about it another time. Then, keep your promise. Set a time and make it soon. As the leader you will need to pace the group discussion. Speed it up if it is getting bogged down on unimportant details. Slow it down if you think they are forgetting some key ideas. Keep them pointed toward the goal for your study. Finally, don't forget that you need to involve yourself in the discussion without monopolizing it. Be willing to answer the same questions that you ask them. You are the key to making the discussion work.

The key ingredient in leading a discussion is the teacher.

There are a couple of keys to remember in your relationship to the group when leading a discussion. First, *respect your students.* Show that respect in the questions you ask and the way you respond to their answers. Be careful not to embarrass students with questions that are too personal. Don't criticize their answers. When someone gives a dumb answer, don't point out the stupidity of it. Imitate Jesus in the way he led a group of disciples that often didn't seem to understand. He mentored them for three years and still they argued over who was the greatest, tried to keep the children from seeing Jesus, were surprised at his power over nature, and were often confused by his teachings. Jesus continued to teach and love these men, making them his disciples.

Second, *listen to the students* and be sensitive to any needs being shown. This includes simple stuff like giving them eye contact, nodding your head, looking interested in what they have to say. Be alert to needs that arise. If you sense that it would be good to get off the subject to talk about another need, do it. Never become so tied to your lesson and schedule that you lack sensitivity to the needs of your students. A small group of college students were meeting in our home for a Thursday night Bible study and fellowship time. We were in the middle of our study when I asked the group about changes in their personal walk with God. Were they still growing? How could they tell? We went around the room each person taking a turn at answering the question. When we came to Keri, her eyes filled with tears as she explained that even though she had grown up in the church, it wasn't until recently that she found a real relationship with Jesus. She had been dating the same guy for about four years. He was a good guy and they had a pretty good relationship, but it wasn't until they broke up that she realized how much she had become dependent on that relationship. She finally needed God. The group listened and identified with her. Others in the group confessed that they had let other people or things take first place in their life too. The discussion turned into a healthy caring support group. We listened and empathized with our friend.

That leads to a third key to keeping the lines of communication open with your students: *show them that you care.* Show them your concern for them in the discussion times. Reach out to them when you need to. If someone becomes embarrassed or emotional, give your verbal support immediately. You may need to give them support physically too: a hand on their shoulder, a pat on the back, or a hug.

Finally it is crucial that every student in your group be a participant in the discussion rather than a spectator. All of them need to be more than just listeners. They are participants. We need to do our best to involve everyone even if it is just in a small way. In a small group, there is no escape from the questions. Don't let them get by with answers like, "I don't know." Communicate that you want their input. Let them know that they are equals. Don't treat one as more important than another. Sometimes it can be hard to get each person involved. There will always be problem participants. Learn how to deal with each type of student, and discussion time will go much more smoothly.

It is crucial that every student in your group be a participant in the discussion rather than a spectator.

Dealing with the Problem Participants

When working with small groups and leading discussions, there may be some students who act as a hindrance to the process. Each one is unique and should be addressed in a particular way. Be advised, you cannot just ignore a problem participant and expect to have a healthy small group or quality discussion.

1. *The quiet kid.* The silent member usually looks bored, but often it is fear that keeps him from getting involved. He doesn't want to say the wrong thing. Encourage him to speak and then give immediate support to his comments. You may need to call on the silent member by name. Ask him a question he can answer. Affirm his answer and then move on to the next person so he is no longer the center of attention. It is critical to involve everyone, especially the quiet kid.

2. *The kid who won't shut up.* (The overbearing monopolizer.) This girl or guy always has something to say on every topic. It can be tough to get her to be quiet. You should never allow one or two people to monopolize the discussion. It kills discussion and group participation and can even cause resentment from others in the group toward the nonstop talker. Compliment her knowledge, but ask her to let others speak. This is easier to do in a small group, but if a problem persists you may need to talk to her one-on-one outside of the meeting time. If you need to confront someone, it is best to do it quickly and smoothly rather than put it off.

3. *The needy student.* This is the kid who sees the small group as his or her own personal counseling session. This person is different from the overbearing monopolizer because he may have some serious problems he is dealing with. You will want to help him as much as possible, but he needs to understand that this is more than a counseling session. It is a time for *all* the students to be actively involved in the learning. You may need to spend some extra time outside of the actual meeting to counsel this student. However, if his or her problems are outside your realm of expertise, seek help. Do what you can, but don't feel that you must do it all.

4. *The peer-pressured participant.* This is the student who never seems to have her own answers. She follows the crowd even in discussions. She gives answers that have already been given or she gives "church answers," that is saying all the answers she thinks you want her to say. Because you are in a small accountability group, you can push for real answers. Just make it a rule that you won't accept repeat answers. Let's say the question is, "Why don't Christian teens speak out concerning their faith more often?" First Rebecca speaks up and answers, "Fear." When Jen also says, "Fear," I ask her to elaborate. "Jen, what do you think they are afraid of?" "Have you ever been afraid to speak up?" "When?" "Why?" The goal is to get her to think.

The Art of Discussion Leading

Almost always the loss of control in a discussion or in a class-room situation stems from the teacher's failure to guide the group effectively toward its goal. Discussion should be used to pinpoint solutions to life's problems and apply the solution personally. There is an art to question asking.

1. *The right setting.* In order to get the most interaction and keep everyone involved it would be smart to make sure everyone is sitting in a circle or some kind of shape where everyone can see and hear everyone else clearly. There needs to be enough light for every-one to be able to see facial expressions, and they need to sit close enough to each other to easily hear each others' words and the tone in which they say them. Sitting around a table works well in a class-room. Sitting in a comfortable living room is even better. Outdoors is good if it isn't in a place that would be distracting. Sometimes it can even help loosen people up to talk a little more if there is some-thing to drink or snack on.

2. *Don't ask questions that have a right or wrong answer.* It is a discussion, not a test. You are looking for life application. If you were to ask, "Who was Mephibosheth?" you would be asking for a right or wrong answer. This doesn't lead to discussion. However, you could come up with a variety of good application and discussion questions about dedicated friendships if you were to tell the story of Jonathan and David's friendship and of David taking in Jonathan's crippled son, Mephibosheth (2 Samuel 9). What does this teach you about friendship? What kind of friendship do you think David and Jonathan had? What relationships could you compare it to today? If someone is truly your friend, how could you show the same kind of love that David showed Jonathan when he took care of his son?

3. *Ask a question that makes them the expert.* This is the best advice I have ever received for asking discussion questions. If the theme is temptation ask, "What temptations does the average guy at your school face each week?" They could then list the temptations because they are the experts in that field. Let's say that your lesson is going to be about having a heart for missions. You could ask, "What are some issues, movements, or causes that teenagers feel strongly about?" If you are studying the Sermon on the Mount you could ask, "What would happen at your school if all of the people that call themselves Christians would begin living by the principles in

Matthew 5, 6, and 7?" One student might think a great revival would break out in their school. Another might think that the non-Christians would be very put off and that the division between Christians and non-Christians would only grow larger. Both answers are correct because the student is the expert.

4. *Don't judge.* Don't evaluate their answers critically or compare. They won't talk if their leader is a judge.

5. *Don't preach.* Don't preach. Don't preach! When tempted to give your opinion, wait 60 seconds. Maybe by then you won't need to talk. Overcome the need to be heard and to have the last word on every topic. This is so difficult for some leaders, but so very critical in getting the students to think for themselves rather than being told what to think.

6. *Be prepared.* Plan ahead. You'll have to be prepared for a variety of questions that may come up. Discussion is often harder to prepare for than lecture because you must be prepared for a variety of thoughts and ideas.

7. *Use humor.* Don't poke fun at their answers, but use humor to liven up a discussion. It is good and even healthy to use humor, puns, exaggerations, and even sarcasm. Make yourself the butt of jokes, not the kids. A young person's feelings can be easily hurt, and chances are you won't find out about it until the damage has been done and the wound is old.

8. *Don't just wind it down, wrap it up!* Be sure to close while it is still hot, not after it is dead. Summarizing everything is not always good as it tends to have a calming effect on the lesson rather than a challenging impact. By trying to summarize a discussion in a few words you miss out on some of the great input that was given. In closing your discussion you want to make sure that you have arrived at your teaching goals for the lesson. Let them help you with the conclusion. Ask them what they plan to do as a result of what they have learned.

There are so many factors to consider in making for a good discussion: the chemistry of the group, the topic of discussion, the setting, time of day, the general mood, etc. At first it may seem difficult to get the group talking. It will take time, but don't give up on it. Don't fall back on lecture simply because it is the safest teaching method. Keep pushing for involvement from your students. Make them think! Small groups are paramount to making inroads into a young person's heart, mind, and life, and teaching through discussion is an excellent way to involve everyone.

Time for Reflection

1. In your opinion, why do small groups have such an important role in making or breaking a youth ministry?
2. Listed at the beginning of this chapter are eight different kinds of small groups. If you were just starting a youth ministry which of these would you try to implement first? Why?
3. Why is the leader such an important role in the discussion? What are the positives and negatives of using students to serve as discussion leaders?
4. Of the eight tips given for leading an effective discussion, which do you think is most important and why?
5. Make a list of two topics you might discuss with high school students and two more topics you might discuss with middle schoolers. Now come up with two or three discussion questions for each topic. Remember to ask questions that make them the experts and not to ask questions with a right or wrong answer.

SUGGESTED READING LIST

Dunn, Richard R., and Mark H. Senter III. *Reaching a Generation for Christ*. Chicago: Moody, 1997.

Griffin, Em. *Getting Together—A Guide for Good Groups*. Downers Grove, IL: InterVarsity, 1982.

NOTES ON CHAPTER SEVENTEEN

1. Jana L. Sundene, "How Can We Make Small Groups Effective in Youth Ministry?" in *Reaching a Generation for Christ*, ed. by Richard R. Dunn and Mark H. Senter III (Chicago: Moody, 1997), p. 653.

2. David Veerman, *Small Group Ministry with Youth* (Wheaton, IL: Victor Books, 1992), p. 18.

3. Jana L. Sundene, "How," p. 653.

4. Ibid., p. 652.

"You can impress people at a distance, but you impact them only close up."
—*Howard Hendricks*[1]

"Mentoring is not an end in itself; rather, it's a process, a means by which students can be equipped and empowered to develop dynamic lives and ministries that are uniquely theirs."
—*Barry St. Clair and Tony Martin*[2]

"At its essence, mentoring is a relationship. It is not primarily a contract, a deal, an agreement, or a legal battle if something goes astray. It is a relationship between two people." —*Bob Biehl*[3]

Chapter 18

Mentoring Students

Kevin Greer

The Need for Relationships

Every person who has been involved in youth ministry for more than two years knows that it takes relationships to see results. In all of our updates and studies of the youth culture, one result is the same. It was the same with Baby Boomers and Baby Busters, Generation X and Generation Y. Relationships are the key to impacting lives in this day and time just as they always have been. It is not a new secret. Each and every generation has needed meaningful relationships in their lives.

Even the studies about Postmoderns emphasize the need for depth of relationships. Leonard Sweet in *Soul Tsunami* gives the following support.

- "Post Moderns are famished for closeness, starved for contact. In a world where touch crimes are increasing, we are a touch-starved people."[4]

- "In the midst of a culture of communal anorexia, there is a deepening desire for a life filled with friends, community, service, and creative and spiritual growth. The church must provide its people with an experience of embeddedness in a community to which one makes valuable contributions."[5]

Youth Mentors Rather Than Youth Sponsors

Life changing stuff happens when you get involved in a person's life. That's why I believe we need youth mentors rather than youth sponsors. If you want to see fired up youth workers, look for those who are actively mentoring students. These are the youth workers who stick around for the long haul. These are the adults in your church that would do anything for the youth ministry at your church. Why? Because they are involved in the lives of students.

So often volunteers in youth ministry are given little more responsibility than a chaperone. The worst thing you can do to an adult volunteer is ask them to come and just pitch in and help wherever they can and mix with the kids. *When little or no direction is given and little or no responsibility is expected, then you really should not be disappointed if you can't hang on to valuable youth workers.* Give them some serious responsibility. Yes, we need someone to run the lights and sound and pass stuff out and help with snacks, but don't you crave youth workers who would do much more? When you see an adult that shows a heart for the students, give them the opportunity to grow. Teach them to be a mentor and give them the opportunity to be one.

The worst thing you can do to an adult volunteer is ask them to come and just pitch in and help wherever they can and mix with the kids.

What Is a Mentor?

Spiritual mentoring is the process by which an older more mature Christian invests his or her life into a younger believer for the purpose of achieving spiritual maturity and accountability in an intensely relational fashion.

A mentor is . . .

1. *An older, more mature friend—an adult friend.* You want the student to understand that you are someone they can trust and seek advice from. Understand that trust takes time. In most cases it won't happen overnight. You may need to spend the first few months simply developing that trust.

2. *A guide.* The mentor has no other agenda than simply to lead the student into a growing relationship with Jesus. Statistically we know that your community is better off when adults take time to

mentor teenagers. "Researchers at the University of California at San Francisco sought to determine why some young people are destroyed by the deficits of their home environments while others seem to thrive under the same set of circumstances. In reviewing these studies Earl Palmer uncovered one constant factor among resilient teens: They all experienced the nonexploitive interest, care and support of at least one adult during their childhood years—a parent or grandparent, uncle or aunt, older brother or sister, coach or teacher, pastor or youth leader—an adult with no hidden agenda or exploitive design on the youngster."[6]

3. *An encourager.* Mentors find ways to encourage. Through positive words, actions, simple rewards, a pat on the back, recognizing special occasions, sending e-mails or letters, and many other ways, mentors must make every effort to encourage the students in their care. I recently did a survey among 1700 high schoolers nationwide and found that 90% of the students believed that 90% of teenagers struggle with liking themselves. The survey also pointed out that 75% of the students hear over 100 obscenities a day, and 75% of them hear 20 or more negative comments, put-downs, or crude jokes in any given day. That's a lot of garbage to overcome.

4. *A confronter.* When an adult invests time and energy into the life of a teen, they earn the right as well as share the responsibility to confront the student when they need it. A mentor won't allow their student to go down the wrong road without putting up a fight for them. For this reason, "teens in a mentoring relationship are 46% less likely to get into drugs; 59% get better grades; 73% raise their goals."[7] Young people need help to battle all the negative pressures they face.

5. *A more experienced, more mature person.* For this reason it is generally not a good idea to use college students as mentors of high schoolers. They simply do not have the life experience to draw from in order to guide teens only a few years younger than they are. There is always an exception to the rule, but 90% of the time it is better to ask college-age volunteers to serve as mentors over junior high rather than high school students.

6. *Someone who has struggled and come out stronger for it.* Mentors are not perfect people. Mentors are growing people. In Philippians 3:17 Paul writes, "Follow my example." Does this mean he has it all figured out or that he has led a near perfect life? By no means. He often admits to his shortcomings and past sins. In verses

10-14 of the same chapter he tells his readers that it is his desire to know Christ and become like him. Yet he confesses that he hasn't attained all of this nor is he perfect. But here is what he is going to do: "I will forget the past and strain toward what is ahead; I will press on toward the goal to win the prize for which God has called me."

Though we aren't seeking perfect people to mentor students, we do seek adults who are, like Paul, confessing their failures and sins, moving past them and pressing on in their growth in Christ.

7. *Someone who sees the need to continue growing personally and spiritually.* You cannot lead a student to an intentional and active relationship with Christ if your walk with Christ is no longer active and intentional. The outcome of any student who is in a spiritual mentoring relationship is that their actions, speech, way of thinking, desires, values, relationships, and everything else about their life is closer to Jesus Christ than when they began. In other words, their life bears fruit of knowing Jesus as Savior and Lord. *A good measuring stick of the students that you mentor is to ask yourself this question: Are they becoming more like Christ or more like you?* One of the greatest temptations in doing any kind of mentoring is the temptation to fill your personal ego needs. It is a wonderful feeling to have a group of students that want to be like their leader. It is powerful to have that kind of control and influence. It is also selfish and wrong. Leaders must get out of the way and let God work. Ego needs must be put aside. *You are not trying to recreate yourself. You are trying to lead students to become more like Christ.* The best Christian mentors are ones that point their students to Christ, even to the point of being unnoticed or forgotten. If you want your students to be spiritual, you must be spiritual.

A good measuring stick of the students that you mentor is to ask yourself this question: Are they becoming more like Christ or more like you?

A Mentor is not . . .

1. *A messiah or savior.* Jesus is their Savior, not you. In your discussions make it clear that Jesus is whom we ultimately turn to for answers and direction. Make it clear to your students that Jesus is the Lord of your everyday life and let them see that in the way you talk, act, think, and live.

2. *A therapist (although at times you may feel like one).* Though you will hope to offer some wise counsel, your relationship

is to be different from that of a therapist and a patient. If you work with a particularly troubled student, you may need to discern when it's necessary to suggest they see a counselor. More often your role is to move your student past the talk of all their troubles and get them to see the world and themselves as God sees them.

3. *A cool peer.* You are a friend, but you are an adult friend. It is tempting to want so badly to be liked by our students that we will strive only to be their friend and altogether cease being the authority. Someone has to be the person who draws the line, and as the adult you are that person. They will look to you to set the boundaries in conversations and in actions.

4. *A parole officer or someone who acts only as an authority figure.* This appears to be in direct opposition to the previous statement. The key is maintaining a balance. If you see your role primarily as an authority figure, then you can count on a very short term as a youth mentor. Rather than drawing students to you and ultimately to Jesus, you will instead push them away.

5. *An ATM machine doling out the funds whenever a kid asks.* It's not your job to fund every activity, pay for every soda pop, or even buy every study book. Though some of this will happen, teaching responsibility is part of your job as a mentor. That includes financial responsibility.

6. *A nice guy who occasionally does something nice for a kid.* Remember the television commercials in the '90s about being a mentor. The picture was usually a blue background with a rainbow and then some actor would come out and implore you to "Take a kid to a ball game. Be a mentor." For crying out loud! That's not being a mentor! That's taking a kid to a ball game, which is a very nice thing to do, but being a mentor is so much more than that. Mentoring involves pouring your life (not an afternoon) into a teenager.

Mentoring involves pouring your life (not an afternoon) into a teenager.

An Investment of Time

The truth is that if a person is going to make a serious impact on another person's life it will take *quality and quantity time*. This is true of any relationship whether it is a husband and wife, a father with his son, a mentor with his or her students, or an accountability group dedicated to helping each other grow in their faith. Quality is a function of quantity. Quality time flows out of large quantities of time. It doesn't just happen in 15 or 20 minute snatches between important appointments or activities. Instead, quality happens within large blocks of time spent together.

Your structured mentoring time may be one and a half to two hours a week. On top of that you will want to have some informal or spontaneous mentoring taking place. It doesn't have to be a specially planned outing. As a matter of fact some of the best relationship building times are when they just come naturally. It might be having lunch together. It may be going to a ball game. Whether it's working on a car together, helping with a project at church, shopping, shooting hoops, or doing some sort of service work for others, find ways to involve yourself in the lives of your students.

The greater the time investment, the greater the life impact.

Understand that being a mentor is different than being a sponsor, chaperone, or even a coach in this: It is long term. It isn't being there for an event or a week or a season. It is dedication to youth over an extended period of time. We're talking about three to four years—spanning the high school years. *The greater the time investment, the greater the life impact.*

An Investment of Your Life

Howard Hendricks writes, "Some have defined mentoring as the process whereby an older person helps a younger person succeed. There's a measure of truth in that, but I prefer to see mentoring in slightly different terms. Rather than being about success, *mentoring is about **significance**. The difference is that success means reaching your goals, whereas significance involves making a difference in the lives of people. How many of us achieve our objectives, yet still are left wondering whether our lives really count for anything?"[8] That's a great quote, but don't move past it too quickly. Stop here. Take a few minutes to answer the question that Hendricks poses, "How many of us achieve our objectives, yet still are left wondering whether our lives really count for anything?" What are you doing with your life that is beyond the here and now? What or whom are you investing yourself in?

You are teaching every day. The job of a mentor is never done. Whether you know it or not, class is in session. Don't be afraid to let them see that you are real and that you fail. But let them also see that you get back up and keep trying. Let them learn grace, love, and obedience not only from your lessons, but also from your life. Mentoring youth is an incredible responsibility. Take it seriously.

- If you aren't in love with Jesus, don't pretend you can lead others to be in love with him.
- If you can't love teens, then find another ministry. It's okay. God has something better in mind for you and for the youth ministry.
- If you can't care enough for kids to be a godly example, to take stands for what is right and pure, to keep it clean, to keep morals that are above reproach, then get out. When it comes to ministry, especially working with youth and children, we cannot allow compromise of morality and ethics.

If you want youth ministry to be your heart's passion, if you desire to make a long term impact, if you want to change lives, determine to be a mentor. Pray for your students, prepare for your time together, be trustworthy, and pour yourself into the young lives entrusted to you. Our time is short. Make the most of it.

They don't need another Program Director. They don't need another Party Coordinator. They certainly don't need another performer or another guy on stage. They need an older, more mature Christian to guide, teach, and love them into a genuine and lasting relationship with Jesus: A Mentor!

Time for Reflection

1. Parents can use all the help they can get with keeping their kids on the right track. Suppose you have a teenager of your own (maybe you do). If you were to choose (hand pick) another adult outside your family to be a mentor to your son or daughter, what kind of person would you pick and why?

2. If you could return to your teen years as an adult and be a mentor to yourself, what kind of advice would you like to have given to yourself? (weird question, huh?)

3. God has given us the honorable task of guiding young people to Him. Make a list of the top 10 most important qualities of a mentor.

4. Which of those qualities seem to be lacking the most today?

Suggested Reading List

Hendricks, Howard. *Standing Together.* Gresham, OR: Vision House, 1995.

Intensive Caring—Practical Ways to Mentor Youth. Loveland, CO: Group, 1998.

White, Joe, and Jim Wideman. *Parents' Guide to the Spiritual Mentoring of Teens.* Focus on the Family. Wheaton, IL: Tyndale, 2001.

Notes on Chapter Eighteen

1. Sermon at a Promise Keepers Rally, Boulder, CO, 1992 (year is a guess).

2. Barry St. Clair and Tony Martin, "Equipping Teenagers to Do Ministry," *Intensive Caring: Practical Ways to Mentor Youth* (Loveland, CO: Group, 1998), p. 31.

3. Bob Biehl, *Mentoring* (Nashville: Broadman & Holman, 1996), p. 21.

4. Leonard Sweet, *Soul Tsunami* (Grand Rapids: Zondervan, 1999), p. 194.

5. Ibid., p. 221.

6. Mark Devries, *Family-Based Youth Ministry* (Downers Grove, IL: InterVarsity, 1994), p. 118.

7. *For Mentors,* http://www.mentoring.org/formentors.html.

8. Howard Hendricks, *Standing Together* (Gresham, OR: Vision House, 1995), p. 105.

Chapter 19

Why Student Discipleship?

Kevin Greer

Christ and Discipleship

How important are the last words a person says before he or she leaves you? Think about it. How important is that last conversation with your friend before he or she moves away? How much thought is put into graduation speeches when the speakers know they will never address this crowd again? Suppose someone you loved was dying and you only had a short time left with them. How important would his or her words be to you?

Before Jesus left this earth in the physical form, He commissioned His disciples to go out and make more disciples. Jesus told His followers, "Go and make disciples of all nations, baptizing them in the name of the Father and of the Son and of the Holy Spirit, and teaching them to obey everything I have commanded you. And surely I am with you always, to the very end of the age" (Matt. 28:19,20). Making disciples should be done purely out of obedience to Jesus' command. No other reason is necessary. Jesus not only told His followers that they should make disciples, He modeled this with twelve men. As their mentor He taught, corrected, encouraged, and challenged them. He saw the need to share His three-year ministry with twelve men, and in so doing He made an investment that lasted forever. He knew that He wouldn't be on this earth forever. Who would carry on the task after He was gone? The work would be continued by the persons He invested His time in: His disciples. These men literally changed the world.

Oswald Sanders gives the following definition for a disciple.

> The word disciple means "a learner." As used by Jesus and by Paul, the word disciple means "a learner or pupil who accepts the teaching of Christ, not only in belief but also in lifestyle. It involves a deliberate choice, a definite denial, and a determined obedience." It is not without significance that the word *disciple* occurs in the New Testament 269 times, *Christian* only 3 times, and *believers* 2 times. This surely indicates that the task of the church is not so much to make "Christians" or "believers" but "disciples." A disciple must, of course, be a believer; but according to Christ's conditions of discipleship (Luke 14:25-33), not all believers are disciples of the New Testament stamp.[3]

Sanders seems to be saying that a disciple will desire more. A disciple wants to give himself over to his Lord. This will only come with a "deliberate choice, a definite denial, and a determined obedience." Choosing to be Christ's disciple is an individual choice, but one that youth leaders can and must help young people to undertake.

In *Successful Discipling,* Allen Hadidian defines disciple making with one sentence. Yet he also includes nine basic principles within the sentence. It is perhaps the best textbook definition of discipling. His definition is as follows:

	Principles
Discipling is a process by which a Christian with a	
life worth emulating	Example
commits himself	Commitment
for an extended period of time	Time
to a few individuals	Numerical Limit
who have been won to Christ	Phase I
the purpose being to	Direction
aid and guide their	Guardianship
growth and maturity and equip them to	Phase II
reproduce themselves in a third spiritual generation.	Phase III[4]

Discipling teens is simply influencing and molding youth to become more like Christ through example, time spent together, and life-to-life teaching. *The major differences between most small group ministries and disciple groups are found in two words: mentoring and commitment.* A deeper level of commitment is necessary in a discipleship group if it is to reach its goals. The leader is a mentor, not just a facilitator as he might be when leading a discussion group or prayer group during other youth ministry programs. Jesus chose twelve men to be his disciples. They were accountable to him. This was not a short-term study group or a shepherding care group. It wasn't even a multiplying cell group. The evangelism was done outside of the group. Others weren't invited to be one of the twelve.

Though discipleship is a life style and not a program, there are methods of making disciples that we can program into our youth ministries.

Look again at Jesus and His group of disciples. They followed Him for three years, listening to His words of wisdom, seeing Him interact with others, enjoying His company, being involved in His ministry, seeing the hardships and the joys. In the end they carried out His ministry after He was gone. This is what a disciple group does. It is a limited number of individuals who are chosen by the leader for the purpose of pouring his or her life into them. They commit to being together for an extended length of time to grow in Christlike maturity.

For our purposes, disciple groups meet weekly throughout the school year to pray, study, encourage, and hold one another accountable in each student's walk with Christ. It is one adult who will mentor two to five high schoolers (all of the same gender), to help them grow deeper in relationship with Jesus, their Savior and Lord.

Reasons for Making Discipleship Groups an Integral Part of Your Youth Ministry

1. Spiritual Growth and Maturity You Can See

Tom Tucker has been a campus minister at Northeastern State University in Tahlequah, Oklahoma, for nearly twenty years now. He told me once that the toughest students that he worked with were the ones who grew up in church and yet remained spiritual infants. All of those years in Bible studies, youth group meetings, church services, etc., and they never learned how to feed themselves. Years of being spoon-fed the Word and never being pushed or challenged to really serve others had resulted in some spoiled young adults. They expected others to feed them and take care of their needs.

Seventy-five percent of college freshman quit church! That's pretty incredible to think about. It seems that their commitment was tied to parents, friends or even a youth minister and the other youth workers at their church, but their commitment wasn't rooted deeply in Christ. Disciple groups are a place where we raise the serious challenges, we ask the probing faith questions, and we make the personal applications of Christianity.

"75% of all children raised in Christian homes who attend public schools will reject the Christian faith by their first year of college."5

2. Stronger Commitments through Accountability

Every summer at a camp or conference there are a large number of students who make public decisions for Christ. However it never fails that many of the decisions made are short lived. In a matter of weeks some of the students are right back to their favorite sins and bad habits. It seems that the commitments just don't stick. They quit the race shortly after getting out of the blocks. How can we keep that from happening? How can we help kids to finish strong? I believe the answer is accountability. *Accountability puts teeth to our commitments.* Make accountability a high priority for your disciple group. Pray for each other. Encourage and challenge each other. Ask each other the hard questions.

3. The Bible Becomes Real

Have you ever taught a lesson with certain students in mind, but never knew if they were getting it? Have you ever looked around the classroom or auditorium and seen some faces that look like they just aren't tuned in? As you were writing your lesson, you came to one part that you just knew Kenny needed to hear. Lesson time comes and Kenny isn't even there, or worse, he's there in body, but his brain is miles away. While you're teaching, he's talking with a friend, hanging on his girlfriend, or sitting in the corner with a glazed look in his eyes as he digs in his ear with a car key.

If you want your students to really understand and remember a lesson, you need to get them involved in it. This can be much more easily accomplished in a small group setting than in a large one. You have the time and opportunity to show how God speaks specifically to them. You can actually turn to Kenny and say, "Kenny, what do you think?" If you don't get much of an answer, you can even say, "Here is how I see it applying to you." In a small group you can involve him in the lesson and even confront him if needed.

Bible study in a small group provides countless opportunities to make personal applications. Take advantage of those opportunities. Get specific and personal in the application of scripture.

4. Meeting Individual Needs with Individual Attention

I wish it were possible to spend quality time with every kid that steps through the doors of the church. Physically it just can't be done if your youth ministry is growing. One person can only personally impact so many lives. This is why we must work together with other adults in order to impact even more students. In my ministry in Colorado I led a disciple group of four to five high school guys each year. More important was the ministry of recruiting, training, and encouraging adults to lead other disciple groups of four to five students. Rather than depending on the paid youth minister to disciple all of the students, volunteers must be brought alongside the youth minister to get the task done. We were able to put together a team of ten adults leading forty plus students in D-groups annually.

It's not just a matter of numbers. It is also a matter of personal giftedness. There are certain students who would be better discipled by adults other than myself. I would obviously want Sally or Jen or Debbie to be discipled by a female rather than putting them in a group with a male leader. I would also look at who could best reach certain students. Drew was a good leader with some guys and Wes was good with some others. It had less to do with ability than it did with relating to particular students. This gives more support to the fact that we must have diversity in our team of youth mentors.

5. Becoming a Place of Refuge

Mark's step-dad could be violent and sometimes he needed to get away. Now and then he would show up on my doorstep asking if he could stay over. I'm not sure how many nights Mark spent on the couch at our home, but he knew that it was always available. Mark knew that our D-group was a place he could talk freely and that my home was a place he could find refuge.

Kendra's step-dad was an alcoholic and abusive. Lyle seemed to have more than his fair share of problems getting along at home. Sara's self-esteem always seemed a bit shaky. Julie was the only Christian in her home. Kirk had a serious problem with caving to peer pressure. Evan was just a quiet kid who needed a close friend. **Everyone** needs a place of refuge. They need a place to come and talk and be listened to without being judged. Disciple groups are meant to be a place where every member can open up, make themselves vulnerable, and know for certain that they can trust the others in the group to support them. From the first meeting of our D-groups we emphasized confidentiality. If conversations are to get deeper than the surface and burdens are to be unloaded, there must be a strong confidence and trust within the group. Over a period of time the small group should come to

The adult leader is the key to vulnerability within the group. He or she must make sure that all of the participants feel that the D-group is a safe and confidential place to talk.

trust and rely on one another. This doesn't happen overnight and it doesn't just happen automatically. It is important to emphasize over and over the need for trust and reliability.

6. Ministry More Than Meetings

A discipleship ministry is both planned and spontaneous. There is the weekly meeting and study time, but there are also spontaneous get-togethers that can be incredible growing opportunities. Our planned meetings would last around an hour and a half every week usually on a weeknight. However, a serious strength of a mentoring relationship is found in time spent outside of the planned meeting. It might be meeting for lunch, shooting pool, running errands together, going to a ball game, volunteering for things together, a road trip, etc. It obviously doesn't need to be every member of your D-group when doing something spontaneous. *As a mentor, you need to look for those unplanned teachable moments. They are all around us.* When one or two of the girls drop by Donna's house to talk, they have a good time together but also have the opportunity to witness Donna's love for her family. A couple of the guys might go to a movie with Kent just for fun. Sitting around at McDonald's afterwards would be another natural teachable moment to talk about some of the stuff in the movie. You are surrounded by teachable moments. The ministry of a mentor is much more than what takes place in a weekly meeting. It is life-to-life teaching.

7. Life-to-Life Teaching

When I was in high school I was involved in a small youth group that met at the home of one of our youth coaches. Her name was

Irma. She was over sixty years old and a widow. She didn't exactly fit the norm that we set for youth coaches. She couldn't shoot hoops or play the guitar, but she sure loved having us in her home. We would meet in her living room, or if it was nice we would meet on the screened-in back porch. She had a pool table in the basement, and we spent a lot of time down there too. Best yet, every Sunday night when you walked in the door you could smell the cookies or cinnamon rolls she had just finished baking for us. I don't recall ever hearing Irma teach a lesson, but that didn't keep her from teaching me how a Christian was supposed to live. Irma invested her heart and life in a bunch of kids who made a mess of her house, ate her food without chipping in to help, and probably never said thank you enough. She showed me what a servant was. She taught me that Jesus is real. She showed me grace on more than one occasion. Most of all, she taught us all about unconditional love. Every Sunday night after youth group was over and it was time to go home, Irma stood near the door and hugged every kid before they could get outside. Even though I didn't comprehend all Irma did for our youth group until years later, it still made an impact on my life. How did this little old lady teach us so much and have such an impact on so many teenagers' hearts? It was life-to-life teaching.

You don't forget those people who came alongside of you and showed you Jesus by the way they cared, the way they taught, the way they talked they spent time with you and with you.

Think back to your teen years in church or school. How many lessons or sermons do you actually remember? Not many, I would guess. As a matter of fact most of us can't remember the sermon from three weeks ago!

How will the kids you are working with remember you? There's that legacy question again! They see a lot more than you think. They notice every time I get a bad haircut or wear something stupid. Do you have kids who love pointing out that kind of stuff to you? They notice how fast you drive, what movies you go to, and the language you use. If they notice the little things like those, they will definitely learn from your life-to-life teaching about how you handle pressure, how you deal with your children, and how you love your wife or husband. The job of a mentor is never done. Don't be afraid to let them see that you are real and that you fail. But let them also see that you get back up and keep trying. Let them learn grace, love, and obedience not only from your lessons, but also from your life.

8. The End Result

Growth is amazing to witness. Don't you wish you could see it as clearly with the students in your ministry? You can, you know. It takes two indispensable ingredients. They are time and relationship. Discipleship ministry is designed specifically for that. You commit an extended period of time to mentor and develop a relationship with a small group of students. Over the year or two or three that you are with them, you will see changes. Sometimes the growth is amazing, and other times it is so small you'll think you need a microscope to detect it. You may just need to give them a few more years to grow on their own. Then out of nowhere, it will just blow you away how much they have fallen in love with God.

The results of leading a small group of students in a deeper walk with Christ are simply awesome. The friendships are long-lasting and go way past the surface. The memories of talks, laughs, and experiences are great. And the results are something you can see over the long haul in changed hearts and lives. It takes a lot out of you as the leader and can be very frustrating at times. There will be nights after D-Group meetings that you ask yourself why you're doing this. The change seems to come so slow or to be nonexistent. But every now and then God lets you see a miracle happen in a heart broken, a life changed, a disciple deepened. That's what it's about: making an investment in this lifetime as well as in eternity.

Time for Reflection ⏰

1. Why are the two components of mentoring and commitment so important in the success of a discipleship ministry?

2. Listed in this chapter were eight reasons for making discipleship groups an integral part of your youth ministry. What other reasons can you think of?

3. Consider the impact that "life-to-life teaching" has had on you. Who do you remember that came alongside you and showed you Jesus by the way they lived and cared, even more than by the lessons they may have taught?

4. Seeing growth happen takes the two indispensable ingredients of time and relationship. What does this say about the value of short-term versus long-term youth ministry?

SUGGESTED READING LIST

Barna, George. *Growing True Disciples.* Colorado Springs: Water Brook Press, 2001.

Greer, Kevin. *Life to Life Discipleship.* Joplin, MO: Christ In Youth, 2000.

Sanders, Oswald. *Spiritual Discipleship.* Chicago: Moody, 1990.

NOTES ON CHAPTER NINETEEN

1. George Barna, *Growing True Disciples* (Colorado Springs: Water Brook Press, 2001), p. 11.

2. Leonard Sweet, *Soul Tsunami* (Grand Rapids: Zondervan, 1999), p. 221.

3. Oswald Sanders, *Student Discipleship* (Chicago: Moody, 1990), p. 8.

4. Allen Hadidian, *Successful Discipling* (Chicago: Moody, 1979).

5. Joe White and Jim Weidmann, *Parent's Guide to the Spiritual Mentoring of Teens* (Wheaton: Tyndale, 2001), p. 317.

Chapter 20

Structuring a Discipleship Ministry with Teens

Kevin Greer

The previous two chapters have been spent primarily on the philosophy of a disciple group ministry. Enough of that! What we really want is the practical, hands-on, week-to-week explanation. How do I make it all work?

So Exactly What Happens in a Weekly Disciple Group Anyway?

The typical D-group meeting will last about an hour and a half. One effective way of using that time would include:

- Hang-out time (about 15-20 minutes)
- Accountability (15-30 minutes)
- Study and homework assignment (30 minutes), and
- Prayer (10 minutes).

As the D-group leader you need to arrive at the place of your meeting a few minutes early. Plan to allow anywhere from ten to twenty minutes for some "hang-out" time. This allows for anyone

Disciple groups are about people more than they are about getting through an agenda. Being flexible and goal driven, both are necessary for an effective leader.

who might be running late. During this time it is good to have some food and drink available and possibly something to do. Whether it's shooting baskets, playing computer games, playing ping pong, or just snacking and talking, the hang-out time is simply meant to ease your way into talking about stuff on a deeper level in the accountability time and study.

Accountability Time

If there is one part of the D-group time that is so critical it should never be skipped, it would be the accountability time. Accountability is the main reason that you are coming together. It is always good to start with the same simple question each time you get together. We'll call it the *life question*. You want to find out what is going on in the students' lives. Ask each person, "What was the high point and the low point of your week?" It is good to find out how each person is doing on a personal level before you move on to anything else. Many times the response will be that nothing much has happened in the last seven days. Don't allow that kind of answer. Push her with a second question: "All right then, what was the best thing about 'nothing much' that happened to you and the worst thing about 'nothing much' that happened to you?" You want them to think a little bit, to tell the rest of the group what is going on in their lives, to open up and get real with the group. Chances are that sometimes the best thing about Andrew's week was that he got a C on a biology test, and the worst thing was that he got a flat tire on the way to work. If that's all, then great. At least you have Andrew involved and talking with the rest of the group. There may come another day though that Andrew is seriously struggling with something. If he has never talked with the group about his day-to-day life before, he may be reluctant to tell them about anything on a deeper level.

Every member of the group needs to talk. This is so important and yet it is so simple that it is often overlooked. You could feel rushed to get to the lesson or all of the other things you have planned. You could even spend so much time on one person that you never get to the others. Don't let this happen. Delay lesson time if necessary, but make sure you get every student to answer those questions.

Once everyone has had the opportunity to answer the initial life question, go on to your list of accountability questions. It would be easy to cruise past these questions really quickly. Don't let that happen. Accountability is central to your purpose for meeting. Determine what the accountability questions will be for your group and review them each week.

Besides integrity issues a disciple group will also hold each other accountable in attendance at church and youth group, memory work, Bible reading, servant leadership tasks, and outreach.

Accountability is central to your purpose for meeting.

When you first start meeting with your group, it would be wise to determine areas that your group needs to be held accountable in. As a group you could come up with a list of five to seven accountability questions to ask at each meeting. Your list of questions might include:

- What are you praying about?
- What did you read from the Bible this week that really hit you personally?
- Did you look at anything that would cause you to have impure thoughts this week?
- Did you find ways to encourage others rather than tear them down?
- Are you respecting your family by spending quality time with them?
- Did you find an opportunity to reach out to a non-Christian this week?

Accountability time usually takes fifteen minutes, but it can easily take up the entire meeting time. If something is important, don't feel bad about putting off the study until the next week. Just remember not to let this happen on a regular basis. If it does, then your group will become more focused on being a support or counseling group rather than deepening and maturing their faith. Teach your students in and through their life experiences that Jesus is real and he loves them and will be with them in their struggles.

The Study

Your discipleship groups are presumably made up of students who want a study that is more than they would get in Sunday school or at youth group. It should be a study that stretches and challenges them. Topics might include:

- Spiritual disciplines
- Pursuing holiness
- Elements of prayer
- Understanding the Bible
- Evangelism
- Leadership training
- Time alone with God
- Scripture memory
- Knowing God
- Service and missions

Your students can hear lessons about sex, dating, alcohol, and getting along with friends or parents at youth group. Don't misuse your D-group time with a topical study on dating. Instead, take a deeper look at pursuing holiness and ask how a person's dating relationships should be affected by this pursuit. *This is a small group designed for spiritual growth, so push them to grow. As their mentor, they should be learning from your life. Share from your experiences, from your knowledge of God's Word, and your relationship with him.*

For a Bible study you look at a specific book (like Philippians or 1 John), a theme (loving others, holiness, servanthood) or a particular person's life (Daniel, Paul, or Mary). Besides a Bible study, there are tons of great Christian books you might choose to read together. Whenever I do Bible or book studies I will assign a chapter to read and then ask the students to mark and highlight their books using the following symbols.

__ Underline everything that stands out to you for whatever reason and be willing to share about what was underlined.

*   Select a key thought or sentence for the chapter.

?   Put a question mark (?) in the margin wherever you read something you don't understand.

➡   Put an arrow in the margin whenever you read something that really seems to be aimed at you.

!   Put an exclamation mark in the margin every time you read what you believe to be a main point in the chapter.

A   Application Statement. Write an application statement at the end of the chapter on how he or she could apply what they read in that chapter.

With all of this we are loaded for discussion when we get together. In addition, you as the discussion leader will need to come up with some good application and discussion questions for the group. Fortunately, a lot of books come with a study guide that can be very helpful.

Another common study for disciple groups is to use curriculum written specifically for small groups. The curriculum studies are meant to be easier for a leader to prepare, but you will usually need to do a lot of adaptation of the study to your group. One helpful idea is to contact some of the companies that publish small group curriculums and ask for their free catalogues.

- Navigators 1-800-366-7788
- Inter-Actions, from Willow Creek Resources 1-847-765-0070
- Serendipity Youth Series 1-800-525-9563
- College Press/HeartSpring Publishing 1-800-289-3300

Finally, be flexible with your study time. The actual study time for your D-group meeting will be around thirty minutes in length. Keep in mind that there will be some weeks that you will not even get to your lesson, although this should be the exception.

Prayer

Always, always, always pray. Never let your D-group time escape without giving a portion of it to prayer. Every book or paper ever written about growing nearer to God emphasizes prayer. You cannot get close to God without prayer. It is our lifeline to him. This must be taught to our students, but more importantly, it must be practiced with them. It ought to be one of your goals that this small group know how to pray before the end of your eight months together. Spending time in prayer is a sign of growth. There are few things more satisfying to a D-group leader than knowing your students are becoming people of prayer.

Every book or paper ever written about growing nearer to God emphasizes prayer. You cannot get close to God without prayer.

Strengthening Relationships through Nonstructured Opportunities

Strengthening and deepening your relationships within the D-group will take place over time spent together. Every week you will have the opportunity to meet with your group for an hour and a half or so. However, your relationships will grow much stronger when you find other opportunities to get together. The more variety in the things you do and situations you are in, the more you will learn about one another. Here are a few ideas you might try.

1. Invite them to your home.
2. Have an all-nighter with your small group.
3. Meet them on their turf (their school, home, or on break at their work).
4. Go to their sport, music, hobby, or school activities.
5. Go to a movie, the mall, or out to eat.
6. Take one or two of them along on a fun day of skiing, golfing, the races, or whatever.
7. Sign up as a group to be on a church softball or basketball team together.
8. Do your own retreat or camp-out, an overnighter at a nearby church camp.
9. Do some service projects and random acts of kindness together.

Each time one of these nonstructured activities takes place, you can count on relationships growing stronger and on being surrounded by teaching opportunities. *Late night talks and conversations on trips are some of the best teaching times you'll have. Often you teach more sharing a cold Dr. Pepper while sitting on the hood of your truck late at night than you could ever teach in a Sunday school class.* That's when you can talk about the future in personal terms. I can't begin to recall how many times I've talked with students about college plans, future careers, ministry options, and marriage during some of those spontaneous get-togethers.

Time for Reflection

1. A common problem with small groups is that they seem to move away from their original purpose of spiritual growth and a deeper walk with God. This happens when groups spend a great deal of time talking and enjoying each other's company and leave little time for study and prayer. How can you be both purpose driven and people oriented?
2. List five accountability questions for your youth ministry small groups to use.
3. List five topics you think your D-group students should consider studying.
4. Think back to your teen years. Can you recall a time when you experienced a strengthened relationship to God or to other Christians through a nonstructured or spontaneous occurrence? What made that event so special?

Suggested Reading List

Fields, Doug. *Purpose Driven Youth Ministry*. Grand Rapids: Zondervan, 1998.

Greer, Kevin. *Life to Life Discipleship*. Joplin, MO: Christ In Youth, 2000.

Notes on Chapter Twenty

1. Richard Wynn, ed., *Successful Youth Mentoring* (Loveland, CO: Group, 1998), p. 51.

2. Amy Simpson, ed., *Intensive Caring* (Loveland, CO: Group, 1998), p. 11.

Chapter 21

Implementing Discipleship Groups into Your Youth Ministry

Kevin Greer

The Purpose for Discipleship Groups

It is absolutely essential that students understand the purpose and plan for disciple groups before they sign up. Put the plan in writing and give it to students at the informational meeting or send it to them in advance of the meeting, or both. This allows students and parents the opportunity to read and understand what D-groups are about and what the expectations are for everyone involved. The following is a model purpose statement for disciple groups.

The Purpose, Plan, and Promise
of Discipleship Groups

The Purpose

We will meet as a small group for the purpose of spiritual growth and accountability in our walk with Jesus Christ.

The Plan

1. We will meet weekly ($1^1/_2$–2 hours) for prayer, study, and deepening of relationships.
2. We will make strong efforts to get to know each other on a personal level, functioning together in trust, support, and Christlike love.
3. We will make strong efforts to get to know our Lord and Savior on a personal level. We will do this by striving to have a daily quiet time of prayer and Bible reading.
4. We will be involved weekly in worship services, Bible studies, and youth group activities.

The Promise

1. After reading "The Purpose" and "The Plan" what is your understanding of what a D-group should be?

2. What do you hope to accomplish by being in a D-group this year?

    I understand that the purpose of Discipleship is to deepen my relationship with Christ. I know that D-group is a commitment, and I will do my best to keep it a top priority. Through it, I will hopefully grow and mature in Christ and help the others in the group to do the same. I also understand that failure to keep the objectives listed in "The Plan" could result in my being asked to leave the group. I will make the commitment to be a part of a Discipleship Group for the next _____ months.

Signed _____

Today's date _____

Requiring a Commitment

If you sincerely are looking for accountability, growth in Christ, trust, and support, then a commitment must be required. When students attend their small group sporadically and only do their assignments occasionally, you don't have the climate needed to accomplish those objectives. *When the commitment level is low, so are the results.* Disciple groups are meant to be something deeper than a discussion group at their Sunday school class or a school Bible club. If you want to see growth in their personal walk with God and stronger accountability relationships, then you must ask for a commitment of priority time to the group.

The students need to understand that the commitment includes meeting weekly throughout the school year. The length of time your group meets is flexible, but running it concurrent to the school year calendar is generally the best design. Canceling for the summer will give your adult leaders a needed break and by the time September rolls around both students and adults are ready to jump back into it.

Even though every Christian teen needs to be discipled, not every one desires to be. Sometimes we might be tempted to assign every teen in our youth ministry to a disciple group in hopes of maturing them in their walk with Christ. The intentions are great, but if a student's heart isn't in it then the results will be frustrating.

Some students are not ready to be called into a committed accountability relationship with a small group. When we try to force the noncommitted person into a group that requires serious dedication and time, frustration sets in for everyone. The others in the group that are serious about keeping all of the commitments get frustrated when they see that not everyone is called to account. The student that isn't ready to make or keep the commitments is frustrated because he feels like a failure. And you the leader are frustrated because you spend valuable time dealing with basic issues of commitment rather than moving forward in mentoring and maturing the ones in the group that want to grow. Because of the goals and commitment level you have set for your disciple groups, they may not be for everyone.

Before implementing a Discipleship ministry commit to spending a good amount of time in prayer. It is significant that Jesus spent the night in prayer before choosing his twelve disciples. Get together with any other adults in your church who would be D-group leaders and ask them to join you in prayer before you inform students of the program, send out the invitational letters, and have any informational meeting. Pray, asking God to convict all who need to be involved in Discipleship.

Getting the Word Out

Once you have decided that you are going to begin disciple groups as part of your youth ministry, you must make a determined effort to promote it and get students plugged into it. Here is a basic schedule for promoting new D-groups.

- Early Summer (or immediately following your big summer conference or camp when enthusiasm is running high)—Begin announcements about D-groups starting in the fall.
- Early August—Send an information letter to every student who has attended the youth program in the last year.
- First weekend after school begins—Sunday morning orientation meeting.
- The next Sunday—Commitments turned in.
- During the following week—Follow up on students who didn't turn in forms. Begin assembling groups. Meet with adult leaders.
- Two weeks after the Orientation Meeting—Begin D-groups.

Making Your Groups

Because these groups are designed to last for an entire school year or more, it is extremely important to show discernment in whom you will group together. Of course, you may not have many options if you only have a few willing to make the commitment. There were years when I was the youth leader at a smaller church that I only had enough students sign up to make one group for the guys and one or two groups for the girls. At a larger church we had forty plus students in ten different D-groups. Making the groups became more challenging. There are several things to take into consideration. You will want to consider size of the group, ages, gender, personalities, and maybe even driving distances of each participant to their D-group meeting location.

1. *Gender Differences.* It is best to keep your groups split up by gender. There are several reasons for this. First of all, it is biblical that older men teach the younger men and that older women teach the younger women (Titus 2:2-6). Secondly, it just makes sense. *If you want the group to get past superficial stuff quicker and get them to open up quicker, it is wise to keep the groups split by gender.* Guys will put less effort in impressing the rest of the group if it is guys only. Girls will be able to get into intimate conversation quicker if it is girls

only. One final reason for keeping groups split by gender is that some may already feel the pressure about what the others in the group think without adding the extra pressure of a mixed gender group. To illustrate this, imagine the social pressures a ninth grade girl would feel being in a group with a twelfth grade guy or vice versa.

2. *Size of Group.* It is wise to keep the group small. This allows for more participation among those involved. Four or five students with one adult leader has proven to be the best combination. I have found that five is a great number for a guys D-group and three to four works great with girls' groups. Generally, girls are better at verbal communication skills, and in keeping your girls' group small you are allowing them more opportunity to share. Guys on the other hand feel more comfortable in a little larger group. Guys are slower to open up and talk and won't need as much time for sharing as girls' groups might.

I realize that some leaders desire a larger group of ten or more. When this happens, it becomes more of a study that the adult leads rather than a time where all of the students are personally involved in the study. This may be because the leader isn't comfortable with an open learning style and would rather have greater control of the meeting time. *The idea behind small group ministry is to allow the participants to discover and learn together. A leader who controls and dominates a D-group is not only unproductive, he can also become dangerous.* Some who prefer leading a larger group will point out that Jesus gave the example of leading a group of twelve disciples. To those persons, I would point out that Jesus could also turn water to wine and raise the dead. Surely a group of twelve or any size wouldn't be a problem for the Son of God. Then again, Jesus seemed to have spent more time with a smaller more intimate circle made up of Peter, James, and John.

3. *Age Differences.* It is wise to never mix junior highers in with high schoolers for D-groups. The difference in physical, emotional, mental, and spiritual maturity ought to be vastly different. However, when you make your high school D-groups, it is actually a good idea to mix the grades a bit. Perhaps include two sophomores, one junior, and one senior. This is good for the mix of ideas and thoughts. Mixing the ages can also actually add to creating unity within your total youth group. Often at a youth group activity you will see small circles or cliques, students only hanging out with their closest friends.

Its only natural for the ninth graders to come in and hang together, while a group of juniors or seniors does the same. Mixing up the ages in your D-group will give students opportunities to build friendships they may have never had.

4. *Personality Differences.* Always keep the purpose in mind when making up your groups. If, by mixing some personalities, you can make it easier to accomplish the purpose then do it. I do my best to break up cliques. On more than one occasion I have had three or four girls come to me and say something like, "We've already got our D-group set and we would like to have Donna be our leader." My response is, "There is a really good chance that none of you will be in the same group and that Donna may not be your leader. Do you still want to be in a group?" If they answer "no," then they were doing it for the wrong reason. It isn't meant to be a club. If they say "yes," I know they are ready. It is good to mix it up some and build some different friendships. It is amazing the relationships that can be built. As a group spends quality time together, prays together, and talks about some heavy stuff together, they will grow in unity.

Adding Students to Your Group

What about adding someone to your D-groups midway through the year? There will be times when a student needs and desires to get involved in a D-group, but all of the groups have already started meeting. It is okay to add someone to the group if you and the group leader agree that it won't have a negative impact. Generally, I would be comfortable adding a person anytime before December. The group has only met for a short time and is still in the beginning stages of opening up, talking, and holding one another accountable. It is after the holidays and into the new year that most groups will move past surface stuff. This is when you can begin to get more personal in your talks and your application of the Word. This is when barriers are more easily knocked down and students are quicker to open up. For these reasons it is generally better not to add someone after the new year begins. Keep in mind this is a generalization. If the leader and the group are open to an addition and the impact wouldn't hinder the group's cohesiveness and growth, then by all means, add the person. There may be other options available. Another group could be started midway through the year or some one-on-one mentoring could be set up. In making the decision, it is wise to keep the best interest of everyone in mind (the leader, the group, and the new student).

What about students who are signing up to be in a D-group a second or third year? Once your D-group ministry is set in place, you will have some students who will begin as freshmen or sophomores and desire to be involved again the next year. This is exactly what you want. If you can mentor a student for several years, your impact on their life will be even greater. I will often have a guy in my D-group three or four years. During that time, the other members of the group changed as some of them graduated or chose not to be in the group the next year, and new ones were added. It's actually good to have a veteran or two in your group each year. They know what to expect and can actually help you lead. When you wrap up your disciple group at the end of the year, encourage your group to do it again next year. Let them know you definitely want them back.

Setting the Time and Place

The optimum time for a D-group to meet is on a weeknight for an hour and a half. Sunday through Thursday seem best. Groups that meet on weekends have less consistency. Select your time and day and stick with it as much as possible. There will be times when you may need to move it, but make those the exception!

The best place to meet is in someone's home. A large church building just doesn't make a comfortable intimate small-group meeting place. However with more and more churches becoming regional rather than community churches, it just isn't feasible to ask everyone to drive long distances to different homes. If you meet in homes, it's best not to move in and take over the house, moving the family to the back room. Choose a place that has an extra room you can meet in that will ensure privacy.

Recruiting and Training D-group Leaders

The leader makes or breaks the disciple group experience. *This is not something that you can just advertise a need for in the church bulletin, take all volunteers, toss in a training manual and some curriculum, and expect incredible results.* Because the leader is so critical to the success of the group, you must spend a good deal of time, thought, and prayer as to whom you will recruit. Obviously you want your leaders to have a heart for youth and be able to comfortably relate to them, but even more, it is imperative that the leaders display a life worth emulating. "A student will not be greater than his teacher" (Matt. 10:24). The leader should be a mature Christian example, a person who is continually striving to come under the lordship of Christ. If you want your students to grow spiritually, then you must be growing too. Look for people who display fruits of Christianity (Gal. 5:22), who have control over bad habits, who exhibit spiritual growth, and have a heart for ministry.

Almost all of my D-group leaders were volunteers that had already been serving in the youth program for a period of one year or more. I knew them personally and could vouch for their character. In approaching them, I would tell them the time commitment involved and would even change some of their other duties in the youth program if necessary. Because leading a disciple group is a huge responsibility, it is wise not to burden your volunteers with too many other time commitments. The last thing you want from your leaders is to set them up to fail by asking for more than they can realistically give.

Because leading a disciple group is a huge responsibility, it is wise not to burden your volunteers with too many other time commitments. The last thing you want from your leaders is to set them up to fail by asking for more than they can realistically give.

In order to increase your number of potential D-group leaders, you will need to increase your total number of youth workers in your overall ministry. Add potential youth workers to your youth ministry team and give them opportunities to work. After watching them for a period of time you will be able to determine if they are ready to lead a disciple group. I also believe that it is important to recruit people who have enough life experience to mentor teens. Generally, college students would be better suited mentoring junior highers rather than high school students that are only a few years younger than they are.

Training doesn't have to be complicated, exhaustive, or drawn out. A good plan would include a solid two-hour training meeting in late August for all your leaders. In two hours you can cover the purpose, plan, and promise, as well as the requirements (or the cost) of being a leader. You will also want to cover what to do on a weekly basis including some ideas for building unity, discussion leading tips, and group study ideas (curriculum). Cover everything necessary to get started. Plan to meet again after the groups have been meeting for one month. By then the leaders will have questions and frustrations, as well as some fun experiences to share. A monthly review meeting for D-group leaders is a great way to encourage your leaders, pray for each other, and just keep everyone on track. Another training method is to match your rookie leaders with some veterans. They would spend the year leading one group together and then each take a separate group the following year.

As with any work, the ministry is only as strong as your leaders. You can't do it alone. Recruit with discernment. Train with practical ideas and realistic expectations. Follow up with encouragement. Pour yourself into the adults who come alongside of you in your ministry. With their help your efforts will be multiplied tremendously.

Time for Reflection

1. Why is it important to have students sign a commitment form before they are assigned a discipleship group? What should go into that form?

2. What happens to the student who was not truly ready to make a commitment to a discipleship group, but who was made a part of one anyway? How does this affect the group? What steps can you take to avoid this unfortunate situation?

3. What are some considerations you must keep in mind when forming your discipleship groups?

4. Think through the adults in your church. Who would you like your students to pattern their lives after? What would it take to recruit this person as a discipleship group leader?

SUGGESTED READING LIST

Greer, Kevin. *Life to Life Discipleship.* Joplin, MO: Christ In Youth, 2000.

Wynn, Richard R. *Successful Youth Mentoring.* Loveland, CO: Group, 1998.

NOTES ON CHAPTER TWENTY-ONE

1. Dick Alexander, "Discipling for Depth," in *Ministering to Youth,* ed. by David Roadcup (Cincinnati: Standard, 1980), pp. 53-54.

2. Tom Bassford, *People and Programs* (Grand Rapids: Baker, 1987), p. 73.

Chapter 22

Mastering the Technique of Student Preaching

Josh Finklea

What Is Student Preaching?

Student preaching is a new term that I want you to become familiar with. The simple definition of it is, "speaking and teaching the Word of God to students." Many of you have sat through several preaching classes while you were in college or seminary. Each one of these classes taught you a formula on how to preach. You learned how to put sentences, phrases, and thoughts together in a way that made sense. You learned how to study Scripture and break it apart homiletically. You learned how to make a central thesis. You learned how to take any Scripture in the Bible and turn it into three points and a poem. You learned the difference between expository, topical, narrative, deductive, and inductive sermons. You prepared sermons and preached them to the class. You learned the nuts and bolts of preaching. But let me ask you, "Did any of your classes teach you the difference between preaching to adults and preaching to students?"

Most college classes focus on preaching to adults. They teach you the nuts and bolts and the right formulas to preach to church congregations. All of that is great if you are preaching to a congregation of adults, but for those of you who are preaching to students, you are left out. There are a lot of principles that carry over from one side to the other. For instance, whether you are preaching to adults or students,

There is a huge difference between adult preaching and student preaching. Therefore, if you are preaching to students master that technique so that the Spirit may prevail.

you'd better know how to study a Scripture and break it apart homiletically and exegetically. But at the same time, there are many differences. The length of your sermons, the type of illustrations you use, the type of sermons you preach, the Bible stories you use, the vocal intonations and body language you use, and so forth, are all different. There is a huge difference between adult preaching and student preaching. Therefore, if you are preaching to students, master those differences so that the Spirit may prevail.

> Effective speaking to youth is 10 percent inspiration and 90 percent perspiration. That's why I'm convinced that there are not very many excellent youth speakers: Few are willing to commit the time and energy it takes to move a youth audience.[3]

Preach in a way that is totally focused on and geared toward students.

All good student preachers have a couple of characteristics in common. They are either humorous, passionate, or sticky. They will grab your attention by making you laugh, by stirring your emotions, or by saying things so well that they stick to your mind. All student preachers must possess at least one of these characteristics, a good student preacher will possess two, and the great ones will possess all three.

If someone gets on stage and tries to preach to students but doesn't possess one of these characteristics, I can guarantee the students won't listen. The great thing about these characteristics is that all of them can be learned. Usually anyone who preaches to students can at least learn all three and easily be good in two and excel in one. The reason this is true is because these characteristics are not limited to a certain personality. Chances are your personality will fit into at least one of these areas, and probably even two. And remember, as Phillips Brooks said, "Preaching is communicating God's truths through your personality."[4]

Characteristic #1: Humor

The first characteristic is that of humor. "Humor can break tension and lower the defenses of your audience."[5] Out of the three this one might be the hardest because this one does play off of your personality a bit. For some people, they have to work at being humorous. If this is you, then don't worry because I'm not saying you have to be funny or be a comedian.

Humor can break tension and lower the defenses of your audience.

And for those of you who are just naturally funny, let me warn you, I said, "You need to be humorous." I didn't say, "You need to be a comedian." The problem comes when there isn't a balance in this area. Some people don't use any humor and others do a stand up comic routine. Both are wrong.

My encouragement would be to use humor a little. Phil Chalmers, a traveling student preacher, says, "I feel like if they haven't laughed, then I have failed."[6] Young people like to laugh. I want there to be several times of laughter/giggling in my sermons. Generally, I will make sure there is humor in my introduction. I want to start them off laughing a little to build a bridge of comfort between the audience and me. Sometimes though, my introduction doesn't allow for humor. I might be starting with a deep illustration or Scripture. When this is the case, I make sure then that there is a time of laughter in my first point. I make sure there is purposefully-placed humor in the first half of my sermon.

I will use humor by telling a story about myself, or by just saying a one-liner. I don't use humor by telling a joke. I have never told a joke during a sermon and I never will for a couple reasons. One, there is a risk of failure. There is no recovery from a joke that has bombed. Two, and more importantly, I don't believe that jokes have a place in sermons. They have no teaching value. By telling a story, especially a personal story, students will go on the journey with you. Your points are much more easily digested when accompanied by a story. I often tell a story from my childhood about my record-breaking year of football. I tell them that, as a running back, I had an outstanding year. I add humor to the story by "hamming" it up a little and by saying the right phrase at the perfect time. I do this by telling them about my glorious year and dreams for the future. Because of this they assume that I'm talking about high school football. When I get to the end of the story I say, "I had the best year of my football career, and the cool thing was the next year I got to play 7th grade football." When I say that, the crowd rushes back over the entire story and realizes that I have been talking about grade school football and they erupt with laughter. By doing that, I've told a story that has an important tie to my sermon, and I have added humor at the same time.

I would encourage the use of humor. I would warn against using comedy. I have seen too many men try to use comedy during their sermons and fail.

My encouragement is to use humor. My warning is to not use comedy. I have seen too many men try to use comedy during their sermons and fail. Oh, they didn't fail to make people laugh. They were great at that, but they failed at presenting the gospel message and bringing about change in students' lives. The guys who use comedy are immediately thought of as good student preachers. People will talk about them for a while and even invite them to speak at retreats and conventions. But shortly thereafter people start to realize that they aren't bringing a message. They are making people laugh but not bringing the students closer to God. These people are like one-hit-wonder musicians. They are gone just as quickly as they came.

There's a place for wit and humor in the pulpit, but there's no room there for a stand-up comic or a show-off. We want to send the congregation home awed by the greatness of God, not laughing at the cleverness of the preacher.
—Warren Wiersbe

The same will hold true for you if you try to use comedy during your sermons. If you do a stand-up comic routine for your students every week, you will soon see your students disappearing. Those that stick around might enjoy the laughs, but their faith will be very shallow. Students want to hear good preaching that challenges them to change. They want to laugh, but they also want to cry. Warren Wiersbe says, "There's a place for wit and humor in the pulpit, but there's no room there for a stand-up comic or a show-off. We want to send the congregation home awed by the greatness of God, not laughing at the cleverness of the preacher."[7] Satan will set a trap for you. He wants you to think that all the laughter is good because he knows that growth won't happen and failure will come if that is all you do. As a student preacher you will start to feel secure in your preaching if they are laughing. You will think that you are hitting the mark. What happens if they stop laughing? Are you becoming boring and dull? Are you not effective? You decide you better make them laugh even longer or more next time. See? It isn't a game you can win. It isn't even a game you should play. Give them laughter. Use humor, but stay away from comedy. Brock Gill, a traveling student preacher says, "I use humor when it is appropriate and natural. I won't tell jokes or use comedy. If you preach with power and conviction you don't need comedy."[8]

Characteristic #2: Passion

When I asked some students about what makes a great student preacher, they all said, "Passion." If you want students to believe, and act upon what you are saying, you have to be passionate.

What is passion? To a junior high student it means one thing, to a godly widow it means another, and to you it might mean something else. In our culture many times passion is thought of in the same light as lust. I would have guessed that to be the first dictionary definition, but I was mistaken—it is one of the last definitions. Webster's defines passion as: "A suffering or enduring; the last suffering of Christ; a strong feeling or emotion; violent anger; ardor; love; vehement desire." This definition can be used to describe exactly how you should preach with passion.

A Suffering Or Enduring

The bottom line is it should hurt to preach. It should hurt your heart and tire your body to preach to students. I know when I am finished preaching that I feel physically wasted. For me, it is like going out on the football field. Any man that says he can play the game of football and not be wasted at the end of the game hasn't really played. Football is a fast-paced, body-slamming game. When the game is over, it should all be left on the field. Preaching is the same in my opinion. Preaching is a mind-searching, heart-sharing, soul-battling event. When the sermon is over, I don't want to have anything left. I want to use all of my energy on that sermon and those students. I know that Satan and his demons are battling God and his angels during the sermon. I can sit on the sideline, or I can get in the game. Let's just say, I've never been one to watch. A friend of mine quit preaching for a while because it caused too much stress in his life. He said that he couldn't handle his heart feeling like it did every time he would preach. I understand his feeling, but the bottom line is, suffering and pain go with the job. If you preach with passion, you are going to have to suffer during the sermon and endure the battle.

The Last Suffering Of Christ

Christ took His passion even a step further. His passion didn't end with the sermon. His passion led him to the cross. Jesus gave up His life so that we could be saved. He gave it all up and then asked us to do the same. If you want to have your sermons filled with passion, you have to be willing to give up your life. I have realized the calling God has made on my life. He has called me to preach to students. When I accepted the call, I gave up my life. Not just my career, but my everyday life. I now go through life looking at people differently, reading things differently, seeing things differently, feeling differently, because I know that I have a message that needs to be heard. Your life should bleed for students.

Something happened in my life when I accepted the call to preach to students. It is hard to explain, but let me try. I go through life now crying all the time. I'll admit it. I'm a cry-baby. When I see things on T.V., I cry. When I see people on the street, I cry. When I see students at conferences, I cry. When I see students come forward, I cry. I can't look at people the way I used to. I see them differently now. I see them needing so much and my heart breaks for them.

"God has called you to preach, so you better get used to it. How can you preach to people if you don't have a broken heart for them?"

One day I was walking through the streets of Atlanta with a friend of mine, and I just started crying. He asked me what was wrong, but I knew there was no way to explain it. I tried, but didn't feel like I was making any sense. But he understood and put it to me in a way I hadn't thought of before. He reminded me about the prophets in the Old Testament. He reminded me that they wept for people. He then said, "God has called you to preach, so you better get used to it. How can you preach to people if you don't have a broken heart for them?" My desire to preach to students has caused me to have a broken heart for them. I'm not saying you have to weep all the time, but you do have to have a broken heart, and you do have to surrender your life for the calling. In order to preach to students I have had to surrender my life. Christ gave it all up, and I have had to give it all up as well. When you surrender your life for the calling, you will find it easy to preach with passion.

Strong Feeling or Emotion; Violent Anger

John Piper has said, "Lack of intensity in preaching can only communicate that the preacher does not believe or has never been seriously gripped by the reality of which he speaks—or that the subject matter is insignificant."[9] He also said, "Compelling preaching gives the impression that something very great is at stake."[10] When you display passion for your message, you are letting the crowd know that what you are saying is of great importance. If you speak in a monotone voice and don't display any emotion, you are just running your mouth. You must speak with emotion to show the crowd that you believe what you are saying and that it is important, even life-changing. Display your strong feelings about your subject, whether that means you cry, whisper, shout, or get angry. When Justin Leonard hit a putt to win the 1999 Ryder Cup, he and his American teammates went nuts. They jumped, shouted, hugged, and celebrated—something you don't see on a golf course very often. The European team and the press had a field day with this. They commented on how rude it was and how it broke all rules of golf etiquette. The U.S. golfers thought differently though and commented that it was a time of emotion. They let their emotions fly, and you need to do the same while preaching to students.

Someone once said of Jonathon Edwards' preaching that he had

> the power of presenting an important truth before an audience, with overwhelming weight of argument, and with such intenseness of feeling, that the whole soul of the speaker is thrown into every part of the conception and delivery; so that the solemn attention of the whole audience is riveted, from the beginning to the close, and impressions are left that cannot be effaced.[11]

It is this kind of emotion that lets your crowd see the importance of your message. Students will listen to a message from a person who is excited, enthusiastic, vocal, or even angry, even if what he is saying isn't the most exciting thing in the world. The benefit is we have the most exciting things to talk about. If we will take our message and mix it with emotions, then people will listen and react. If your sermon doesn't excite you and stir your passions, then go back to your study because it isn't worth preaching.

Ardor and Love

Ardor? Now there is a word that I don't use every day. It means a warmth of emotion. Maybe I could reword it to a warmth of love. Passion is developed out of a warmth of love. Not a hard or abrasive love, but a warm love.

If you don't love the students your preaching to then you won't have passion.

Passion isn't always displayed in a loud voice, but in a warm voice of love. Passion, when thought of in the context of preaching, is developed out of a warm love for people. I wouldn't be passionate about what I'm saying if I didn't look into the eyes of students every time I'm on stage. I asked Mark Moore, a well-known traveling preacher and college professor, what made his heart tick for ministry and for preaching. He replied, "That's easy. The Holy Spirit has placed a burden on my heart for people. I see people and I want to help them and minister to them."[12] If you don't love the students you're preaching to, then you won't have passion. You must have a warm love for them that carries you through your preparation, prayer, and presentation. The evangelist Charles Simeon said, "Let your preaching come from the heart. Love should be the spring of all actions and especially of a minister's."[13] Look into the eye of every student you come in contact with, let that warm love for them build up, and you will find it easy to preach with passion.

Vehement Desire

There's another word that I don't use often: vehement. Vehement means "eager" or "urgent." Wow! Now that definitely closes the chapter on passion. Why should I speak with passion? Because my message is urgent. I have an urgent desire to make sure that everyone I ever speak to comes to Christ. I know that not all seed is going to fall on fertile soil, but I pray that it will. You need to look at students and see their souls and want them to be saved. Jesus could return at any moment, therefore my message is urgent. Brock Gill said, "I realize that there is a crowd of people in the audience who are lost and dying. It is like seeing people in a burning building. I have to show them the door to safety. I let what is in my heart pour out."[14] Students are dangling their toes over the fire. Are you going to let them get burned or save them? Jude 23 says, "Snatch people from the fire." You have the most urgent message in the world. Life is a mist that appears for awhile and then is gone. For all I know, I have one sermon with each student. I don't want to waste time or to dillydally on stage. I have an urgent message and that is what I'm going to preach.

"If I have no passion, I might as well just sit down."
—Mike Baker

Passion is an essential characteristic of good student preaching. Without it you are wasting time. As Mike Baker says, "If I have no passion, I might as well just sit down."[15]

Characteristic #3: Sticky

When you first see that word "sticky" as a characteristic of student preaching, you might not understand. You might be asking yourself, "What does he mean by 'sticky'?" Sticky means that what you say has a way of sticking in students' minds and on their hearts. Some guys just have a way of saying things, of putting thoughts together, of using objects, of changing their voice, that makes what they say stick. Jeff Walling, a preacher in North Carolina who does a lot of student preaching, is a speaker that is sticky. Students love to listen to him preach because what he says sticks. He doesn't use a lot of humor or passion, but he is very effective because what he says sticks. There are many things you can do to be sticky, but the two most important ones are to be intentional and purposeful.

To be sticky you must be intentional. Carefully plan out your words. Intentionally use body language. Purposefully use object lessons. You must be intentional in your preparation. If you fly by the seat of your pants then there is no way that you can be sticky. You must plan in advance for it. But it doesn't stop there, it continues all the way to the stage. Many student preachers will stand on the stage and say things that don't have anything to do with their sermons. Maybe it is the introduction, or maybe it is a time-out in the middle. You must realize that these are meaningless words that cannot be used. God may move you in a different direction during the sermon, but he won't move you off track. Stick to the game plan and be intentional.

To be sticky you must also be purposeful. Too many guys fill their sermons with too much information. The goal of student preaching is to say one thing and say it well. William Shakespeare summed up student preaching the best when he said, "Speak plain and to the purpose."[16] The goal of student preaching is not to educate. That is what Bible studies, accountability groups, and Sunday school are for. The goal of student preaching is to challenge and enact change. When I first started preaching, I would give my students three to five things to think about and work on for the coming week. I quickly realized that if I could get my students to do one thing better for Christ this week, then they were

The goal of student preaching is not to educate. That is what Bible studies, accountability groups, and Sunday School are for. The goal of student preaching is to challenge and enact change.

doing well. Therefore, I learned that my sermons should be clear and concise and focused on one thing. Winston Churchill once said, "A speech is like a symphony. It may have three movements but must have one dominant melody."[17]

Student preaching is one of the best tasks that anyone could ever be given. It is the best because you are given a sacred trust. You have the ability to share the very words of God with students. Students who are moldable. Students who are looking to change. Students who are ready to accept God. That is an awesome task. As one student preacher said, "Consider each opportunity to talk for God as a trust from Him to you. You must be faithful to speak for Him—anything else is failure."[18] Master the technique of student preaching.

Time for Reflection

1. How is preaching to students different from that of preaching to adults? Or is it? What do they have in common?
2. What are the three main characteristics of effective student preachers?
3. What is the difference between including humor in your sermon and simply telling a joke? Why is this difference important?
4. How do you develop "passion" in your preaching?
5. What does it mean to be a "sticky" preacher? What are some ways to accomplish this?

NOTES ON CHAPTER TWENTY-TWO

1. Dewey Bertolini, *Back to the Heart of Youth Work* (Wheaton, IL: Victor Books, 1989), p. 38.
2. Dan Webster and Jana Sundene, "Speaking to High School Students," in *The Complete Book of Youth Ministry*, ed. by Warren S. Benson and Mark H. Senter III (Chicago: Moody, 1987), p. 340.
3. Jim Burns, *The Youth Builder* (Eugene, OR: Harvest House, 1988), p. 193.
4. Warren Wiersbe, *The Dynamics of Preaching* (Grand Rapids: Baker, 2000), p. 16.
5. Webster and Sundene, "Speaking," p. 338.
6. Personal interview.
7. Wiersbe, *Dynamics*, p. 16.

8. Personal interview.
9. John Piper, *The Supremacy of God in Preaching* (Grand Rapids: Baker, 1990), p. 103.
10. Ibid., p. 103.
11. Ibid., pp. 49-50.
12. Personal interview.
13. Wiersbe, *Dynamics*, p. 45.
14. Personal interview.
15. Personal interview.
16. James C. Humes, *Speak like Churchill, Stand like Lincoln* (Roseville, CA: Prima Publishing, 2002), p. 25.
17. Humes, *Speak*, p. 28.
18. Personal interview with Mike Baker.

Chapter 23

Ministering to Junior High Students

Josh Finklea

The Often Overlooked Ministry to Junior High

If you want to change the world, start with your junior high kids. If you want to bring life into your church, start with your junior high kids. If you want to grow your youth ministry, start with your junior high kids. Junior high students are often overlooked in our youth ministries. They are overlooked because the word on the street is that junior high students don't care about God, are too shallow to learn about him, and are too hyper to go deeper. Most churches write them off until they get to high school. This is evident because the majority of all youth ministers who have the responsibility of working with junior high and high school students spend most of their time and money on their high school students. Why is it that year after year junior high students are overlooked and put to the side? Is it because they make you want to pull your hair out? Is it because they are the hardest to find teachers for? Is it because they are shallow? Is it because they smell? Is it because they are hyperactive? Is it because it is extremely hard work? Or is it because people remember what they did to their teachers when they were in junior high, and they know that history repeats itself?

Junior high ministry is hard but it is also the most rewarding because junior high students are moldable.

Answer: All of the above. Junior high ministry is hard, but it is also the most rewarding because junior high students are moldable. If you will take time to minister to them, you will help change a life, a ministry, a church, and a country.

Junior high ministry is not rocket science. On the contrary it is actually very simple. It is a mere three-step process: 1. Love them. 2. Minister to them. 3. Program for them. If you will do those three things in that order, you will have a junior high ministry that is a spiritual and numerical success.

Love Them

The most important thing you can ever do in your junior high ministry is love your students. If your students know they are loved by you, they will follow you wherever you lead them. The number one difference between a high school student and a junior high student comes down to this idea: High school students ask, "Do I like the youth minister?" Junior high students ask, "Does the youth minister like me?" If junior high students feel liked or loved by someone, then they will hang out with him. As a leader, if you show your junior high students that they are loved by you, then they will want to hang out with you and they will follow you.

The most important thing you can ever do in your junior high ministry is love your students.

true

Junior highers are extremely vulnerable. They can be hurt. But on the positive side, it means they are very open and can be influenced in positive ways. They have not yet set themselves in concrete. They are willing to change, to experiment, and to discover all God has in store for them. They are quite flexible, giving junior high workers a unique opportunity to play an important role in the shaping of someone else's life.[3]

You can express your love to them through many different vehicles. Love them verbally. Each year I put on conferences for junior high students that CIY calls, "Believe." Over the last few years I've been in front of thousands of junior high students. I've said many different things to them, but the most important thing I say to them happens in the first five minutes of every conference. When I come out on stage at the beginning of a conference, I welcome them and then tell them I love them. I want to do it up front because I know that if I can get those students to believe that I do truly love them, they will listen to anything I have to say. If you want your students to know they are loved by you, you must say it out loud to the group and to individuals. A friend of mine who is a youth minister in Missouri concludes every youth group by saying, "See you next week, and remember I love you." You must also tell individual students that they are loved. There will come times when you are talking to students one on one. When this happens, take time to look straight into his eyes and tell him that you love him. You might be the only person that he hears those words from all week.

Love them through your touch. Junior high boys equate how much you love them by how hard you hit them in the shoulder. Watch junior high students, and you will notice that they are always beating on one another. That is the way they express love. Now, don't get me wrong. I don't want you to go out and beat on kids, but you do need to love them through meaningful and proper touch. A handshake, a pat on the back, or a hug expresses more than words ever can. In the book, *The Gift of The Blessing,* Gary Smalley said, "In a study at UCLA, it was found that just to maintain emotional and physical health, men and women need eight to ten meaningful touches a day."[4]

The act of touch lets kids know they are accepted and loved.

The act of touch lets kids know they are accepted and loved. I know that in today's society you have to be careful in this area. But I want you to know that I hug the guys and girls that I minister to. They need a place where they can feel love. I have had several people tell me that when they came into my youth group, they felt loved just through my handshake. They later told me that when I shook their hand and said that I was glad they were there, they could tell I genuinely meant it. One night while I was worshiping at a conference I felt the need to pray for Allison, a girl from my group who was sitting in front of me. When I started praying for her, I reached out and touched her shoulder. When the service was over, she came up and said to me, "I don't know if you knew what I was struggling with in there, but when you touched me it was as if God was reaching out to me and helping me." There is power in touch.

Love them by encouraging them. Junior high students are in the midst of change—physical change, social change, and for many, family change. You have the opportunity to be a blessing to your students by being a source of encouragement. One way to encourage them is to place value on them. You need to verbally communicate to each student in your group that they are valuable to you, to your youth group, and to God. When encouraging a student, find something that he does for your ministry and let him know how crucial he is because of what he does. But don't stop there; next you need to encourage him by letting him know that God is going to use him. I will often tell a kid that if she follows God, then He will do something great with her life. Love your students by encouraging them and placing value on them.

Love them by playing with them. In every Youth Ministry 101 class you will hear that you need to hang out with your students. This is especially true when it comes to junior high ministry. If you want them to know they are loved, you must hang out and play with them. With junior high students this is easy because they have more time on their hands than high school students. Their practices don't go as long, they don't work, and they don't date, but they want to be busy. Take advantage of this by hanging out with them.

One way to do this is by having them over to your house or the church. I call this "being open." If you will open your home and your office to your kids, you will be bombarded with students. Invite your students over for dinner or for a movie. Have them go to the church to play some ball or even to work. Wednesdays in my office was student workday. Every Wednesday ten to fifteen students would show up after school. I knew this was going to happen every week, so I started making a stack of tasks for them to do. Phone calls, copies, cleaning, organizing, setting up, etc. These are all things that I could delegate to my students, so I did. Wednesday workdays became crucial to my ministry because it made me more productive on Monday and Tuesday. If a task came up that could wait until Wednesday, I would put it in my student's file. As beneficial as it was for me, it was even more so for my students because it helped them to realize that they were important to the ministry, valuable, and loved.

Most kids want boundaries. They do not mind being disciplined because it shows them that you love them.

Love junior high students by disciplining them. Many junior high students don't have any boundaries. Their families don't give them the boundaries they are looking for. They translate this to mean that their parents don't care. Most kids want boundaries. They do not mind being disciplined because it shows them that you love them.

The first thing you can do is discipline your kids respectfully and carefully. Whether it is a core kid or a visitor, you must discipline them, but do so respectfully and carefully. One way to stop someone who is talking while you are teaching is just to walk towards the student while you are talking. When you get close to him, he will naturally stop talking. If that doesn't work, you can gently place your hand on his shoulder. That is a simple way of saying to the person, "I care about you and want you to hear this."

Sometimes though you will have to call a person out by name. There are several ways to do this without embarrassing them. Say things like, "Sara, you need to hear this," or "Sara, check out what God is saying to you." Or you can ask them a question like, "Sara, when was the last time you . . . ?" When asking a kid a question, don't surprise him. Don't ask him things that you know he didn't hear because he was talking. Ask him something he can answer. Remember you aren't trying to embarrass him; you are trying to get him back on track. Sometimes you might have to kick a kid out of class. Kicking kids out should be a rarity and reserved for core kids. In all of my years of youth ministry I have only done this three times. You must treat non-Christians and visitors differently from core kids. Discipline them as necessary, but do it very carefully. You cannot expect as much out of them as you do your core kids.

Another thing you need to do is let the kids know what your expectations and rules are. Make sure they know your rules, and keep them to a minimum. I know youth ministers who make all kinds of rules about everything under the sun. When I was a youth minister in Indiana, my kids knew my basic rules: Honor God and others by your actions. Now that is pretty simple, isn't it? I can ask them if their actions honored God or others. They know that if the answer is "no," they need to change their behavior.

Make sure that your kids know exactly what your rules are and keep them to a minimum.

Every youth minister has been faced with problems that arise while on the church van or bus. In order to minimize problems in the van, I keep the dome light on at all times. If it is dark outside, my teens know the light is shining inside. This keeps the guy/girl thing from happening. It also keeps a lot of other little things from happening as well. You can see things and stop them before they become a problem. I have also noticed that it helps the teens socialize more. If you adopt this policy, you must realize a couple of things. Your

If you never discipline, it is going to be tough to do it when you really need to.

teens will give you every excuse in the book to turn the lights off (they want to sleep, it's illegal, there are no couples in here, etc.). Just tell them that they can ask all they want, but you will under no circumstance turn the light off. Once they hear you say this a couple of times, they will quit asking. If you make a commitment to do this, stick with it. If you ever turn it off, they will always try to get you to turn it off. (If you do this, make sure that you turn it off when you park. I speak from experience.)

One philosophy in the teaching field is, "Don't ever smile until Christmas." The reason for this is because it is easier to lighten up than to tighten up. This is true in youth ministry as well. If you never discipline, it is going to be tough to do it when you really need to. Discipline your junior high students so that they will know they are loved.

Minister to Them

Once you have convinced your students that you love them, they will be open for you to minister to them. The junior high years are crucial spiritual development years. It is during these years that the highest percentage of people accept Christ. It is also the age when many students either get on fire for God or start to walk away from him. With this in mind you have to know the best way to minister to them. Minister to them by: giving them God, offering times for decisions, teaching short and simple, leaving room for discussion and plugging them into adults.

First, give them God's love and Christ crucified. Because of their need to feel loved, when it comes to ministering to them you must show them that they are loved by God. Teach them about the cross. Don't overemotionalize it, but do give them the straight-up facts and details of what happened that day on Golgotha. Don't just plan it into one lesson. Teach on it every week. A common mistake that youth ministers make is that they teach something one time and think that they are done with that topic for a year. You have to repeat themes, especially with junior high students, if you want them to truly grasp them. The cross should be talked about every time you teach. Sometimes give the cross a full lesson, sometimes just a sentence. But always bring it up because your junior high students are at a point in their lives where they are searching for love, meaning, and God.

Another thing you must do to minister to junior high students is offer times of decision. Because junior high kids are at the point in their lives where they are ready to accept Christ, you must give them opportunities to do this. It isn't something you have to do every week, but it is a necessity. *If you don't ever offer times for decisions, they won't make them.* Offer decision times during youth group, at a retreat, or at a conference. I tried to offer some sort of decision time once a month. You can make this an informal thing by saying, "When youth group is over, I'm going to be sitting here on the stage, and if anyone needs to talk to me about giving your life to Christ, feel free to come talk to me." Or it can be formal by having kids stand up, come forward, go to the back, etc. during your meeting. If you don't ever offer times for decisions, then they won't make them.

Keep it short. A junior high youth meeting can go anywhere from forty-five minutes to two hours and be effective as long as each segment of that meeting is short. Junior high students can handle long meetings as long as they consist of short segments. I believe you need to have a change every fifteen minutes, twenty at the most. (I will talk about ways to do this later in the chapter). When it comes to teaching/preaching seventeen minutes is the maximum. A preacher can say everything he needs to in seventeen minutes or less. If it takes you longer than that, you have too much fluff or too much to digest. Keep it short for junior high students.

Keep it simple as well. There is a big difference between simple and shallow. For too many years people have considered junior high students to be shallow, thus their teaching was shallow. Junior high students can handle complexity. They can handle the meat of the word. But you must give it to them in simple and small portions. Don't downgrade your students. Don't keep them in the shallow end of the faith. Give them depth, but give it to them in simple terms and measures.

Always leave room for discussion. Junior high students can get lost or sidetracked with one little statement you make. They can also grab ahold of what you are saying and want to apply it in their life, but need a few more details. Because of this you must always leave room for discussion after a time of teaching. These students need a forum where they can ask questions. Sometimes the questions are off in left field, but many times the questions are what lead to their growth. After teaching you can ask the group as a whole if there are questions, but the best way to do it is to get in smaller groups (5-10 students), so they can ask questions in a comfortable and intimate setting.

Plug them in to other adults. You cannot do youth ministry alone, especially with junior high students. You can't because you won't have enough time, energy, and love. You *One adult can effectively disciple and love five junior high students. Don't try to do more.* must find other adults who will authentically love your students. I believe in the "Give 5" method. This is a method of discipleship and love. One adult can effectively disciple and love five junior high students. Don't try to do more. If you can find one adult who will pour his life into five junior high students, then you will find five junior high students who are growing in their relationship with God.

Program for Them

Most youth ministries and parachurch organizations program for high school students and incorporate junior high students into that program. Recently I looked through several publications to see what conferences and programs were being publicized for junior high students. Christ In Youth's "Believe" was the only one I could find. No one else is targeting junior high students. There were several organizations that allow junior high students to attend their conferences, but they don't program for them. I've been to those events and it is obvious that they program for high school students. And many youth ministries across America do the very same thing. They incorporate junior high and high school students together, but miss their junior high students because they program for high school students. Junior high students have some basic differences from high school students. Program for these differences and you'll find success.

One major area of programming is worship. Junior high students love to worship. They love to dance with God and get intimate with him. One year during our Cincinnati "Believe" conference the worship band led the students in a song that involved a lot of dancing. The students got so into it that they almost brought the building down. The city fire and police departments rushed into the room and shut us down for a while. The students had danced so enthusiastically that they had shaken the building and caused part of a first floor ceiling to fall in. Junior high students love to dance in worship.

The next year in Cincinnati I watched as over 2,000 junior high students danced to the song "Undignified." I witnessed a 2,000-member mosh pit and thought we had lost all control. If you want your junior high students to worship, you must provide them with some energetic, action-oriented songs. Any song that has dancing or motions is always a hit with junior high students. These songs are great because they help expel some energy. They also help those who are non-Christians or those who don't like to sing, because they can still participate by dancing or doing the motions.

When planning for a worship service for junior high students I encourage a 75% upbeat rule. Seventy-five percent of the songs you do should be of an upbeat nature. If you give them songs they can dance to, you will notice that their walls come down and they become comfortable. It is at that point that you can come in with some deeper songs and take them to an intimate level. That is where they want to go. They just need help getting there. One year I did a theme called "The Cry" for Believe. It was a theme based on the concept of worship. After we had broken down the walls and helped students to feel comfortable we did an intense, hour-long worship set. This set was very free and personal. We told students they could sing with the band or go to different stations during the songs for personal worship through prayer, creativity, and Scripture reading. The first time I tried this, I didn't know what to expect. I anticipated that kids would sing for a while and then go to stations after they had gotten in the mood. That isn't what happened. The band started playing and immediately the kids got up and scattered. I thought I had just started an hour of total chaos. But God revealed something different to me. The students immediately started getting in groups and reading their Bibles together. They sat down and drew pictures and wrote poems to God. They found corners where they could privately pray and sing. After some time of this many came to the front of the stage and poured out their hearts in worship to God. That night God broke my heart and taught me about true worship. And that night junior high students showed me that they love to dance in worship and at the same time love to get intimate with God. Give them both experiences.

When programming for junior high students you need to keep things changing.

When programming for junior high students you need to keep things changing. This generation of students live in a fast-paced, information-overload, ever-changing society. They are used to things flashing before their eyes and changing every minute. You don't need to go to those extremes, but you do need to change something every fifteen minutes. This can easily be done by offering a variety of events during your meeting. Dramas, special music, video clips, discussion groups, games, teaching, dance routines are all things that can be used to bring about change. Put a video clip in the middle of worship, or a special song in the middle of your teaching time. Change things up each night and change things up each week. Don't use the same order of service each week. Keep them guessing.

When programming use your junior high students. Don't let your adults do everything. Get your students involved, and let them do the dramas, play in the band, run the production table, and sing. Chances are you can make a band out of adults or high school students who will sound better than your junior high students. But the point is not to have an awesome band, but rather to have a decent band that can get the job done and provide a place for junior high students to be involved. When I was doing youth ministry in Indiana, the leader of our worship band was an adult and everyone else was students.

Another way to get your students involved is to let them run the production table. Junior high boys don't always like to sit and sing, but they love to run sound boards, make light cues, and play with the computer. Chances are they can do it better than your adults. One day I gave a brand new video mixer to a seventh grade boy. I asked him to figure it out and have fun with it. To him it was like a video game. He came back the next week and worked magic with that mixer. He, like most of your junior high students, has the time and desire to be involved in production. Plug them into your ministry and your junior high ministry and your church will benefit from it for years.

When programming for junior high students you also need to plan plenty of activities/social events. When it comes to high school ministry, I think six social events a year is plenty, but for your junior high ministry ten is a better number. Junior high kids love to hang out, and they have more time to do it. These social events don't have to be big events. If you just have a gym night, tons of kids will show up. These events are great for the evangelism of your youth group. Junior high kids are the most evangelistic people in the church. They don't evangelize based off of a spiritual need though. They evangelize by inviting their friends to hang out with them at activities.

Therefore, if you want your youth group to grow, then provide activities for your students to attend.

When it comes to programming, the age-old question is, "Should I keep my junior high and high school students together?" I believe if you program properly, this is very possible. For most activities like, Sunday school, accountability groups, and events, I separated my students. But during our student worship service I kept both groups together. Junior high and high school students can worship together, but you need to program certain things into the service for both groups. Don't gear your ministry for high school students and allow junior high students to attend. Focus on your junior high students by loving them, ministering to them, and programming for them, and you will bring growth to your youth group, church, and the kingdom.

Time for Reflection

1. Is your junior high ministry a priority or just an "add on?"
2. How do you program differently to meet the needs of your junior high students as compared to your senior high students?
3. What do you do that specifically communicates love to your junior high students?

SUGGESTED READING LIST

Rice, Wayne. *Junior High Ministry.* Grand Rapids: Zondervan, 1987.

Shaheen, David. *Growing a Jr. High Ministry.* Loveland, CO: Group, 1986.

NOTES ON CHAPTER TWENTY-THREE

1. Wayne Rice, "Junior High Ministries," in *The Complete Book of Youth Ministry,* ed. by Warren S. Benson and Mark H. Senter III (Chicago: Moody, 1987), p. 481.

2. David Shaheen, *Growing a Jr. High Ministry* (Loveland, CO: Group, 1986), p. 11.

3. Rice, "Junior High," p. 483.

4. Gary Smalley and John Trent, *The Gift of Blessing* (Nashville: Thomas Nelson, 1993), p. 40.

Chapter 24
Evangelizing Young People

Josh Finklea

A Walk Down Bourbon Street

I met Alice on the streets of New Orleans. She was a homeless woman who lived on Bourbon Street. The first encounter I had with her was when she came up and asked me if I would buy her and her boyfriend a beer. I gave the boyfriend enough money to buy the beer, and while he was gone, I sat down and talked to Alice. We talked about her life in New Orleans. The parties, the history, the atmosphere, and life on Bourbon Street. After we talked for a while I took off and let them enjoy their beer.

Some of you are struggling with the thought that I bought someone a beer, but please understand the spiritual state of non-Christians. Others of you are wondering why I didn't say more to her about Christ. You need to understand love and proper timing. This story is about evangelism, and one that might bring you new insight and understanding.

Christians talk about evangelism frequently, but often do nothing evangelistic. Youth ministers talk about having evangelistic youth ministries but really don't know where to start. Students talk about bringing their friends to Christ, but are clueless on how to do it. If you want to have an evangelistic youth ministry, it comes down to your heart bleeding for people, your ability to create a climate for evangelism, and your ability to teach the method.

God Breaks My Heart in Ybor City

Does your heart break for lost people? Do you weep for people that you encounter who are hurting? Do you feel an overwhelming burden to love people and tell them about Christ? Jesus' heart broke for lost people. When he was making his triumphal entry into Jerusalem, he broke down and wept. In the midst of a party he fell apart because he hurt so much for lost people (Luke 19:37-41).

Does your heart break for lost people? Do you weep for people that you encounter who are hurting?

God doesn't see non-Christians as dirty, rotten sinners. He sees them as lost children. He sees them as His kids and His heart breaks for them. I remember the night God helped me to see past the sin into the person. It was the night I went to Ybor City in Tampa, Florida.

I stepped onto the streets of Ybor City and couldn't believe my eyes. Sure I had been warned about the sin that filled the city like thick fog on an early spring morning, but I was not ready for the overwhelming sense of evil that hit me as I walked out onto the street. Ybor City is filled with nightclubs, strip joints, bars, black magic shops, and more. The streets were packed with people from every walk of life. The homeless and the rich. Teens, college kids, and older adults. Drug users and pushers, religious fanatics and Satanic followers. You name it, they were there. And they were caught up in sin. Everywhere I looked sin looked back at me.

I first saw the sin in a fourteen-year-old boy. He had dark eyes and matted hair. You could tell that he hadn't slept in a bed in a long time. He was a runaway. We talked a little and then he left. He continued to come back throughout the night for more conversation.

I then saw the sin in a couple of teenagers. They were walking by "putting up a front" as they called it. I stopped them and asked them what they were doing in Ybor City. They said, "We come here every night and put up a front. You know—put on a show. We do it in hopes of getting something—either some girls, some drugs, or some alcohol." When they left me, I wondered if they had gotten anything from me.

I then saw sin in the eyes of a worn-out woman. She worked in a strip joint. I saw her standing in front of her club, so I went up and talked to her. She thought I might be coming to talk to her for some business, but I quickly informed her that wasn't why I wanted to talk.

I was weeping because my heart had been changed and rather than seeing sin with my eyes I saw a multitude of people who were lost.

I asked her if I could ask her a question. With hesitation she said, "Okay." I asked, "Why do you work here?" She simply responded, not out of pride or passion, but out of sadness and oppression, "I have a three-year-old daughter and a bad habit that I must support. This puts money in my pocket and bread on my table."

I stood in the middle of the road at the main intersection of Ybor City as I was getting ready to leave. When I looked around, I caught myself weeping. I was weeping because my heart had been changed, and rather than seeing sin with my eyes, I saw a multitude of people who were lost. I saw people who needed the grace and compassion of Jesus.

I went to Ybor City that night because I heard it was a great place to people watch. I left Ybor City that night with a burning passion in my heart for lost people who were in the death clutches of sin. I decided that night that I'm not going to judge people who are stuck in sin, but rather I'm going to give them compassion and point them to the grace and the love of Jesus. "Our generation wants and needs a gospel that addresses the human condition with both truth and hope and that allows room for the mystery of suffering."[4]

Evangelism, Discipleship, or Missions

If your heart is not broken for lost people, you will not be an evangelistic person. If you don't see them the way God sees them, you won't have an evangelistic youth ministry. And that is okay. Not everyone is built with an evangelist's heart. I've met too many youth ministers who say they want to have an evangelistic youth ministry, but the reality is that their heart beats for discipleship.

Every youth ministry is built on one of three building blocks: evangelism, discipleship, or missions. You can look at any decent youth ministry and pick out which one they are built upon. This isn't a bad thing; it is a necessity. You can't excel at all of them, and you can't sell all of them. Pick one and build upon that. That doesn't mean you are forgetting the other two, it just means they aren't your foundation. An evangelistic youth ministry will naturally create disciples who are growing in their relationship and wanting to serve others. A discipleship-based youth ministry will teach students to be evangelistic and serve. A missions-minded youth ministry will focus on serving which leads to discipleship and evangelism. All are good, but only one is your heart. Youth ministries that build upon the one that is closest to the youth minister's heart are youth ministries that succeed. But if you let your heart be broken for lost people and see them the way God does, you will become an evangelist, and so will the teens in your youth ministry.

Creating a Climate for Evangelism

Now that the preparations for evangelism have been made, you need to set the table. There are certain things you must do to create a climate of evangelism.

Evangelism is too often approached as a separate program that has to coexist with other activities of youth ministry. Rather than setting evangelism aside as a concern to address from time to time, it should be the seasoning that flavors all we do in youth ministry. Evangelism should permeate every program, activity, and emphasis in youth ministry.[5]

Cast the Vision

I remember the first day that I walked into the church in Danville, Indiana, to become their youth minister. I immediately told the elders that I was different, and I was going to be bringing in a lot of different kinds of kids to this church. I told them to be ready for sinners to be walking through the halls. I also immediately went to my new group of students and said, "I'm here to bring people to Christ. You have friends who are lost and need him. I'm going to help you bring them to Christ. If you don't want to have a youth group of over a hundred kids next year, then tell me now so that I'm not wasting my time." At that point there were fifteen students in the youth group. I didn't know them. They didn't know me. But they quickly learned what we were going to be about.

If you want your students to be evangelistic, you have to cast the vision. You have to let them know what you expect and what God can do through them. I challenged my students to become evangelists. I encouraged them to share Christ with others. I let them know that they had the keys to life that people are looking for. I also revealed to them that God was going to use them to bring hundreds of people to Christ.

However, don't stop here. Keep casting the vision. Rick Warren, the lead pastor of Saddleback Community Church, calls this the Nehemiah Principle. Nehemiah gathered the Israelites and rebuilt the wall around Jerusalem in fifty-two days. Halfway through the project they became worn out and were ready to quit, so Nehemiah reminded them of the vision. Your students will get worn out and want to quit. Evangelism is hard work. Sometimes you see a lot of fruit quickly. At other times you feel as if all you are doing is planting seeds. Keep your students refreshed by casting the vision every twenty-six days.

Provide a Dynamic Worship Service.

Create a climate by providing a worship service that non-Christians want to come to. Don't be seeker-sensitive. Don't be visitor-friendly. Be outreach-oriented. This means that you do every thing with a non-Christian in mind. This doesn't mean that you are shallow, that you avoid using Scripture, that you shy away from preaching, or that you don't worship. It actually means just the opposite. Non-Christians come to your program because they want to have fun and expect to hear from God. Too many churches and youth ministers think outreach means games, laughter, and swimming in the shallow end. It is the exact opposite. If you want to have an evangelistic program, you have to give non-Christians worship, the Word, and the gospel. But you do it in a way that they can digest it.

Don't be seeker-sensitive. Don't be visitor-friendly. Be outreach-oriented.

Make Sure People Feel Loved

Dawson McAllister writes,

Teenagers are crying out—or wanting to cry out but are afraid no one is listening—as never before for meaningful relationships.

They crave genuine connections based on real love. This craving drives them to substitute sexual encounters and the many forms of escape when the pain of isolation is too great. Youth ministry can step into the void and become a surrogate family for these young men and women longing for love.[6]

The first thing a non-Christian should feel when he comes to your program is love. Students are crying out for love. Many of them aren't getting it at home or at school, so make sure they get it when they come to your program. Position your adult and student leaders throughout your room and tell them it is their job to love people as they show up. I told my leaders that they had to "Give 5" every week at our program. They knew this meant they had to go and talk to five people every night, preferably people they weren't really close to. I also used this phrase as a red alert. If I ever said, "Hey, everyone go give five to someone" through our sound system, then my students would start giving high fives, but my leaders knew that meant there was someone in the room who needed some love. They would immediately start looking for a new kid who had just walked in or a person sitting in a corner by himself. Be outreach-oriented by giving love.

Good Idea

For those raised in the church, a youth group may not *feel* like a private club with its own culture, rules, and norms, but to many of those on the outside that's how it has felt for decades. As the secular culture becomes increasingly post-Christian, the gap widens between those who feel qualified for membership and those who don't.[7]

Be Encouraging—Not Judgmental

Create a climate by providing a place where non-Christians can come and be encouraged, not judged. Jesus never judged lost people. He encouraged them. He forgave the adulterous woman and encouraged her to "go now and leave her life of sin" (John 8:11). He forgave the prostitute and said, "Your faith has saved you; go in peace" (Luke 7:50). You and your students must realize that your youth group is for hurting lost people. Our churches have turned into rehabilitation rooms rather than trauma centers. We tell people to start to get healthy and then come to The Physician, rather than taking them to The Physician to get healthy.

Our churches have turned into rehabilitation rooms rather than trauma centers.

AMEN

When I was sixteen years old, a girl invited me to attend her youth group. I didn't want to know anything about church or God, but I went anyway. I was shocked that I had had such a good time, so when she invited me the next week, I went again and enjoyed it again. The next Friday I went out with some friends and got drunk. Sunday rolled around and I anticipated another call and another invitation to youth group, but the call never came. When I got to school the next day, I saw the girl and told her I was disappointed that she didn't invite me to youth group. That's when she quickly replied, "It is obvious that you don't want to have anything to do with God because I know what you did Friday night." And that was the last time I went to her church.

I wasn't a Christian, yet she was expecting me to act like one. If you want to create a climate for evangelism, you can't expect your non-Christians to act like Christians. They are sinners who need to be encouraged, not judged. There were many Sundays when I would look out into my youth group and see non-Christians who on Friday were having sex, doing drugs, and flirting with homosexuality. I didn't judge them. I didn't kick them out for smoking cigarettes on the sidewalk. No, I encouraged them with the love of Christ.

Understand the Problem of Sin

The secret to this is understanding sin. If you have never accepted Christ as your Savior, then your sins aren't forgiven. Romans 6:23 says, "the wages of sin is death." Therefore, the sin you committed when you lied to your mom at the age of ten is going to send you to hell before the sin of doing drugs at the age of seventeen will. If you haven't ever asked for forgiveness for your first sin, then what is one more? By keeping this in mind it will allow you and your students to look past the vast sea of a person's sins. You won't see every little thing he is doing wrong. You won't judge him for his lifestyle. You'll see his soul and want to encourage him into loving Christ. I bought Alice and her boyfriend a beer, and it didn't bother me. It didn't bother me because I wasn't focused on her individual sin problem, but rather her whole sin problem. Until she repents of her sins, it is the first one she committed that is going to send her to hell. Don't judge them, rather encourage them to love Christ.

Make Non-Christians Feel Welcome

Create a climate by doing certain things in your program for the non-Christian. Play proper secular music to help them feel at home and comfortable. Don't play it on a treble-filled little radio. Play it through a good system with some good bass and volume. Provide snacks and drinks beforehand to help make the environment informal. If you do this, don't serve generic chips, cookies, and soda. Our God deserves better than that. Give them Doritos, Oreos, and Mountain Dew, not tortilla chips and Green Lightning. Non-Christians will equate that to mean that our God is a second-rate God. Play some games occasionally and have some fun, but don't be cheesy. Most importantly talk about the cross weekly and provide opportunities for decisions.

Always Preach the Cross

If you have an outreach-oriented meeting, then you have to assume that non-Christians are going to be there. When a student sits down in your youth group, you never know if he will ever be back. You must talk about the cross in some form every night so that he will hear the gospel. You can't say, "I'll talk about it next week," because he might be dead by next week. Sometimes you will give whole lessons on the cross, but mostly it will be just thirty seconds to a minute of your talk. It doesn't matter how long you talk about the cross as long as somewhere within your talk you say at least this much, "Jesus loves you so much that he died on the cross so that you could be forgiven of your sins." I believe it is a sin to preach a sermon or teach a lesson and not mention the cross. Your non-Christians must hear it weekly.

Provide Opportunities for Decisions

You also must provide opportunities for decisions so that they will know what to do with the knowledge they are learning. This generally doesn't have to be an "invitation" although they are good to do occasionally, but more often it is simply words spoken. "If you need to talk about what God is doing in your life, I'll be sitting on the stage when we are done," or "If you need to accept Christ into your life, please come see me after we dismiss." The best way to provide this is through examples though. If you have kids who are giving their lives to Christ and are getting baptized, encourage them to do it during youth group. Bring them up front at the end of the service and allow them to talk to the group. Have the whole group watch them get baptized. By doing it during youth group, your non-Christians get an eye-witness account of how to accept Christ.

Teach Students How to Be Evangelistic

If your heart bleeds for evangelism and you've created a climate for it, the final thing you need to do is teach your students how to do it. I came up with a simple method of evangelism that I believe is the best way to teach evangelism and more importantly live evangelism. It is called the S.T.A.R. Method.

Shine

If you want to bring someone to Christ the first thing you must do is shine. You must live the life in front of them. Jesus said in Matthew 5:14 that, "You are the light of the world." He also said in Matthew 5:16 "Let your light shine before men, that they may see your good deeds and praise your Father in heaven." If you will live the life in front of non-Christians, they will take notice of your joy, service, love, and compassion and ask you about God.

The problem is most students haven't figured out how to shine all the time. They are more like lightning bugs. They will shine for a second and then go out, shine, go out, shine, etc. A lightning bug only gives you a glimpse of the light for a second. The only way for a lightning bug to stay lit is for it to die. Take it and smear it across the sidewalk and it will shine for a long time. Christians need to take a lesson from the lightning bug. The only way for a Christian to shine all the time is to die. You must die to yourself and live for Christ, and by doing so you will reveal God to the world. Live a life of goodness, righteousness, and truth, for in this way you will shine. (Eph. 5:8-9)

Talk

To live a good life and to shine in front of people is where you start, but if that is all you do, you have done nothing because all you have done is teach people how to be a good person. There are a lot of good people in the world who are on their way to hell. I've heard many youth ministers take the easy road and tell their students all they have to do is live the life in front of people. "How, then, can they call on the one they have not believed in? And how can they believe in the one of whom they have not heard? And how can they hear without someone preaching to them?" (Rom. 10:14).

If you are going to be a star, you must talk. You must open up your mouth at some point and tell people about Christ. When Peter and John were in prison, the Sanhedrin said they would release them as long as they never talked about Jesus again, and they replied, "for we cannot help speaking about what we have seen and heard" (Acts 4:20). Peter and John said that there was no way for them not to talk. They had a message in them that had to get out because they had seen God and heard God. They knew that they would not be able to be quiet. Jeremiah 20:9 says, "But if I say, 'I will not mention him or speak any more in his name, his word is in my heart like a fire, a fire shut up in my bones. I am weary of holding it in; indeed, I cannot.'" We need to recapture that intensity.

To talk doesn't mean that you stand on a street corner and shout out Scripture all day. What it means is that you look for every opportunity to bring God into your conversations with others. Many times it will be little hints of God. But by doing that you will be ready when the time is right to challenge someone to think about their relationship with God.

One way that I talk to a non-Christian is I often leave him with a thought. When I've met a non-Christian and I am finished talking to him, I will always say, "I want you to know that I love you and God loves you." I purposefully say this and in that order. People are used to hearing that God loves them, but they aren't used to hearing a guy they hardly know say he loves them. By saying, "I love you," I immediately catch him off guard and hit him in his heart by attaching value to him. Then I come in with, "and God loves you." Since his heart and mind is open, I notice that he actually hears me say, "God loves you," rather than just letting it come in one ear and out the other.

Action

If you want to be a star you have to be ready for action. You must be ready for who God is going to bring into your life today. First Peter 3:15 says, "Always be prepared to give an answer to everyone who asks you to give the reason for the hope that you have. But do so with gentleness and respect." Every morning you must wake up knowing that God is going to bring someone into your life today to whom you are going to have the opportunity to witness. It might be a stranger on the street, a lady at a cash register, or your best friend. If you're not ready for action then you will miss this moment in eternity's timeline.

I missed an opportunity to witness to a waitress, Amy, at Chili's once. One night after I had preached at a youth rally, the worship band and I went to get something to eat. While we were there, our waitress started asking us several questions. They weren't deep spiritual questions, but they were searching questions. As we pulled out of the parking lot that night, I saw Amy standing in the window watching us drive away, and that is when it hit me. I saw right through her eyes into her heart and saw a girl crying out. I lay in my hotel bed that night and wept because I missed an opportunity. I gave her some answers but I didn't give her God.

Be ready for action by being ready to answer people and do so with gentleness and respect. I've heard students defending their faith to their friends. They raise their voices and act irritated that they would question them on why they do certain things. If you are acting like a star, you will be questioned. That is the whole idea. Therefore, make sure when you answer people, you do so with gentleness and respect. Don't be mean. Don't raise your voice. Don't make them feel ignorant. Realize that they are non-Christians, and this is your opportunity to talk to them.

Reason

The reason you evangelize people is that if you don't, they will burn in hell. There are people you come in contact with every day who are on the road to hell, and it is your job to save them. Jude 23 says, "snatch others from the fire and save them." God has entrusted his people to rescue sinners from the fires of hell. Students need to be taught that they need to reach out to everyone, no matter what they are like, because they shouldn't want anyone to burn. Let's quit reaching out to white, middle class America only and start reaching out to everyone: friends, family, rich, poor, tattooed, homeless, enemies, sick, and addicts. Hell is real, and you need to save people from it.

I have written a poem entitled, "I'm a Star" that sums this all up. (Inspired by "The Fellowship of the Unashamed," author unknown.)

I am a star . . . not the type of star you are used to seeing. I am not famous. I am not popular. I am not the best at anything. I am not the strongest, smartest, richest, best looking, or best dressed. But I am a star.

I am a star because I shine. I have turned the switch on, plugged the power source in, turned the brightness up, and I am going to blind people with my light. People will see God through me because he is in me.

I am a star because I am going to talk. I cannot keep it in. I have a message in me that is a burning fire. My message gives hope for the hurting, grace to the ungodly, and life to the lost. My message is found in the Word. My message is in my hand, and I am holding it out there for everyone to see, and I will preach until everyone has heard. I will not shut up.

I am a star that is always ready for action. I am not sitting on the shelf. I am not plastered to the pew. I am not saving it for Sundays. I am lighting it up. I am going where he sends, listening to his voice, following his call. I am ready to make ripples in this world. I am ready for action.

I am a star for a reason. I have a passion for lost people. I must save them from the fire. I will not let them ponder on possibilities. Death is certain. Heaven is perfect. Hell is pain. Judgment is permanent. I will save my friends, my family, my classmates, and my enemies. I will save the good people and the bad ones, the athletes and the geeks, the prom kings and the street queens. I will love the unlovable, touch the untouchable and serve the unservable. I will save people from the fire.

I am a star because I have been delivered. My body has been bought. My foul-ups have been forgiven and my soul has been sealed. My Deliverer is sending me out to deliver a message of deliverance.

Therefore I will be a star in the face of fear, in the midst of martyrdom, and in the presence of the principalities of this present world. A star has been born and I am going to shout it out . . . I am a star . . . for the SUPERSTAR![8]

Paul challenged us to be stars in Philippians 2:15. Teach your students to be stars and you will teach them how to live a life of evangelism.

I saw Alice and Travis several more times that weekend in New Orleans. Each time I saw them, they sought me out and we talked some more. I talked to them about the beautiful Catholic church that we stood in front of. I was able to tell a store manager that Alice was a friend of mine when she tried to kick her out of her store. We had many conversations, and during the last one she asked me, "What type of minister buys a homeless person a beer?" That was the moment I had been waiting for. I replied, "Alice, the type of minister that wants you to know that he loves you and God loves you." And with that tears of joy came to her eyes and a kiss of love was planted on my cheek. I didn't have to judge her for her lifestyle, but rather encourage her to love Christ.

Time for Reflection

1. Does your heart break over the sin of the world? Can others see your passion to win the lost? If others can't see it, then it doesn't exist.
2. Do you purposely put yourself in places to feel the needs of a lost youth culture, or do you live a sheltered, protected life? What can you do to change? Where would you go to best understand teen culture in your town or city?
3. Does your youth program welcome newcomers? Do you have a specific plan in place to be sure they are recognized and welcomed?
4. Do you have a specific plan to teach your young people how to evangelize such as the S.T.A.R. method?

SUGGESTED READING LIST

Hahn, Todd, and David Verhaagen. *GenXers after God*. Grand Rapids: Baker Books, 1998.

McAllister, Dawson. *Saving the Millennial Generation*. Nashville: Thomas Nelson, 1999.

NOTES ON CHAPTER TWENTY-FOUR

1. Todd Hahn and David Verhaagen, *GenXers after God* (Grand Rapids: Baker Books, 1998), p. 68.
2. Jim Burns, *The Youth Builder* (Eugene, OR: Harvest House, 1988), p. 71.
3. Rick Caldwell, "Evangelism through Youth Ministry," in *The Complete Book of Youth Ministry*, Warren S. Benson and Mark H. Senter III (Chicago: Moody, 1987), p. 313.
4. Hahn and Verhaagen, *GenXers*, p. 41.
5. Wesley Black, *An Introduction to Youth Ministry* (Nashville: Broadman Press, 1991), p. 209.

6. Dawson McAllister, *Saving the Millennial Generation* (Nashville: Thomas Nelson, 1999), p. 124.

7. Chap Clark, "The Missional Approach to Youth Ministry," in *Four Views of Youth Ministry and the Church,* ed. by Mark H. Senter III (Grand Rapids: Zondervan, 2001), p. 79.

8. Unpublished poem by Josh Finklea. Used by permission.

"Ministry, least of all youth ministry, was never intended to be a service profession. Ministry is the grateful response of God's people, whose activity in the world and with one another suggests a new way of being alive. Ministry is not something we 'do' to someone else. It is a holy way of living toward God and toward one another."
—*Mark DeVries*[1]

"Youth ministry begins when a Christian finds a mutually comfortable way to enter a young person's world. Ministry starts with a relationship. The youth ministry models of the later twentieth century have, for the most part, been 'come' models, in which students have brought peers to Christian adult-sponsored activities." —*Chap Clark*[2]

Chapter 25
What Does a Youth Ministry Look Like?

Dr. Gary B. Zustiak

Programs in Youth Ministry

A philosophy of ministry must be developed before serious programming can take place. Programming will flow out of the youth minister's philosophy of ministry. There are a number of different programming models that have been used in the church. There is no "one" right model for every church. The programming model that you choose should flow out of your philosophy of youth ministry and take into consideration the needs of the youth, your resources—both staff and facilities, and the strengths and spiritual gifts of you and your staff.

Realize that whatever program you choose, it is simply a vehicle. It is a means for you to meet and develop caring relationships with young people.

The most effective way to meet kids one-on-one is to go places they go, and do things with them. Many youth pastors are just hirelings—they produce a program. A youth pastor with a shepherding mentality, rather than that of the hireling, will produce a ministry. He wants to accomplish several things. First, he wants to give his young people a taste of what he has—a personal faith in Christ. Secondly, he wants to help them mature and begin grooming them for the future—training and developing them so that they, too, can minister.[3]

Understand that the youth ministry models that will be presented may not all be appropriate for every situation. Even if you are very sincere and enthusiastic, you could still fail miserably in attempting to implement the model of your choice for several reasons. First of all, the situation may not be appropriate. In choosing a youth ministry program which best fits the church where you are called, you must take into consideration your personal philosophy of ministry, the demographics of the community, the church, resources, needs of the community and church, and the overall philosophy of ministry of the church as a whole.

Your abilities and gifts might not be suitable. You may have a desire to implement a discipleship model of youth ministry, but your interpersonal skills may be such that you are just not adept at leading in a small group setting. You may even choose the Hero or Bright Light approach, but find that you don't have the personality to pull it off.

The Holy Spirit might be working to bring about something unforeseen by either the youth minister or the people in the church. God is not bound by any of the boxes that we want to put Him in. While you might think a particular program is the answer, God may have something totally new and exciting in mind for you and your church if you will only be open to His leading.

Understand, also, that while I use the term "program," youth ministry is really a strategy, not a program. This applies to every aspect of youth ministry, such as Sunday school or Friday nights. They are not programs—they are part of the strategy. The "program" is to influence the lives of young people towards Christlike living. The only basis of effective ministry is within the context of relationships. Youth programs must be designed to foster relationships between young people and their friends, the youth leaders, and other significant adults who have input in their lives. Programs and structures are only important insofar as they promote relationship building between teens, God, and one another.

Youth ministry is more about ministry than about youth, for Jesus Christ calls young people—like all of us—into ministry and not into a youth program. Authentic ministry with youth is not just about spiritual discipline; it is a spiritual discipline. Youth ministry, like all ministry, requires and provides spiritual nourishment for pastors as well as for young people. In practice, this means that when our own life with God catches fire, the souls of youth and our congregations ignite as well.[4]

The Hero Model

What are some typical programs that form the basis of a youth ministry? Duffy Robbins lists several of the main designs found throughout the evangelical world.[5] The first he calls "The Hero." This is also referred to as the "bright light" approach and is found among many parachurch youth ministries. It's based on the theory that on a dark night, the brightest light in the neighborhood will attract the most moths. This model suggests that we build youth programs around a central personality, a charismatic figure who naturally appeals to teenagers. As this "Bright-Light Knight" attracts students, those students will in turn attract other students, and so on.

The strength of this model is that it is incarnational and relational. The Hero is an individual who is willing and able to get close to kids and to build significant relationships with them.

Several weaknesses are inherent in this model. It often breeds mavericks, Lone Rangers—people who tend to shine better and brighter when they work on their own. "That means it will be very difficult to build any kind of effective team ministry into the program."[6] Without a diversity of adult models, it will be limited in the number of kids it can reach. Lone Rangers often lack in accountability as well. And finally, a program built around a personality may fail quickly when that person leaves.

The Involvement Model

The "Involvement Model" is very common. There are a number of ways that a church can get students involved in some kind of a program—everything from puppet ministries, ministry teams, clowning, drama teams, youth choirs, Bible bowl, and various athletic programs. Some programs are focused on the group, such as praise teams, multimedia teams, while others are aimed outside the group in terms of outreach.

One strength of this model is that it makes belonging to a youth group more than a spectator event. The teens are active members of the church body. It can give the church a powerful outreach into the community which translates into a positive evangelistic impact.

A weakness of this model is that it doesn't adequately attend to nurture and discipleship, so the result is that we occasionally end up sending out half-filled Christians who are trying to overflow. Students, especially those in leadership, may make the mistake of equating involvement with spirituality. One can be involved in a good number of activities and still neglect his/her spiritual life.

The Spring Break Model

The "Spring Break" model emphasizes a host of exciting activities: bowling, Six Flags, bungee jump, burger bash, kidnap breakfasts, mud wrestling mania, etc. These bring in big crowds, are high profile events, and produce a lot of excitement. But the down side is that they are weak on content. Plus there is the time-proven adage: "You win them to what you win them with." When the fun and games cease and the challenge to discipleship and commitment starts, how many of these kids will walk out the door because they only came for the "fun stuff?"

"You win them to what you win them with."

The Discipleship Model

The Discipleship model emphasizes heavy-duty discipleship and Bible study. These are the folks who may not have a big group, but the kids who are there are getting serious in-depth, teaching. The focus is to train students to be God's people in an ungodly world, equipped with Bible study and prayer skills developed in a caring atmosphere with a view to reproducing their Christian lives in others. This includes weekly Scripture memory, workbooks, accountability groups—the works. The Wesleyan tradition is founded on this model. The Navigators also use the same strategies.

Small group meetings are the basis of the discipleship model. These usually consist of four to six students and an adult leader. These D-groups meet weekly to hold members accountable for Bible study, prayer, Scripture memorization, and evangelistic efforts. D-group group leaders meetings are used to keep the ministry headed in a unified direction.

Sometimes youth ministers who follow this model take it to the extreme. You might hear one say something like: "We don't have time to mess around with fun and games, Mickey Mouse activities. If kids don't want to get serious about Jesus, they can go elsewhere."[7]

The positive side of this is that these kids are into hard-core, industrial strength discipleship. The weakness is that it has little outreach appeal. Many kids do go elsewhere . . . and not always to another church, but to something fun the world has to offer.

The Ministry Model

The Ministry model has emerged in recent years with an emphasis on work projects, missions, and service. "The Ministry model develops student ministry skills and a context in which to use those skills through carefully planned exposure to human and spiritual needs outside the cultural context of the church, enhanced through meeting similar needs to the community surrounding the church and supported by accountability groups within the youth group."[8]

This is the youth group that runs a Kids' Club in the inner city, raises money for a mission trip to Haiti, sponsors three Compassion children, and serves as peer counselors at the local crisis pregnancy center. The emphasis of the Ministry model is the opposite of the Spring Break model. Instead of a "me-centered" fun and games approach, the Ministry model's purpose is to involve young people in worthy projects and take the focus off of themselves. The Scripture motto for this model would be, "Be *doers* of the Word and not just hearers only."

One of the obvious advantages of the ministry model is its focus on serving others, rather than gratifying the teens' desires and wants. It is also a great witness to the community at large, for it shows the world that not all teenagers are selfish, drug using, party-crazed animals. The danger of this model is that you may have young people who are involved in worthy projects, without really understanding *why* they should be involved in the first place. The involvement level needs to be balanced with teaching and discipleship, otherwise you may end up with a group of teens who are trying to minister to others while their own spiritual lives are suffering or in danger. Genuine service should flow out of a solid theology and biblical understanding of the needs of the world and the Christian's obligation to meet those needs.

The Purpose-Driven Model

By far the most popular model at this point in time for youth ministry is the "Purpose-Driven"[9] model developed by Rick Warren, senior minister at Saddleback Church, and adapted by Doug Fields, his youth minister. This model is based on the concept of concentric circles representing different groups of people with increasing levels of commitment and involvement.[10]

Those five groups are: The Community, The Crowd, The Congregation, The Committed, and The Core. This model aims to draw people from the outside through to the center. The decreasing sizes of the circles indicate the decreasing numbers of people in each level, as the required commitment to the church increases. The Purpose-Driven model also includes five main

purposes of the church. These purposes should be in evidence throughout every ministry of the church, although some ministries will focus more specifically on certain purposes more than others. Additionally, different purposes are emphasized at the different levels of commitment and involvement (although all purposes are relevant at all levels). The five purposes are: Evangelism, Worship, Fellowship, Discipleship, and Ministry.

There are several advantages to this model. First of all, it has a clear plan on how to reach out to the lost (the community). Once an interest is shown, there are specific steps set in place to move them toward a Christian commitment, discipleship, and eventually leadership. Secondly, the purposes for the church that are identified are very biblical. You don't have to worry that your program may not be in accord with God's will for the church.

The only real criticism I have of this model is that it does not seem to have an adequate emphasis on missions—foreign outreach. It has a concern for the lost in the community and a plan to reach them, but doesn't address the issue of the lost in foreign lands.

The Commitment-Level Model

Another model which is similar to the Purpose Driven model is "The Commitment-Level Model."[11] Rather than using concentric circles, this model uses a funnel to illustrate its purpose and function. Obviously, you start at the top and work your way down. The different levels in this model are the Pre-Christian, Seeker, New Convert, Believer, Worker, and Leader. Similar to the Purpose-Driven model, more commitment and participation is required of people as they go deeper into the funnel. The funnel gets smaller as it gets to the bottom in order to show that less people will be involved at higher commitment levels. Worship services planned for and led by young people are at the heart of the model. Worship teams composed of young people prepare the component parts of the worship service, which could include music, drama, dance, media, Scripture reading, and other forms of visual art. Shepherding groups provide a way for all who attend the youth church to be present or accounted for.

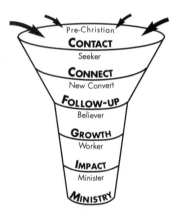

Much like the Purpose-Driven model, the commitment-level or funnel model starts with outreach and has a specific plan to move people toward a greater commitment to Christ and involvement in the ministry of the church. But it doesn't really address the problem of what to do with those people who have grown up in the church and are either callused to ministry or simply satisfied with their spiritual level of maturity and have no desire to grow. It is also somewhat vague as to what exactly should be done at each of the levels of ministry and how distinct these activities should be.

The Competition Model

The competition model uses natural leaders from the high school subculture, who are trained to serve as servants and motivators to their teams in the context of team competition, to attract and hold high school students for a confrontation with a biblical message.

The premier example of this kind of program was the Son City program of Willow Creek. For many years this was considered the "ultimate" youth ministry model because of its ability to attract large numbers of kids.

Major activities would be weeknight meetings using team competition, music modeled after the current popular music, dramatic vignettes related to the theme of the evening's talk, media presentations, and low-key sermons based on some topic that the majority of kids could identify with, such as "getting along with your parents," "developing a healthy self-esteem," or "love, sex, and dating," etc. It was basically a "seeker-service" for teens with an emphasis on evangelism.

For a more in-depth study, discipleship meetings were provided for those students who wanted to experience more of the biblical "meat." These were offered on a different night than the team competition nights.

One of the strengths of this program is that, if it is done correctly, it has the ability to attract large numbers of teens. The program offers a high level of excitement and the multimedia is very attractive to the techno-minded teens. The down-to-earth talks make the Bible seem relevant to the millennial mind.

It also does a good job of involving the youth as student leaders. They are not left just to sit and watch the adults do the program, they have an active role. It rewards them for being evangelism minded. For every friend they invite who comes to a meeting, they receive extra points for their team.

One of the negative aspects of the competition model is that it requires a significant financial investment. Sound systems, media equipment, athletic paraphernalia, and staff salaries are just a few of the costs the competition model will incur.

An even more serious criticism is that students can end up feeling "used." They come under the guise of being wanted and loved, and then find out they only mean 500 more points to someone's team. An increase in attendance is not worth the price that you pay in authentic relationships. When the students figure this out, they will begin to vote with their feet. One young person who left a growing ministry because of the focus on team competition wrote his youth ministry and said, "If you ever stop playing games and start caring about people again, let me know. When I became a number and not a person, I felt like it was time to find another church family."[12]

Preach

It son.

A fear of mine

If students can only attend one youth group meeting a week, then the constant diet of "church lite" is not going to ground them doctrinally or help prepare them for the attacks on their faith they are sure to encounter when they enter college.

The Safe-Place Model

The safe-place model uses the equipment and facilities of a church or parachurch organization in conjunction with the presence of loving Christian adults who spend time with them and earn the right to be heard. The adults then have the opportunity to reach out to the kids and build spiritually accountable relationships with them.

YMCA and YWCA were among the first to use this model. Safe places take the forms of group homes for young people, tutoring labs, skateboard parks, gyms, and Christian coffee houses. The major activities of this model stress using a ministry vehicle such as a recreation room, gym, weight room, coffee house, or a group home to provide an opening to build relationships with students who may otherwise remain untouched by the church. The activities are not an end in themselves, but are an opportunity to gain a hearing for the gospel.

"The effectiveness of these ministries is built upon the ability of the leadership to remain focused on the power of the gospel to transform lives."[13] The place where this model is especially useful is the inner city where physical safety really is an everyday issue for the children growing up in the neighborhood.

One of the positive aspects of this ministry is that it is usually a parachurch organization that follows this model. The staff does not have to dress and look like "typical" ministry staff. They can hang with the kids and not stick out like a sore thumb. Their work hours and methods can be unorthodox and no board member is going to become unglued.

Because inner city kids do not have many resources of their own, the gym and recreational center have a built-in attraction. Kids with nothing else to do are naturally going to hang out at the center. This gives the staff ample opportunity to build relationships and to invite them to Bible studies.

There are several drawbacks to this model. The first is that many of the parachurch organizations that I am familiar with who operate under the "safe place" model do not do a good job of integrating the young people into a local church. Also, what does a young person do when he grows up and is too old to attend the "youth club" at the local center? It is also possible that, while relationship building is an important aspect of youth ministry, the safe-place model may place too much emphasis upon this aspect of ministry without balancing the need for solid Bible teaching in the life of the young person.

The Family-Based Model

The importance of this model is seen in the fact that I have deemed it necessary to include an entire chapter on family-based youth ministry. Please refer to the following chapter for more pertinent details. In the family-based model, parents accept the responsibility for the spiritual growth and character development of their children. They do not try to do this in isolation, but in the context of the extended family of the church.

Bill Gothard, with his *Institute for Basic Youth Conflicts*, and James Dobson's *Focus on the Family* were a few of the first to again emphasize the priority of the family in youth spiritual formation. Mark DeVries book, *Family Based Youth Ministry,* was the first to challenge the traditional model of youth ministry and to give a detailed account of the importance of family-based youth ministry.

In order for this model to work, the parents must be sold on the importance of their involvement with their own children and be willing to put in the extra time that it will take to pull it off. They must be willing to coordinate their family schedules with the activities of the church and youth group. Obviously this is not a program that you can force parents to participate in. It also has the unique problem of what to do with the students whose parents are not Christians or do not attend church.

The Christian-School Model

With the spread of Christian schools across the country, some believe that the need for the traditional youth group has decreased. Proponents of the Christian-school model believe the following to be true:

The Christian school model builds young people into well-rounded Christian adults using the Christian high school as a social, academic, and spiritual laboratory, shaped by Christian teachers and administrators who share and foster a Christian worldview, so that as adults the graduates will live as Christians in a non-Christian world.[14]

The relational aspects of some churches' ministry to students has shifted to the Christian high school. The negative aspect of this model is the lack of attention to the young person who is enrolled in public school, but who attends a church whose main emphasis is its Christian school and not a dynamic youth program. This student gets the short end of the stick and is the one who probably needs the in-depth Bible training more than any of the others.

The idea is that the Christian high school provides a Christian worldview as well as social activities for the majority of students from Christian homes, which decreases the need for traditional youth functions. Again, this is great for the students whose parents can afford to pay the tuition for a private school, but what about the student who chooses to attend public school?

In this model, the principal of the school and the faculty have the primary role of discipleship. Parents provide support for the ministry and the youth minister participates by helping bridge the gap between public and private school students.

The Inclusive Congregational Approach

The inclusive congregational approach to youth ministry believes that youth ministry should not be separate from the main church body. It should not take place in isolation, creating a youth ministry ghetto. "Youth ministry is not about finding an extra place for yet another ministry, but about finding a place for youths within every ministry and among the people that the ministries are designed to reach and serve."[15]

The strength of this approach is that it recognizes that youth are important and should not be marginalized when it comes to genuine ministry opportunities within the life of the body. It has a noble premise, that of including the youth in all aspects of congregational life.

But I fear the weakness of this approach is that a church's efforts to include youth may be reduced to tokenism, in which the youth only appear to have a genuine stake in the various ministries. It is probably easier to talk about including youth in the life of the church than actually doing it. The congregation may truly want the youth to participate with them, but they may want them to participate *as adults.* In other words, do it the way we would do it and like the forms of ministry that we like. This ends up stifling the introduction of any new worship material and making young people feel rejected because they are not allowed to have input on the kind of worship style or preaching they would prefer.

Conclusion

Understand that one programming model is not necessarily better than others. They all have their distinct strengths and weaknesses. What you need to strive for is developing a balance. A healthy model is one that is able to meet the diverse needs of teenagers at various levels of Christian commitment. A common error in developing a program is trying to come up with one program that meets the needs of all the students in one event a week. It simply won't work. If you program to meet the needs of your deeply committed kids, you run the risk of running off the seekers. If you try to make it too entertaining, the spiritual kids starve to death. Realize that you will need multiple levels of programming, and recruit the kind of staff that can make it happen.

Time for Reflection

1. Which model of youth ministry best fits your situation and gifts?
2. If you were to build your own model of youth ministry, what would it look like?
3. Does every church have to follow the same model of ministry? Why or why not?
4. Do you have to limit your program to following just one model, or is it possible to mix several models? If so, which ones would you like to mix together? Why?

SUGGESTED READING LIST

Fields, Doug. *Purpose Driven Youth Ministry.* Grand Rapids: Zondervan, 1998.

Rice, Wayne, Chap Clark, et al. *New Directions for Youth Ministry.* Loveland, CO: Group, 1998.

Senter, Mark H., ed. *Four Views of Youth Ministry and the Church*. Grand Rapids: Zondervan, 2001.

Notes on Chapter Twenty-five

1. Kenda Creasy Dean and Ron Foster, *The Godbearing Life* (Nashville: Upper Room Books, 1998), p. 9.

2. Mark H. Senter, "Introduction," in *New Directions for Youth Ministry*, ed. by Wayne Rice, Chap Clark, et al. (Loveland, CO: Group, 1998), p. 8.

3. E.G. von Trutzschler, "Youth Ministry Is More Than a Meeting," in *The Youth Leader's Sourcebook*, ed. by Gary Dausey (Grand Rapids: Zondervan, 1983), p. 39.

4. Dean and Foster, *Godbearing*, p. 17.

5. He cites the Involvement, Relevancy, Spring Break, King James, and Boot Camp as common youth ministry models. See: Duffy Robbins, "More Than a Meeting: Programming as Discipleship," *Youthworker* (Summer 1992).

6. Ibid.

7. Ibid.

8. Mark H. Senter III, "Basic Models for Youth Ministry," in *Reaching a Generation for Christ*, ed. by Richard R. Dunn and Mark H. Senter III (Chicago: Moody, 1997), p. 180.

9. Illustration taken from Fields, *Purpose Driven*, p. 87.

10. See Ibid., pp. 95-97.

11. Illustration taken from Mark Tittley, **http://www.sonlifeafrica.com/model/main.htm**.

12. Doug Fields, *Your First Two Years in Youth Ministry* (Grand Rapids: Zondervan, 2002), p. 85.

13. Senter, "Basic Models," p. 187.

14. Ibid., p. 166.

15. Malan Nel, "The Inclusive Congregational Approach to Youth Ministry," in *Four Views of Youth Ministry and the Church*, ed. by Mark H. Senter III (Grand Rapids: Zondervan, 2001), p. 6.

Chapter 26

Family-Based Youth Ministry

Dr. Gary B. Zustiak

The Power of the Family on Character Formation

Historically youth ministry has been carried out in isolation from the family. The youth minister was seen as the "professional" who understood the needs of youth, talked their language, liked their music, and communicated God's word to them in exciting and creative ways. Parents were often left out of the picture. The task of educating and training young people for Christian service was turned over to the "expert." Parents were even occasionally portrayed as hindrances to effective youth ministry because they opposed some of the new ideas and changes that the youth minister wanted to introduce into the youth program. Parents were only valuable for their monetary support and providing transportation to and from youth events. The youth minister was in charge and he took total control.

The error and failure of this model in its ineffectiveness and inability to produce long-lasting spiritual results wasn't seen until a number of the young people had graduated from the youth program. The lack of long-lasting change and commitment in the lives of many young people forced youth ministers to reevaluate their effectiveness.

They found that they were not as powerful an influence as they had once hoped and believed. Indeed, over and over again the research showed that it is the *parent's* values, attitudes, and relationship that have the greatest long-term effect on youth.

> Youth workers are becoming increasingly aware that a student-only youth ministry is less effective than a family-friendly youth ministry. Because we rarely see students in their family context, we often underestimate the power of the family. Each student in our youth ministry is the product of a unique family system, a system responsible for forming beliefs, values, and actions. If we plan to effectively minister to students over the long haul, we must sincerely desire to minister to entire families, because a youth ministry that excludes parents is about as effective as a Band-Aid on a hemorrhage.[4]

In a survey of *Teenage Magazine* readers, 66% of the teens surveyed said their family had the most influence on their lives while only 27% said that peers did. Youth ministers weren't even on the list![5]

While the youth themselves are not always aware of just how important their parents are in influencing their values and choices, and parents question their own effectiveness, the fact is that parents are the primary influences of teenagers, both now and in later years when the youth minister is long gone. In light of this, it is my conclusion that the critical test of a youth ministry's long-term effectiveness is the ability of the youth minister to develop an effective family ministry as an integral part of the total youth program.

In a survey of Teenage Magazine readers, 66% of the teens surveyed said their family had the most influence on their lives while only 27% said that peers did. Youth ministers weren't even on the list!

One of my working assumptions is that the contemporary crisis in youth ministry has little to do with programming and everything to do with families. Our culture has put an incredible amount of emotional weight on the shoulders of the nuclear family, a weight which I believe families were never intended to bear alone. One of the secrets to a lasting ministry with teenagers is to find ways to undergird nuclear families with the rich support of the extended Christian family of the church and for these two formative families to work together in leading young people toward mature Christian adulthood.[6]

The importance of the family in the moral and spiritual development of teens cannot be overstated. Consider the impact the family has on the development of teens from the following:

- Search Institute, in a broad-based 1990 study of Protestant congregations, found that the level of the "family's religiousness" was the single strongest predictor of faith maturity in young people.
- In families where neither parent attends church regularly, only 6% of the children will grow up to be faithful to Christ. If only mom attends regularly, 15% remain faithful. If only dad is consistent in his attendance, 55% remain faithful. But in families were both parents are regular in attendance, 72% of their children remain faithful.
- A *USA Today* survey found that 76% of 1,200 teens surveyed *wanted* their parents to spend more time with them.
- Young people who are fortified with significant relationships with adults are consistently the ones who are able to resist involvement in negative behaviors and are highly resistant to peer influence.
- While peers sometimes exercise more control over a teen's choice of dress, music, entertainment, etc., only when parents are extremely negligent do peers exercise more control over the teen's choice of beliefs and values. Parents are still the number one influence.
- National Merit Scholars looked for common factors that influenced teen's development of high achievement. One common factor: They eat dinner with their families almost every day.
- According to the 1990 Search Institute Report only 15% of men between the ages of 40–59 have a mature, integrated faith. In other words, 85% of our young people come from homes without a father to set an example of faithful discipleship.
- Teens who are living with both of their original parents are two to six times more likely to be involved in church than young people who live with single parents or a step-parent.
- In 1940 at least one grandparent was a full-time, active member of approximately 60–70% of all households. Today, fewer than 2% have a grandparent available as a resource.
- A 1995 federally funded study of more than 12,000 7–12th grade teens published in *The Journal of the American Medical*

Association found that the more teenagers feel loved by their parents the less likely they are to have early sex, smoke, abuse alcohol or drugs, or commit violence or suicide.

Why the Previous Neglect of Family Ministry?

If the influence of the family is so powerful, why have youth ministers been so reluctant to incorporate parents into the overall youth program? There are several reasons. Historically the first wave of youth ministers came out of the late '60s and early '70s. Culturally this was a period of rebellion, the generation gap, and the mentality "don't trust anyone over thirty." Unwittingly, many youth ministers reflected and incorporated this spirit of rebellion into their philosophy of youth ministry. So a kind of "me-versus-them" mentality developed which pitted the youth minister against parents and authority.

A kind of "me-versus-them" mentality developed which pitted the youth minister against parents and authority.

Youth ministers were often afraid or intimidated by parents because of an earlier experience where a parent had attacked and criticized them (whether justly or unjustly) over some aspect of the youth program that did not meet with their approval. This left the youth minister "gun-shy" and wary of any involvement or input from parents.

Pride was another issue. When parents questioned the value of a particular program or event, the youth minister took it as a personal attack upon his leadership skills and ability. After all, he was the "expert" on youth, and who were they to challenge his ideas?!

Many youth ministers viewed parents as simply "out-of-touch" with the youth culture and didn't see them as having anything of value to offer the program. All of these negative attitudes seriously impaired the effectiveness of youth ministry. If youth ministry is to be redeemed, it will take place when the youth minister learns how to minister to and listen to the concerns of parents.

Chap Clark lists eight mistakes that a traditional youth ministry often makes which hurt families.

1. Not considering family times and needs when scheduling youth events.
2. Assuming the role of parents.
3. Making parents look bad.

4. Not keeping parents informed.
5. Not encouraging or offering support for families.
6. Undermining parents' judgment or authority.
7. Not including families in youth events.
8. Failing to connect teenagers with the extended church family.[7]

The Purpose of Family-Friendly (Family-Based) Youth Ministry

The youth ministry program in the local church must see its purpose as supporting the family, not as a replacement for the family. Although some parents would gladly give their responsibilities to the youth minister and let the church do the rest, this does not serve the best interests of any of the parties involved. "The church, the youth group and the youth worker never can be adequate substitutes for parents. Most children grow in their faith more from watching and living with models of that faith at home *The youth ministry program in the local church must see its purpose as supporting the family, not as a replacement for the family.* than they ever will from youth group meetings, retreats and sermons put together."[8] Dewey Bertolini has said, "Youth workers are to function as 'paraparents.' From the Greek preposition *para*, paraparents defines our role as that of literally 'coming alongside' the parents, offering the best source of support they will find anywhere."[9] The youth minister must not merely do for the youth what their parents cannot, or will not, do for them. Instead, the youth minister must endeavor to equip those parents to communicate the faith and to minister to the spiritual and developmental needs of their teenagers themselves.

As families are ministered to and strengthened, the individual development and quality of the teenagers' lives improves. Research has shown that the strength of the relationship between parents and their teenagers fortifies teenagers with the courage to make wise choices. The study found that teenagers from close families were the least likely to be involved in high-risk behavior.[10]

While you wait for your teenagers to grow up, you can take comfort in the fact that by the time young people reach their midtwenties, their lines are almost always identical to the lines their parents drew. Even those who do not like certain attributes of their parents find themselves following their parents' patterns. So perhaps the point is not how we can get our kids to behave as we want them to, but how we can be the kind of parents we ought to be so that when our kids are like us, we'll like what they are.[11]

Ways to Implement Family-Based Youth Ministry

I believe the biggest change will be in attitude rather than in direction or program components. Be advised that neither parents nor students want a totally integrated parent-teen youth ministry. Although parents are more open to a family-friendly youth ministry than students, most appreciate a youth ministry *for* their kids and not *with* their kids. And it is no surprise that most students prefer the traditional compartmentalized youth ministry where they can have an autonomous church experience away from their parents.[12]

When beginning a family-friendly youth ministry, understand that the change should not be sudden or all at once. It should take place gradually with a series of progressive steps that build on one another and lead toward a stronger family focus. There are several different ways that it can be approached. *The first thing that needs to happen is for youth ministers to come to the realization that parents are not the enemy!* That may come from education, maturity, or parenthood on the part of the youth minister.

The next step is to *get to know the parents.* The youth minister should make a concerted effort to meet parents and learn their names. In fact, part of the youth minister's calling time in the home should be directed towards getting to know the parents better, their dreams, frustrations, and areas where they need to be ministered to. Visit them on their job site, take them out for coffee, or eat lunch with them.

You can't be a family-friendly youth ministry and demand that students be out of the home several nights a week.

The next thing that can be done on the part of the youth minister is to *develop a youth ministry philosophy and schedule that is sensitive to family priorities.* Families are already pulled in many different directions. Often the church only adds to the fragmentation while outwardly professing to support the importance of family time together. "You can't be a family-friendly youth ministry and demand that students be out of the home several nights a week. Teach your students to always check with their parents to decide what programs they will attend."[13]

A very important and practical ministry to parents is to *provide classes and programs which equip parents to effectively nurture their children in the Christian faith.* Another idea is to provide opportunities for teenagers to interact with their parents and other adults and learn through observation and modeling. This interaction is sorely needed and desired by teenagers. A survey in *USA Today* of 1,200 teenagers found that 76% *wanted* their parents to spend more time with them.[14]

What are some specific measures that the youth minister can take which will support the concept of a family-based youth ministry? First, he can *make sure that the parents are informed* about the purpose, goals, and events of the youth program. This can be done through quarterly parent meetings, a parent newsletter, a youth group hot line, and regular calling in the homes of the families.

Next, the youth minister can focus in on *assisting parents.* Most parents are concerned about their child's welfare, moral choices, friends, education, and problems. The youth minister needs to sensitively assist parents in their task of raising their children. This must be done without coming across as a "know-it-all" or implying a judgment upon their parenting abilities. Special parenting seminars, support groups, opportunities for guided interaction, family counseling, occasional Sunday electives for parents of adolescents, and the development of a parents' resource library are all practical ways that the youth ministry program can assist parents.

Parents need to be encouraged. Usually the only time that the spotlight is upon them is when their child has done something wrong! Make it a regular habit to sponsor parent-appreciation events, send thank-you notes, make phone calls that highlight something positive about their teen, and attend special events (recitals, concerts, athletic events) which focus in on the accomplishments of the teen.

Involve parents. Involve them by having a core group pray for the youth program and the families involved in it. Organize a parents' council, utilize parents in short-term service projects and programs, and involve them in regular teen meetings. Find and utilize "been there" parents who can serve as a resource for other parents who are experiencing a frustration with one of their teens in a particular area such as curfew, dating issues, jobs, etc.

Build relationships with parents. Be sure to call on families and spend time getting to know the parents and their needs and struggles, not just those of the children involved in the youth program. Work together on a common project, whether it is something around the home or for the church.

Allow families to spend time together. Be careful not to over-program youth activities so that there is no time left for families to interact. Every school holiday or free afternoon does not have to be taken up with some kind of youth activity.

Model the importance of family ministry in your own life. While it would be easy to schedule seven days a week with different youth and family programs, the youth minister must make the spiritual well-being of his own family a priority. (Learn the lesson of Eli and Samuel.) The most important youth group that the youth minister has is the one found under his own roof. This means the youth minister must be careful not to overcommit himself and to schedule his time wisely.

While it would be easy to be scheduled seven days a week with different youth and family programs, the youth minister must make the spiritual well-being of his own family a priority.

Help the family make some traditions. Traditions are important to families. The Jewish culture included many important traditions concerning the worship of God that families did together, such as the Passover and other feast days. I would encourage you to start some traditions in your own family and to help the families in your church start some of their own.

Our family started some unique traditions that are still special to our children. We have even passed them down to the grandchildren. Several of them revolve around the Christmas season. When the children were young, my wife bought an advent calendar and each day before Christmas the boys took turns opening the door and discovering the prize and verse behind it.

On Christmas Eve my wife started the tradition of serving a clam chowder dinner. There is nothing biblical or particularly spiritual about clam chowder, but it became special to our family. It was easy to fix and warm on a cold winter's night. Now it doesn't seem like Christmas if we don't have clam chowder on Christmas Eve.

After eating dinner we loaded the kids in the car and drove around to look at all the Christmas decorations. The first year I got a computer, I made some award certificates for such categories as "best theme," "neatest," "most interesting," etc. for outdoor lights and decorations. The family would vote in the car and when we had a winner we would send our youngest up to the house. He would place the award in the mailbox, ring the doorbell, and run! I still wonder what the people thought when they found those awards.

After viewing the lights and decorations we returned home to sing Christmas carols and to read the Christmas story. As the boys all got old enough to read, we would all take turns reading a portion of the story. My wife would put a cassette tape in our recorder and she would record the boys singing the Christmas carols and reading the biblical narrative. We would leave it running while the boys opened their presents to record their excitement and comments about each gift. Our boys are all grown and married. When they bring the grandkids over for Christmas Eve, Mary puts in one of those old cassettes and the boys' wives get a real kick out of listening to them. They also gain a sense of history and insight into our family.

One tradition that became a favorite of our boys actually started out of a practical need. When I was in graduate school we didn't have a lot of money, so when the boys would invite their friends over for a birthday party, it didn't take them long to open the three or four presents we could afford. So, in order to extend the present opening time, Mary would hide the presents in the house and give the boys clues. They would have to figure out the clue, go look in that place, and find their next clue. Eventually the clues led to a present and another clue. The kids in the neighborhood thought our birthdays were the most fun because they got to play Sherlock Holmes. There were times they didn't even stop to take time to open the presents because they were only interested in finding the next clue.

When we took family vacations and long trips, we would play certain car games such as the sign alphabet game, the 50 states license plate game, or other car travel games. When PBS did a special on the first *Star Wars*, Mary taped them all and the boys would sit and listen to them spellbound for hours. We would try to stop at as many Historical Markers as we could and we kept a travel diary of all the places we stopped.

There are a number of things you can do to facilitate families having fun together. The following is a list of suggestions. You can modify, add to, or create your own.

- Build something together—model, birdhouse, bookshelves, etc.
- Visit—Museums: Natural History, Science and Industry; Library; Zoo; Parks; Caves; Flea Markets; etc.
- Story time—Lewis's *Chronicles of Narnia*, Tolkein's *Ring Trilogy*, Peretti's spiritual warfare series, the *Little House* series.

Make your own adventure books. Write your own story. Take turns reading to each other.

- Meal times—help prepare, humor, daily jokes, events of the day—"deep thoughts," "Rush Reports"
- Games—card, board, computer, skill, drawing, guessing
- Plant a garden, give each child a section, weed, water, plant, etc.
- Date Nights with each individual child, money, let them choose.
- Pictures—Make an album, video 9 to 5—take your child to work with you if permitted, go to school with them for a day
- Sports—coach, travel together, videos, professional, books, skate, bowl, golf, putt-putt, go cart, basketball, bicycle, tennis, fishing, swimming, Frisbee golf, etc.
- Map—push pins, birthplaces of family, relatives, Bible events
- Zoo—photo contest, imitate the animals, feed the animals
- Tour the City! (Fire station, police station, city hall, historical monuments)
- Cemetery—Historical, tombstone rubbings
- Adopt a grandparent
- Role Reversal
- Runway Runaway—guess what airline, kind of plane, tour the control tower
- Collections: rocks, stamps, coins, baseball cards
- Interior Decorator—Holidays, seasons
- Tour a factory, chocolate, bakery, dairy, etc.
- Have a picnic: At a park, on the floor in the house (any room), in the snow, at the river, etc.
- Cook: a foreign meal together—use Spanish, French, Italian accent while preparing and eating the food! Eat by candlelight, make ice cream, roast marshmallows in fireplace.
- Create: crafts, talent show, joke night, write a silly story together, silly song, write a rap (complete with sound effects), create commercials, slogans, a movie, a comic book
- Active: Charades, play "oldies" and teach your kids the twist, the jerk, the skate, the Freddie, the hustle, the hokey-pokey, etc. Exercise together, take a walk
- Star Gaze—Find the constellations, tell mythology behind them
- Make History—Tell kids about what you were like when you were their age, interview grandparents, do a family tree, research your name, names, ancestry

SUGGESTED READING LIST

Clark, Chap. *The Youth Worker's Handbook to Family Ministry.* Grand Rapids: Zondervan, 1997.

DeVries, Mark. *Family-Based Youth Ministry.* Downers Grove, IL: InterVarsity, 1994.

DeVries, Mark, and Nan Russell. *Bridges.* Downers Grove, IL: InterVarsity, 1996.

Thomas, Steve. *Your Church Can Be Family Friendly.* Joplin, MO: College Press, 1996.

NOTES ON CHAPTER TWENTY-SIX

1. Mark DeVries, "What Is Youth Ministry's Relationship to the Family?" in *Reaching a Generation for Christ,* ed. by Richard R. Dunn and Mark H. Senter III (Chicago: Moody, 1997), p. 481.

2. Chap Clark, *The Youth Worker's Handbook to Family Ministry* (Grand Rapids: Zondervan, 1997), p. 22.

3. Dub Ambrose and Walt Mueller, *Ministry to Families with Teenagers* (Loveland, CO: Group, 1988), p. 14.

4. Doug Fields, *Purpose Driven Youth Ministry* (Grand Rapids: Zondervan, 1998), p. 251.

5. "World Youth Survey Results," *Teenage Magazine* (April–May 1986), pp. 52-53.

6. Mark Devries, *Family Based Youth Ministry* (Downers Grove, IL: InterVarsity, 1994), p. 18.

7. Chap Clark and Pamela J. Erwin, "Reconstructing Family Life," in *New Directions for Youth Ministry,* ed. by Wayne Rice, Chap Clark, et al. (Loveland, CO: Group, 1998), pp. 49-52.

8. Ambrose and Mueller, *Ministry,* p. 49.

9. Dewey Bertolini, *Back to the Heart of Youth Work* (Wheaton, IL: Victor Books, 1989), p. 103.

10. Merton Strommen and Irene Strommen, *The Five Cries of Parents* (San Francisco: Harper, 1985), p. 72.

11. Jay Kesler, *Energizing Your Teenager's Faith,* quoted in *Family Based Youth Ministry,* ed. by Mark DeVries (Downers Grove, IL: InterVarsity, 1994), p. 76.

12. Fields, *Purpose Driven,* p. 252.

13. Ibid., p. 255.

14. Quoted in *Parents and Teenagers* (August–September 1988), p. 8.

"While all of the activities and excitement assured that no one questioned my work ethic, I questioned everything. In the midst of all that was happening, I couldn't shake the emptiness of all I was doing. I was distant from the Lord and my heart was slowly hardening."
—*Doug Fields*[1]

"I realized I was running on empty, and I vividly saw my need to feed my forgotten soul. I wanted to move back to the point where I was serving others from an overflowing spirit, not an overtaxed one." —*Paul Borthwick*[2]

Chapter 27

Developing a Balanced Youth Program

Dr. Gary B. Zustiak

The Importance of Balance

In the movie, *The Karate Kid*, there is a scene about halfway through the movie where Mr. Miyagi takes Daniel out in a small rowboat and instructs him to stand in the bow of the boat and to practice his defensive moves. Daniel wants to know when he is going to learn how to punch. He is anxious to prove himself to the bullies that torment him. Miyagi answers, "Must first learn balance. If balance is good, karate is good. If balance is bad, karate is bad. Everything in life depends on balance."

As it is in karate, so it is in ministry. The key building block of a long and healthy ministry is the ability to maintain balance—balance in every aspect of one's life. There are several Scriptures that direct our focus to the key areas that should be considered. All of these Scriptures teach us something about the importance of balance.

- Luke 2:52: And Jesus grew in wisdom and stature, and in favor with God and men.

Notice the four areas of personal growth that are mentioned: cognitive, physical, spiritual, and social. A healthy youth program is going to offer the young people help in their cognitive development, opportunities to exercise their physical needs, spiritual instruction, and opportunities for social interaction. The fault of most youth programs is that they focus in on just one aspect of growth. Either they have a heavy focus in the cognitive area, e.g., Bible Bowl, but low in meeting physical needs. Or they are great in meeting physical needs offering all kinds of sporting and recreational opportunities, but very little in the way of spiritual depth.

- Acts 2:42: They devoted themselves to the apostles' teaching and to the fellowship, to the breaking of bread and to prayer.

We see that the early church did not focus in on just one aspect of the Christian life or ministry, but their experience was one of balance in the area of instruction, fellowship, communion, and prayer.

- Romans 12:6-8: We have different gifts, according to the grace given us. If a man's gift is prophesying, let him use it in proportion to his faith. If it is serving, let him serve; if it is teaching, let him teach. If it is encouraging, let him encourage; if it is contributing to the needs of others, let him give generously, if it is leadership, let him govern diligently; if it is showing mercy, let him do it cheerfully.

Paul shows that a healthy church is made up individuals who use their different gifts for mutual edification. It takes everybody using his or her gifts, not just one person doing all the work no matter how talented or gifted. The church is balanced by the variety of gifts given to the members of the congregation.

- Ephesians 4:11: It was he who gave some to be apostles, some to be prophets, some to be evangelists, and some to be pastors and teachers, to prepare God's people for works of service, so that the body of Christ may be built up until we all reach unity in the faith and in the knowledge of the Son of God and become mature, attaining to the whole measure of the fullness of Christ.

In this passage we see balance in the various ministry positions that God has created for the church. The purpose for these ministry positions is to help raise up mature Christians who are grounded in the faith and can withstand the temptations and persecution of the world.

- Matthew 22:37-40: Jesus replied, "'Love the Lord your God with all your heart and with all your soul and with all your mind.' This is the first and greatest commandment. And the second is like it: 'Love your neighbor as yourself.' All the Law and the Prophets hang on these two commandments."

- **Matthew 28:19-20:** Therefore go and make disciples of all nations, baptizing them in the name of the Father and of the Son and of the Holy Spirit, and teaching them to obey everything I have commanded you. And surely I am with you always, to the very end of the age.

Doug Fields uses these two passages as the foundation for a balanced approach to youth ministry in *Purpose Driven Youth Ministry*. He teaches that a healthy ministry will have a balanced emphasis in: worship, ministry, evangelism, fellowship, and discipleship.

Balance in the Life of the Youth Minister

The youth ministry "salvage yard" is full of run-down, rusted out, and busted up youth workers who may be guilty of only one thing; they neglected their *own* spiritual, physical, emotional, and mental needs. Remember: You cannot give away that which you yourself do not possess. You cannot impart a passion for evangelism if you do not have a burning desire to reach the lost. You cannot teach your kids about the importance of prayer, if your own prayer life is negligible. "To attempt to lead a person spiritually while at the same time neglecting your own spiritual life would be a travesty. Any leader who fails to take nourishment daily from the Word of God will most certainly degenerate into a voice from a vacuum."[3] Paul Borthwick agrees,

You cannot give away that which you yourself do not possess.

> I have often told my youth team that a healthy staff begets a healthy youth group. When the leaders are growing, the youth find it easier to follow suit. The principle is basically that of being a model. The inner life of the leader will either make him or break him. If he neglects the cultivation of purity, humility, and faith, he is in for big trouble.[4]

In Mark 1:35 Jesus rises early in the morning to go off to a solitary place to pray. He balances his time of ministry to others with a personal devotion time. In Mark 6:30-31 Jesus instructs the disciples to get away by themselves to a quiet place for a short period of resting after a demanding time of ministry to others. In Luke 5:15-16 after a time of great ministry and healing, the crowds are demanding more ministry time from Jesus. Think of the pressure of this situation. People are being brought to Jesus to be healed of ailments and diseases such as leprosy, blindness, lameness, and demon possession. These are legitimate needs. There is no other place in the known world where they can go to be cured. Jesus is their only hope. But even in this situation Jesus says, "No." He withdraws from the crowds, seeks out a lonely place and begins to pray.

Did Jesus turn down their requests for healing because he was not compassionate? No! Once again we see that ministry time must be balanced with personal time spent with God. Jesus has given us the perfect example. Jesus' ultimate goal or mission was to be sacrificed as the spotless lamb of God so that he could redeem the whole world. His main purpose was not temporary healing, but eternal healing, and if he didn't keep his life in balance by keeping his spiritual life strong there was always that chance that Satan would take advantage of extreme fatigue and weakness and tempt him beyond what he could bear. Jesus teaches us that sometimes the most spiritual thing we can do is to say "No" to requests that may be good in and of themselves but may have the ultimate effect of detracting from our main purpose and goal.

Jesus teaches us that sometimes the most spiritual thing we can do is to say "No" to requests that may be good in and of themselves but may have the ultimate effect of detracting from our main purpose and goal.

> You and I are called to exert a godly influence in a decadent society. We are called to set a godly standard in a very ungodly world. We are called to communicate a godly message to a sadly deceived people. Question: "How can we exert a godly influence if we ourselves are not godly?" Answer: "We can't." Question: "How can we set a godly standard if we ourselves are not godly?" Answer: "We can't." Question: "How can we communicate a godly message if we ourselves are not godly?" Answer: "We can't."[5]

The youth minister must take special care to nurture his own soul. If he neglects his soul because of the demands of ministry, not only is his own spiritual life in danger, he runs the risk of losing all that he has worked so hard to build. The effectiveness of his ministry will be in direct proportion to his own spiritual health. If he crashes and burns spiritually, so will his ministry. "Carefully guarding our own spiritual health and nurturing our spiritual growth are the best things that we can do to prevent burnout, spiritual apathy, or hostile

Developing a Balanced Youth Program

withdrawal from God or ministry."[6] Listen to the words of Kenda Creasy Dean as she shares about the dangers of spiritual fatigue that she encountered early in her ministry.

After a few years in ministry—three, to be exact—the program I worked with began to seem weary. If God made me gung-ho, God also made me *tired*—and not just because I needed more sleep. My soul was on empty; I was running on fumes, and the ministry entrusted to my care was too. The depressing truth was that youth were not the only ones who needed more substantial faith; *so did I*. Here I was, supposed to be teaching them to pray, immersing them in Scripture, involving them with the poor—and when was the last time I did any of that for the sake of my soul and not for the sake of my job? God knew I was faking it and I knew I was faking it, but I didn't know how to stop faking it without dropping out altogether.[7]

Unfortunately, her experience is not uncommon.

Not only do youth workers need to feed their own soul, they also need to spend time with their own peer group. You must not overinvolve yourself in the lives of young people to the neglect of your own. By spending short periods of time away from the youth group, you fill your cup and are able to go back to them with something of significance to offer. If you never "fill your cup" then you find yourself in the frustrating position of trying to quench their spiritual thirst from an empty well. It just won't happen.

It should go without saying, there needs to be balance between ministry time and family time. If our relationships at home suffer because of neglect, you can be sure that our entire ministry will suffer. Too many ministers have assumed that God would watch over their marriage and family because they were doing the Lord's work. They end up working 70-80 hours a week spending time with other people's kids, while neglecting their own families. I know too many in this situation who have ended up bitterly disappointed when the wife files for divorce and runs off with another man.

On the other end of the spectrum, I have met some youth ministers who have almost turned their family into their own personal gods. They inform the church board that they can only be out two nights a week because they do not want to neglect their family. The result is that they slowly lose touch with what is happening in the life of their teens because of the lack of contact. The entire program suffers because the minister has not put in enough time to build relationships, either with the volunteer staff or the youth. This minister will soon find himself without a job.

If our relationships at home suffer because of neglect, you can be sure that our entire ministry will suffer.

Learn to walk that delicate line of balance between spending enough time with your teens and volunteer staff in order to develop genuine relationships with them and to gain insight into their pastoral needs without neglecting your own family's needs. Ridge Burns suggests the following ways to strengthen your marriage and family life while being involved in ministry.

1. Take time to talk with your spouse and family. Fill them in on the intimate details of what is going on in your life and ministry.
2. Put your family on the church and high school student mailing list so they can help you with scheduling conflicts.
3. Schedule a sabbatical weekend each year during which you and your spouse or family go some place by yourselves.
4. Schedule a three-month sabbatical every four years of ministry.
5. Set aside an evening each week for you and your family to ask the question, "How are we getting along?" This time of sharing gives each person the opportunity to express affirmation or displeasure.
6. Do something outside your ministry realm that is fun to do as a couple or family, like jogging, biking, playing golf, or playing tennis.
7. Travel together. If you speak at conferences or attend conventions, invite your spouse or family along. The fellowship will be great.[8]

Balance between Programs and Relationships

Programs may *attract* youth, but it is relationships that *keep* them. This has been a recognized foundational truth of youth ministry for years.

Programs and relationships are two necessities in youth ministry. You need programs that will meet people's needs and challenge them towards a goal. But at the same time you want people to participate in and support your programming. Programs without people are lonely affairs. In the same way, programs that ignore the needs of the people they seek to serve are equally lonely affairs.

Programs may attract youth, but it is relationships that keep them.

Balance in the Program Areas

There are a number of problems with an unbalanced program. Unbalanced programs don't minister to the total student. They tend to focus in on just one aspect of their growth, either cognitive, physical, social, or spiritual. But growth in only one area leaves a person deficient in all of the other important aspects of his life. Having a strong Bible Bowl program challenges the cognitive and spiritual needs of young people, but doesn't address their need for social interaction, ministry to others, or their need to participate in some kind of physical activity such as church-league basketball, volleyball, or slow-pitch softball.

Students need an opportunity to give as well as receive. Many youth programs are set up to "minister to the needs of youth." They offer discipleship programs, Friday night socials, and small group activities. But all of these are student focused, and they subtly reinforce a selfishness that seems to pervade youth culture. Teenagers need to be challenged to look outside of themselves and see the needs of others. A healthy youth program will provide opportunities of service through mission projects, local ministry opportunities such as soup kitchens, homeless shelters, and after-school tutoring.

When the youth program is only one dimensional, such as a social or athletic program, important evangelistic opportunities are lost. A variety of students will have a variety of interests. Not all of them will be interested in joining a Bible bowl team and memorizing the entire book of Leviticus and being able to answer any trivia question concerning Jewish worship customs in less than a tenth of a second. But they might be interested in some aspect of the fine arts, such as playing in the praise band. Perhaps they love athletics and can't get enough opportunities to play. They would love to join the church basketball team.

Growth opportunities are lost if the program is not balanced. If the program is centered on social activities, then the young people may not have adequate opportunities to be challenged spiritually. Growth comes from both being challenged cognitively (learning correct doctrine and theology) and from participation in ministry opportunities that meet the needs of others.

When the youth program is only one dimensional, such as a social or athletic program, important evangelistic opportunities are lost.

The solution is to build a youth program that offers opportunities to participate in the five areas of study, fine arts, socials, service, and athletics. This would meet the various growth needs of students and provide adequate opportunities for outreach and service. A balanced youth program is one that is designed to meet all the needs of youth: spiritual, social, physical, and cognitive. (See Chart)

STUDY	FINE ARTS	SOCIALS	SERVICE	ATHLETICS
Sunday School	Drama	Car Rally	Yard Work	Bowling
VBS For All Ages	Puppets	Crisco Party	Visitations	Aerobics
Mid-Week Youth	Painting	Bike Hike	Letter Writing	Jogging
Group Meetings	Chalk Drawing	Blue Gnu	Office Help	Volleyball
Release Time	Cross-Stitch	Polaroid Hunt	Baby-sitting	Flag Football
Discipleship	Praise Band	Scavenger Hunt	Camp Crew	Karate
Groups	Choir	Kidnap Breakfast	Table Setting	Tennis
Worship Services	Clown Ministry	Kite Flying	VBS Helpers	Basketball
Church Camp	Crafts	Train Trip	Junior Church Helpers	Soccer
Prayer Breakfast	Sculpture	Swim	Sharpen Pencils	Bicycling
Noon Bible Studies	Hand Bells	Backwards Night	Snow Removal	Slow-pitch Softball
Bible Bowl	Magic	Backpacking	Communion Help	Water Skiing
Bible Club	Mime	Rafting/tubing	Card Making	Snow Skiing
Evangelism	Skits	Video Mania	Flower Bed	Fun Runs
Outreach Studies	Christian Video	Secret Destination	Habitat For Humanity	Triathlon
Serendipity Studies	Movie Making	Go-Karts	Food Pantry	Fast-pitch Softball
Devotions	Airband	Sleighride/Hayride	Bulletin Help	Gymnastics
Retreats	Ensemble	Funhouse	God Squad	Racquetball
Lock-ins	Guitar	Concerts	Centerpieces	Weight Lifting
CIY Conferences	Murals	Nerd Nights	Community Help	Swim Teams
Personal Devotions	Poetry	Progressive Dinner	Dorm Preparation	Water Aerobics
Book Club	Creative Writing	Pizza Party	Litter Cleanup	Open Gym
	Decoupage	Caroling	Painting	Field Hockey
	Sewing	'50s Social	Gleaners	Ice Skating
	Multimedia	Fifth Quarter	Youth Paper	Ice Hockey
	Readers Theater	Nutsville Dinner	Mission Project	Curling
		World's Largest (anything)	World Vision	Wally Ball
		Mini-golf	CIY Missions Trip	Golf
		Bigger and Better Hunt	Deaf Class	Badminton
		Sweetheart Banquet	Refugee Help	Frisbee
			Adopt a Grandparent	Sailing
				Floor Hockey

There are a number of advantages to a balanced program. First of all there are more opportunities for service—both for students and sponsors. The more activities you offer, the greater the opportunities for involvement and growth. When you program to meet the physical, spiritual, social, and intellectual needs of young people, it is inevitable that you will have greater program variability and creativity. You have a peace about your youth program knowing that you are meeting *all* of the student's needs instead of just focusing on one.

Offering a balanced youth program helps to make the year's planning easier. When you know that you are going to offer a mission trip during spring break, slow pitch softball in the summer, basketball in the fall, discipleship groups in the spring, a praise band for youth church, a drama team for Wednesday night, church camp and CIY Conference, then it becomes much easier to fill in the blanks.

A balanced program offers something for every interest group. The kids who love an intellectual challenge can join the Bible Bowl team. Those who enjoy the arts can help with the praise band or the drama team. The jocks can play church league basketball or softball in the summer. The spiritually mature can participate in a student led Bible study or attach themselves to a mentor. Those who are evangelistically minded can travel to foreign fields or the inner city with the mission outreach group.

Balance in Varying Levels of Spiritual Maturity

Not only do you need to have balance in the types of activities you offer your students, but you must also balance your program to meet the varying levels of spiritual maturity that are found in the young people. You want to program for growth. The way to accomplish this is to take students where they are and lead them to maturity in Christ. This means that you must have something that would interest the seeker without intimidating him, but also offer opportunities for spiritual growth for the kid who has been in church all his life and is thinking of entering the mission field.

Don't expect every student to be involved in every program. This would be very unhealthy for a number of reasons. First of all, you do not want the youth program to be in competition with the family, but to support the family. Encourage students to limit the number of programs they are involved with. Have them choose according to their interests and needs. Since you are purposely offering programs of varying spiritual intensity, it goes to reason that not every program is going to be desirable from the standpoint of the student. You should offer some low-key, evangelistic programs to interest and win the non-Christians, and also offer some in-depth study and service programs that require a great deal of commitment and stretch the teens spiritually. The idea is to take kids where they are and move them up the scale to your final goal which is maturity in Christ (see chart).

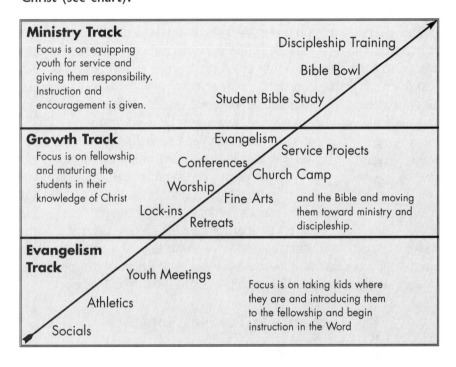

Balance in the Volunteer Staff Involvement

The youth minister cannot and should not try to manage and direct the student ministry alone. He needs the gifts and abilities of a volunteer staff. When recruiting a volunteer staff, he should seek out people who are willing to commit to the youth program on a full-time basis. These are people who are willing to teach a Sunday school class every week or be in charge of a small group every Wednesday night. They show up at every youth function and go out of their way to invite young people into their home. They may even serve as staff at a week of church camp.

Not everyone is willing to commit to being a full-time student volunteer, but they will offer some part-time help. These people may help with junior church one week a month or teach for a week of VBS. They are willing to help with a social event as often as their schedule permits. Utilize these people as often as you can. They may love what they do enough to commit to being full-time volunteers. Even if they don't, their involvement is good for the students who need to make healthy relationships with Christian adults.

You will also need to recruit some specialty people. Specialty people do not teach on a regular basis, but have a particular skill that is needed. This skill may be in the area of crafts or the arts. Perhaps the person is a drama teacher or music teacher at a local school who can offer some special insight, help, or training with your praise band or drama team. You might have someone who loves to camp and who has all of the equipment needed, i.e., tents, lanterns, canoes, etc. This person may be willing to help with a wilderness retreat or a father-son weekend camp-out.

Students do not want to be reduced to spectators; they want opportunities for genuine involvement.

You must also balance your adult involvement with student leadership. Students do not want to be reduced to spectators; they want opportunities for genuine involvement. If the students are to have ownership of a program, they must be given opportunities to have input in the planning of programs and leadership of them. Ownership leads to growth and support.

Balance in Teaching Topics

When you are planning your Sunday morning Bible school lessons or your midweek youth group study, you must be careful to avoid needless repetition. Needless repetition is most likely to take place when you wait till the last moment to prepare your lesson. Your temptation will be to fall back on a topic that you feel the most comfortable with or have taught before, but the result is that it is not new material for the young people. For a generation that is known for its "been there—done that" attitude, this could be the death knell for that night's study time. Repetition can also occur if you are not wise in your curriculum choices. Many publishing houses will repeat favorite Bible passages from year to year or certain popular topics.

You must also be careful that you don't end up using your study time to ride all of your favorite hobbyhorses. In other words, be sure you teach on a balance of topics, not just the ones that are your favorites, e.g., end times, sex and dating, or self-esteem.

A good example of a nice balance in topics for study can be found in an old youth publishing company called "Success with Youth." Here are the ten areas of study they suggest:

1. Faith in Jesus Christ
2. Growth in the Holy Spirit
3. Love to Others
4. Response to Scriptures
5. Effective Prayer
6. Ethical Behavior
7. Church Participation
8. Responsibility to the World
9. Family Life
10. Personal Development

Balanced Programming Helps to Avoid "Just Winging It"

One common danger of many youth ministers is the temptation to wing it in their teaching and planning. They can even find ways to rationalize and justify this lack of planning on their part. They have so many demands that they just don't have the time to put in to planning their lessons or programs.

When the youth minister gives in to this temptation, the members of the youth group notice. So do the adult volunteers. It is seen in the fact that the overall quality suffers. The temptation to wing it can become habitual. When this happens, the whole ministry program begins to deteriorate.

There are many benefits to preparation. You can be more sensitive to your youth. Better programming meets kid's needs. If you will discipline yourself to plan ahead and to plan a balanced program and balanced lessons, you will grow professionally and personally as you meet the challenge.

Worksheets to Help in Preparing a Balanced Youth Program

The following worksheets are provided to help you with designing a balanced youth program and balanced lessons.

You should plan out your entire program for a year. In a large church, you can fill each area of need every month of the year. In a smaller or midsized church, you may need to stagger some programs, e.g., fine arts in the spring and athletics in the summer.

	STUDY	FINE ARTS	SOCIALS	SERVICE	ATHLETICS
JANUARY					
FEBRUARY					
MARCH					
APRIL					
MAY					
JUNE					
JULY					
AUGUST					
SEPTEMBER					
OCTOBER					
NOVEMBER					
DECEMBER					

Not only do you need to plan your programs for a year, but you should also plan out your teaching. Be sure to think through both what you would teach in the morning during your Sunday school hour and what you would teach during your midweek youth meetings. Think through the spiritual needs of those most likely to attend. Generally speaking you should cover deeper topics on Sunday morning and lighter ones during your midweek meetings.

	STUDY TOPIC	1ST WEEK'S LESSON	2ND WEEK'S LESSON	3RD WEEK'S LESSON	4TH WEEK'S LESSON
JANUARY					
FEBRUARY					
MARCH					
APRIL					
MAY					

JUNE					
JULY					
AUGUST					
SEPTEMBER					
OCTOBER					
NOVEMBER					
DECEMBER					

Here is an example of a midsized church with a year's programs planned out. The study is divided up between Sunday school and midweek youth meetings with the idea that the midweek is going to be lighter as it is geared for evangelistic outreach.

	STUDY	FINE ARTS	SOCIALS	SERVICE	ATHLETICS
JANUARY	Parables of Jesus Situation Ethics	Reader's Theater	Blue Gnu	Shovel Snow	Volleyball
FEBRUARY	Parables of Jesus Self-Esteem	Reader's Theater	Sweetheart Banquet	Make Cards for Nursing Home	Volleyball
MARCH	Parables of Jesus Love, Sex & Dating	Reader's Theater	Movie Night	Write Letters to Missionaries & Servicemen	Volleyball
APRIL	Psalms Death and Dying	Video production	Bigger and Better Hunt	Wash Windows	Basketball
MAY	Psalms Cults	Video production	Progressive Dinner	Paint Classrooms	Basketball
JUNE	Psalms Creation vs. Evolution	Video production	Kidnap Breakfast	Yard Work	Basketball
JULY	1 Peter Family Life	Web site design	Luau	Mow Lawns	Softball
AUGUST	1 Peter Drugs & Alcohol	Web site design	Nerd Night	College Dorm Preparation	Softball
SEPTEMBER	2 Peter Apologetics	Web site design	Bike Hike	Litter Cleanup	Softball
OCTOBER	OT Heroes War	Praise Band	Hayride & Funhouse	Food Pantry	Bowling
NOVEMBER	OT Heroes Comparative Religions	Praise Band	Lock-in	Survey Work	Bowling
DECEMBER	OT Heroes World Hunger	Praise Band	Christmas Gift Exchange	Fruit Baskets	Bowling

1. Is your ministry balanced, or are most of the activities focused around a particular need? Do you offer anything for the young person whose main interest is fine arts? Athletics?
2. Does your own life reflect balance in terms of ministry and family life?
3. What do you learn from the life of Jesus about the importance of balance in terms of ministry and personal devotional life?
4. Do you offer something for the seeker as well as the mature Christian?

SUGGESTED READING LIST

Borthwick, Paul. *Feeding Your Forgotten Soul.* Grand Rapids: Zondervan, 1990.

Dean, Kenda Creasy, and Ron Foster. *The Godbearing Life: The Art of Soul Tending for Youth Ministry.* Nashville: Upper Room Books, 1998.

NOTES ON CHAPTER TWENTY-SEVEN

1. Doug Fields, *Purpose Driven Youth Ministry* (Grand Rapids: Zondervan, 1998), p. 29.
2. Paul Borthwick, *Feeding Your Forgotten Soul* (Grand Rapids: Zondervan, 1990), p. 18.
3. Dewey Bertolini, *Back to the Heart of Youth Work* (Wheaton, IL: Victor Books, 1989), p. 19.
4. Paul Borthwick, "The Person of the Youth Minister," in *The Complete Book of Youth Ministry,* ed. by Warren S. Benson and Mark H. Senter III (Chicago: Moody, 1987), p. 101.
5. Bertolini, *Back,* p. 23.
6. Borthwick, *Feeding,* p. 18.
7. Kenda Creasy Dean and Ron Foster, *The Godbearing Life: The Art of Soul Tending for Youth Ministry* (Nashville: Upper Room Books, 1998), p. 42.
8. Ridge Burns, *Create in Me a Youth Ministry* (Wheaton, IL: Victor Books, 1986), p. 117.

ABOUT THE AUTHORS

Gary B. Zustiak, D. Min.

Gary Zustiak has served as the Director of Youth Ministries and Resources for Christ In Youth since 1999. Prior to coming to CIY he was the Professor of Youth Ministry and Psychology at Ozark Christian College for 13 years. He has also served as adjunct professor at Lincoln Christian Seminary. Gary has held ministries in Illinois and Idaho. He and his wife, Mary, have three sons, Joshua, Aaron, and Caleb, and three grandchildren. Gary loves going to movies, playing his Taylor guitar, and hugging on his grandkids. He has authored two books, *The NeXt Generation* and *Reasons to Believe.*

John Mouton

John Mouton has been an Associate Director in the Missions Department at Christ In Youth since 1991. Prior to that he spent seven years in youth ministry at the Fairview Christian Church in Carthage, Missouri. He is married to Nancy, and they have three children: Joshua, Jonathan, and Sarah.

Josh Finklea

Josh Finklea is a veteran in the field of youth ministry and speaks on behalf of Christ In Youth and Compassion International. He is a highly sought after speaker for conventions, conferences, retreats, and school assemblies. He is passionate about preaching to students and loving lost people. Currently, Josh works with Christ In Youth where he is the director of the Junior High "Believe" program. Josh and his wife, Krista, have four children, Clay, Mackenzie, Tate, and Abby.

Kevin Greer

Kevin Greer has been an Associate Director at CIY since 1996. He oversees and directs the Discipleship Retreats and assists in the direction of Summer Conferences. Prior to coming to CIY he spent 17 years as a youth minister in Oklahoma and Colorado. Kevin is also the author of *Life to Life Discipleship.* His driving purpose in youth ministry is to instill in youth workers the desire to mentor and disciple their students to grow stronger, deeper, and more real in their relationship to Christ. Kevin and his wife Debbie have three sons: Jay, Levi, and Ethan.

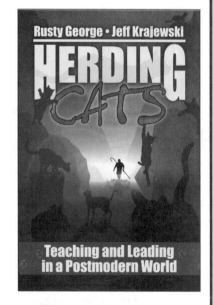